Confessions
of a
price controller

Confessions of a price controller

C. JACKSON GRAYSON, JR.

with

LOUIS NEEB

1974

Dow Jones-Irwin, Inc. *Homewood, Illinois 60430*

First Printing, May 1974

Printed in the United States of America

Library of Congress Cataloging in Publication Data

Grayson, Charles Jackson, 1923–
    Confessions of a price controller.

    1. Wage-price policy—United States. 2. Price regulation—United States. I. Neeb, Louis, 1939– joint author. II. Title.
HC110.W24G72   353.008′26   74–3246
ISBN 0-87094-075-9

TO

Barbara, Christopher, Michael, Randy Grayson

Jean, Michael, Kelly Neeb

for "Helping it happen"

. . . AND TO

*The Price Commissioners,
The entire staff of the Price Commission,
and the American People*

for "Making it happen"

Preface

If you read this book expecting a kiss-and-tell exposé of shenanigans in high places, you're going to be disappointed.

True, the title says "confessions."

And the word suggests dark secrets, intrigue, and revelations of naughty things in the dead of night. Or payoffs. Or sex.

Sorry.

Nothing so exciting as that. But perhaps more important.

These are the confessions of an economic czar—who, as Chairman of the Price Commission in Phase II, controlled the nation's prices for a period of 15 months, from November 1971 to January 1973. They reveal what was learned about our economic system, government, and price controls.*

It began on August 15, 1971.

"What! Price controls?" was the incredulous reaction of most Americans (and the rest of the world) to the dramatic announcement by President Nixon on that summer Sunday evening. The

---

* None of the six Price Commissioners or any other Stabilization officials read this book in advance. The observations and views are strictly personal and may or may not coincide with others' recollections of facts, opinions, or conclusions.

President was ordering, for the first time in American history, peacetime wage and price controls.

"What price *controls?*" soon became the question as people tried to understand and comply with the myriad of regulations, rulings, and orders pouring out in the early days of Phase II.

"*What* price controls!" complained disillusioned people in early 1972 as they watched the price bulge flow through the economy.

"What *price,* controls?" was finally asked by business and labor as they witnessed the costly and distorting effects of controls on the economy and their freedom.

Though this book focuses mainly on this period, now known as Phase II of the Economic Stabilization Program, it is really not a history. It is a report of the interaction of wage-price controls, government, the public, politics, and markets—and what all this could mean for the future of our economic system.

As Leonard Silk of the *New York Times* once characterized the period, "The dismal science of economics became the black art of controls."

It is not a book *of* economics.

The "economics" of price controls is a scholarly, mind-boggling study involving complex theories, mathematical equations, tables, graphs, statistical tests, and all that. Such economic studies are being done, and will continue to be for years to come as scholars pour over statistics to sort out what happened and guess what might have happened without controls.*

This book involves none of that.

It reports, instead, what happened when an "economic jury" (the Price Commission) got together—a lawyer, an accountant, two economists, a business school dean, a businessman, a politician—and substituted their collective judgment for that of the marketplace.

Instead of their being (as many people presumed) a group of

---

* Those wishing to read more detailed historical descriptions and economic reporting of the entire Stabilization Program should obtain various issues of the *Economic Stabilization Program Quarterly Report* and the *Economic Report of the President,* available through the Government Printing Office. Also, The Brookings Institution in Washington has various published studies of the program.

Solomon-like, objective, dispassionate, omniscient people, they were just ordinary citizens, subject to the usual errors of judgment, sinking feelings, doubts, fatigue, disappointments, fears, and anger.

Running a control system, it was found, was not a calm, orderly application of economic theories, but an eclectic mixture of economics, power, pressure, and politics. It was a drama of trivial and major events, a clash of personalities, brinksmanship, day-to-day craziness, improvisations, and squabbles. It involved all the problems, challenges, and pitfalls of creating and operating a large new organization—whether in the public sector or in private industry—in a volatile, high-pressure situation. It included recruiting and organizing staff, setting goals, building morale, planning and participating in meaningful productive meetings, establishing and maintaining internal communications and public information . . .

It is also not a book *by* economists.

It is by two people—Jack Grayson and Lou Neeb—who directed the administration of the price controls in Phase II. Jack Grayson was Chairman of the Price Commission and Lou Neeb was Executive Secretary.

Neither were economists.

Neither had written about, nor had done any research in economics. However, we had a diverse set of experiences—administering a government agency, newspaper reporting, farming, university teaching, FBI Special Agent, business management, and consulting.

It is not a book *for* economists, either.

There is no analysis of whether inflation was caused by excessive money supply, fiscal irresponsibility, structural blocks, business and labor power, devaluation, new social contracts, or combinations of these factors. Certainly, it is hoped that this book will be of use to economists in studying theories and in making future economic policy recommendations for price stability.

But it is written *primarily* for our fellow citizens to give them insight into the real process of price controls—how they work and what they do to and for our country. Average people do not ask whether the Phillips curve has shifted to the northwest corner, or whether M_1 and M_2 are too high. They ask:

What was it really like? How did you get started? Who did you recruit? What did you *do?* Did the White House interfere? How did you operate? What were the pressures? Why did you do (this) (that)? Should we have ever started this business? Will we ever get out?

These are good questions.

Inflation is the number one problem for the American people and for the world. It disrupts economic, social, and political systems. And if not checked, it increases the cry for a shift from a market driven economy to one that is more centrally directed—to one where price and wage controls are not intermittent or in phases, but continuous as a part of an overall planned, mixed economy.

It is the citizens who face the increasingly critical choice as to whether the United States will operate with a competitive market system or with some form of permanent wage-price controls. In a democratic society, this issue will ultimately be settled, not by economists, but by people at the ballot box. Therefore, it is important for them to know just how a recent price control system designed to control inflation really was created and operated.

Though we both administered the price control system vigorously, it is no secret that each of us is a strong believer in the merits of the private enterprise system. Some people, notably Professor John Kenneth Galbraith, believe that controls should be run "by those who believe in them." This is true if one wants a more permanent system of wage-price controls. But if the objective is to use controls for the limited purposes that they can serve for a short period of time, and then to drop them—then it makes sense to put in charge of the program people who want to work themselves out of a job.

Just that was done.

These, then, are the "confessions" in this book: A tell-it-like-it-was personal view of the way price controls were created and operated in Phase II.

We bet it's not like you thought it was.

Dallas, Texas　　　　　　　　　　　　　　JACK GRAYSON
April 1974　　　　　　　　　　　　　　　LOU NEEB

Contents

Playbill

It is easy to get lost in the book without a player's guide to key people and Washington alphabetese. Here is a guide.

Price Commission

Commissioners   the seven members of the Price Commission, six part time and one, Chairman Grayson, full time

Detailees   government employees temporarily assigned away from their "home agency" to the Price Commission

Staff   every member of the Price Commission organization (about 700 at the end)

Key Staff Members

Bert   William B. Lewis, Executive Director

Lou   Louis Neeb, Executive Secretary

Pete   Peter Carpenter, Deputy Executive Director

Stabilization Program

CEA   Council of Economic Advisors

CLC   Cost of Living Council

CSC	Civil Service Commission
IRS	Internal Revenue Service
JEC	Joint Economic Committee
OMB	Office of Management and Budget
PC	Price Commission
PB	Pay Board

Stabilization Officials

Burns	Arthur Burns, Chairman, Federal Reserve Board
Connally	John Connally, Secretary of Treasury and Chairman of the CLC, from beginning of Phase I to May 1972
Rumsfeld	Donald Rumsfeld, Director of CLC
Shultz	George Shultz, former Director of OMB, Secretary of Treasury, and Chairman of CLC from May 1972 to end of Phase II
Stein	Herbert Stein, Chairman, Council of Economic Advisors

Prologue

"The President of the United States has asked me to call you to be the Chairman of the Price Commission," George Shultz said on Friday, October 14, 1971. Hearing from him was a surprise since we had really not been together since we worked closely on a task force that produced a report for the Ford Foundation in 1967.

"The what?" I said.

"The Price Commission. You know, Phase II."

I vaguely remembered hearing something about it.

"The Chairman?"

"Yes."

He offered a few more explanatory words, and I said, "I'll call you back tomorrow."

The next day I said "No."

Then I spent a sleepless night. "What in the world have I passed up! How could I be so stupid! A chance like that will never come again." It was too much.

I called back the next morning.

"George," I said, "is the job still open?"

"I don't know."

"If it is, I'll take it." I held my breath.

"I'll contact some people and let you know."

That was Sunday morning. No reply Sunday, none on Monday.

"That job is gone," I said to my wife Monday night. "I'm stupid. I've blown it—a chance at the greatest challenge I could ever have." I moped.

On Tuesday morning, the phone rang.

"The job is yours if you still want it."

"Yes."

Part one

The beginning

To place in perspective my feelings for the free market (now much stronger than before my time as Chairman of the Price Commission) you need to understand my perception of the fifteen months of Phase II. The first three parts of this book provide that background. The fourth part looks ahead at where we may be headed.

Part One focuses on the sixteen hectic days when the basic policy that guided Phase II was laid down. During most of these sixteen days, we were concerned primarily with policy and not implementation. The Cost of Living Council and the Office of Emergency Preparedness were still running the Phase I freeze. The pressures of the public and political environment only touched us in a light way, and the full impact of what we were creating was beyond real comprehension. But it was to come on November 13, 1971, the end of Phase I and the beginning of Phase II.

Given the gift to see what happened later, I think we still would have reached most of the same decisions.

1

The sixteen days

Good evening Dr. Grayson. You have before you the vital statistics of the world's largest economy. According to informed economists and advisors to the President, the U.S. economy is suffering from a near spiraling inflation. Without a decrease in the rate of inflation and an increase in productivity, the government will lose its competitive position in the world market. Your mission, should you choose to accept it, is to develop a comprehensive and equitable plan to stop the high rate of inflation while at the time insuring the health and progress of a trillion-dollar economy. You have exactly sixteen days to develop your plan.

As always, should you or any of the PC staff be caught or killed, the Secretary will disavow any knowledge of your actions.

This tape will self-destruct in five seconds.

Good luck, Jack.

That's not exactly the way Phase II was born, but almost. Back in October, 1971, the enormity of the task ahead did seem like a Mission Impossible.

When George Schulz called me to tell me I had the job, I was Dean at the Southern Methodist University Business School in Dallas. Within forty-eight hours after that call, I resigned my position, appointed an Acting Dean, said goodbye to faculty and students, put my wife and two children on a plane to Mexico, packed a few suitcases, and headed for the airport. Television cameras, bright lights, and several reporters were waiting at the departure gate.

"What are you going to do when you get to Washington?"

"I don't know. I'll talk to the President and Secretary Connally and see what they want me to do."

"What do you think is causing this inflation?"

"I don't know."

"Senator Proxmire says that he thinks that you should be confirmed. What do you say?"

"Whatever the Congress wants."

It was the first of many exposures to the media, and I wondered if I would be able to handle it—particularly the Washington press corps.

It was both exhilarating and frightening. Sixteen days were left before the freeze ended, and the seven-member Price Commission had to:

--Create price policies to run Phase II;

--Organize the functioning of the seven-member Price Commission;

--Recruit and organize a staff, then estimated to reach 450;

--Create operating and policy links with the Pay Board (PB), Cost of Living Council (CLC), and the Internal Revenue Service (IRS);

--Organize and secure policy recommendations from the Rent Board and the Health Services Industry Committee;

--Build an operating budget and secure approval; and

--Write and publish our legal regulations.

Flying to Washington on the night of October 20, I assumed most of these tasks were already well under way . . . that a partial staff had been assembled, that policy recommendations for Phase II were already roughed out, that spaces were ready for occupancy, and that someone would show me the ropes around Washington and provide some pointers about price controls—past and future.

Somehow it just didn't work out that way.

I was met at Dulles airport at 9 P.M. by two staff members of

6

the Office of Emergency Preparedness (OEP). I was handed a thin briefing book, taken to the Shoreham Hotel, and told to come at 9 A.M. the next morning to the White House office of Don Rumsfeld, then Director of the Cost of Living Council. Before falling asleep that first night I glanced at the briefing book, which consisted of statements by the President, a transcript of a press conference by Secretary Connally, copies of the Economic Stabilization Act, and some background information on the freeze. There was nothing in them that I had not read in *Time, Newsweek,* or *U.S. News & World Report* on the plane.

I was exhausted and quickly fell asleep.

My two-hour meeting the next morning with Don Rumsfeld was cordial. Our conversation consisted mostly of talk about the difficult job ahead, my family, the rivalry between the Dallas Cowboys and the Washington Redskins, and the upcoming meeting with the President and members of the Price Commission/Pay Board on Friday, October 22. He indicated that visits the next day with Paul McCracken and Herb Stein of the Council of Economic Advisors might be helpful. (The next day both McCracken and Stein said: "Not much in classical economics seems to be working, why don't you come up with something on your own rather than be prejudiced by our views.")

It seemed incredible—and frightening—that so little had been done in advance. True, the overall organization structure had been designed, and the broad mandates had been stated by the President; but none of the details had been completed in either policies or personnel. There was no staff. No recruiting plan. No policy recommendations. No background papers on prior price control programs. Office spaces were not ready—I was told to find an empty desk somewhere in the CLC's cramped spaces until permanent offices were ready in two weeks. And there was still the Phase I freeze to run, which occupied the attention of the OEP and CLC.

Clearly, if the Phase II price program was to get off the ground, the Price Commission had to move—and move fast!

The assignment of Bob Kagan as my first staff member was a fortunate break. A 33-year old Yale Law School graduate who had returned to Yale to study social sciences, Bob had come to Washington only sixty days earlier to do his dissertation on Phase I. After joining the staff of OEP on a part-time basis, he was assigned to me largely because he was the easiest to spare. Though he lacked experience in Washington, he was intelligent, energetic and dedicated to excellence of results—and he had a clear sense of the importance of the mission. (These characteristics were typical of many of the people added to the staff of the Price Commission throughout its life.)

Bob and I agreed: If we spent our time planning what to do, worrying about Washington protocol, making visits, securing clearance for actions, and collecting data, we would never get the job done in time. The only way to begin the journey—literally—was to put one foot in front of the other. So we walked to the CLC building at 1717 H Street, found a deserted office, secured a Washington telephone directory, borrowed a typewriter, a few pieces of paper, and some pencils.

And so we were finally, actually under way.

The next few days and weeks were kaleidoscopic. There were swearing-in ceremonies . . . a meeting with the President . . . my first White House Press Conference . . . phone calls to friends all over the United States ("Can you come to Washington to help?") . . . meetings with Cabinet members . . . interviews with prospective staff members . . . hurried readings of data and position papers . . . day-long meetings of the Commission followed by long evenings of recruiting . . . stacks of unreturned phone calls . . . bundles of unanswered mail . . . moves into new spaces and above all, the ticking of the clock and the crossed-out blocks of a wall calendar approaching the red-circled date of November 14—the end of the freeze.

The very first meeting of the Price Commission was held on Tuesday, October 26, 1971 in a conference room on the fourth floor of the Old Executive Office building in the White House. The meeting opened with a brief swearing-in ceremony. The press took pictures and silent film. This was followed by a few words from Don Rumsfeld, who repeated the importance and urgency of the task. I recall thinking that I should be more sober, more nervous, more in awe of what was about to begin. Instead, I was excited, impatient with the ceremonial time wasted, anxious to get the agenda covered so I could go back to recruiting, and concerned about coffee and lunch. (My agenda for the day was written at breakfast on the back of my napkin.)

8

Over the preceding weekend, I had body-snatched ten young people who had lived through the freeze at OEP; and two of them, Lou Neeb and Nona Slutsky, joined the seven Commission members for the first meeting. After the press and Rumsfeld left, the nine of us settled down to design a price control program to cover the entire economy. The first week of the Price Commission had arrived.

Where do you begin?

You could go back and examine the policies and the records of prior price control programs in the United States. There were controls during World War II (OPA: Office of Price Administration) and the Korean Conflict (OPS: Office of Price Stabilization). You could examine the extensive history of controls in Europe (often called "income policies" in the post-war period). But time was running out, practically no staff was aboard, my fellow Commissioners were far more experienced professionals in their fields, most had served on governmental commissions, and my knowledge of economics and past price control programs was abysmal.

Instead, the first thing we did was to establish a procedure and style of operation that lasted throughout the program:

- --A quorum consisted of four people.
- --A majority vote prevailed.
- --No alternates were permitted.
- --Some staff were present at all discussions, except a few Executive Sessions.
- --An agenda for each meeting was prepared by the Executive Secretariat and the Chairman.
- --Individual Commissioners could request any information or studies.
- --Policy issues, but not individual cases, were brought before the Commission.
- --Votes would not be taken until it was clear that we could not find a consensus position.
- --Discussions were triggered by "Option Papers" prepared by staff members. The format consisted of:
  a. Issue
  b. Pro and con arguments
  c. Recommendation

The first alternative the commission seriously debated was *extending the freeze* beyond November 14.

It was an appealing thought. It would buy time for us to create better policies. It was simple. Draft No. 1 of proposed PC policies therefore started out:

> Present ceiling prices will continue in effect until changed in accordance with the guidelines in this statement and regulations subsequently issued.

Then we changed our mind.

Lou Neeb presented a paper to the Commission entitled "Legacy of the Freeze" (which is Appendix A of this book), outlining pluses and minuses of the freeze, problem areas needing immediate attention, and transition problems. This was backed up by a 400-page black book containing specific problems of industries, firms, and individuals being squeezed to the point of bankruptcy, shortages, and law suits when freeze prices were set below the costs of production. Spectres of the disappearance of peanut butter, applesauce, lumber, frozen foods, and other commodities were all in the book of "horror stories" of what happens when tight clamps are applied to the economic arteries of a dynamic economy.

That led us to explore some variation of continuing the absolute freeze.

We considered "normalizing" the freeze until January 1, 1972, by permitting relaxation of the rules in specific cases where the worst inequities were occurring. That idea was shelved for the moment to consider what kinds of policies we might apply, whenever the freeze ended.

To scan a variety of alternatives, I distributed to the Commissioners a report that Secretary of Commerce Maurice Stans had given me the previous day. It was a report of about sixty pages, prepared by a small group of distinguished CPAs, outlining their views of all major approaches that could be taken in price controls. These approaches, and combinations of them, proved to be valid assessments throughout Phase II.

Near the end of that day, we were visited by three officials of the Canadian government, headed by John Young, Chairman of the Canadian Prices and Incomes Commission. They were in

Washington observing the effects of our Phase I freeze, and Herb Stein suggested that we might benefit from their experience. We did. It was helpful listening to their prior experiences in Canada with controls, and the alternatives they currently had under study. Many parts of the program we later adopted were similar to some of the policies they considered most feasible for Canadian adoption.

We adjourned at 6:35 P.M.

The Commissioners returned to their hotel rooms, laden with stacks of material for night reading.

Lou and I headed for our CLC offices, planning the agenda for the next day's meeting while we walked and outlining the necessary staff work and position papers that had to be completed and reproduced for the next morning. Upon our arrival we began interviewing people stacked up in our offices, returning "urgent" telephone calls, placing telephone calls to government officials and friends across the nation, giving staff directions, scrounging supplies, space, favors, and following up on our myriads of "action" notes scribbled to ourselves during the day.

That evening ended at 2:30 A.M. . . .

The three days remaining in that first week were spent discussing various control techniques, internal operating procedures, and relationships with other agencies in the Stabilization Program (the CLC, PB, and IRS). The staff presented a helpful matrix during this first week. The matrix (shown below) arrayed various degrees

Level of Price Commission Control

Structure of Control	Location of Control		
	All in Commission	*Mix of Commission and IRS*	*All in IRS*
Severe Controls	1a	1b	1c
Mixed Controls	2a	2b	2c
Voluntary Controls	3a	3b	3c

of control, ranging from voluntary to severe, by (*a*) the Commission only, (*b*) the Commission and the IRS, and (*c*) the IRS alone. This matrix thus enabled us to debate the severity of the price standards and the strength of the enforcement effort, without arguing specific policies and enforcement methods.

If the Commission adopted the severest of controls without the collaboration of the IRS (alternative 1*a*), the fear was that many firms would be thrown into bankruptcy, industrial investments would dry up, and unemployment might increase. At the opposite extreme, if we cooperated with the IRS in imposing moderate controls (alternate 3*c*), the fear was that inflation would continue, public support would erode, and the inflationary "psychology" would not be curbed.

The final consensus centered on 2*b*—the middle ground.

Relations with the CLC were somewhat delicate. Though a CLC representative was present during our early PC meetings he was usually silent, while Lou Neeb and I maintained links through telephone calls and visits with Don Rumsfeld.

The CLC was anxious not to "intrude" on our deliberations because of the "Meany memo," the summary statement extracted from the President at the last minute by George Meany that guaranteed the policy and case independence of the Price Commission and Pay Board from CLC domination. This was Meany's final condition for the AFL-CIO's participation on the Pay Board. The memo stated that while the PC and PB would have case and policy independence, the CLC would have the authority to determine coverage—that is, which areas of the economy would be controlled and which exempted. And within the controlled areas, CLC would also determine classification—that is, what size firms, or "tiers," would be subject to various degrees of control for prenotification, reporting, and surveillance. The Commissioners asked Lou to request the CLC to consult with us as they deliberated on coverage and classification, so that we could make recommendations and also not waste time on areas likely to be decontrolled. (Various messages flowed back and forth all during the program as sectors of industries were included or excluded.)

A series of events concerning the coal industry developed that first week, straining our working relationship with the CLC.

12

When I first met with Rumsfeld the week before, he had handed me a manila envelope, bearing on the outside a red metal bar. (The "red slug," I learned later, meant "for eyes only" and confidential.) It was a two-paragraph informational memo saying that negotiations between the coal companies and the coal unions were stalled; that a strike was likely if no settlement could be reached soon; and that if the strike occurred, there was a danger of heating coal shortages that winter and electrical "brown-outs." (The energy crisis was still a future problem.) No action was requested.

On Tuesday, in the middle of a meeting, a phone call came in from Secretary of Labor Jim Hodgson. Secretary Hodgson wanted the PC to concur in a statement to be issued by the CLC that whatever was agreed upon in the current coal negotiations and approved by the Pay Board, could be passed through as price increases by the PC.

The Commissioners objected to any statement, feeling that we should not commit ourselves in advance and risk a precedent-setting policy. I was asked to inform Secretary Hodgson and Rumsfeld that we would not concur in such a joint statement.

Hodgson was disappointed and requested we review the decision in light of the fact that a strike might result. The next day, the Commissioners reaffirmed their position. Hodgson and Rumsfeld then came to my office to present personally the situation and its dangers, and to be sure that we had considered all aspects. I restated our position and said we would consider each company on a case basis, but only *after* adoption of our standards and *after* the settlement.

On the last day of that first week, Hodgson called again to say that he was going to try to get CLC to issue a statement on its own. When I informed the Commissioners, they unanimously agreed that in the event of such an action by CLC, the PC would issue a statement making it clear that it had not approved any statement guaranteeing the "pass-through" of labor costs from any labor settlement.

Our position was an early assertion of the promised independence, and signalled the beginning of a tension in relationships between the Commission and the Council that lasted throughout

13

Phase II. Though there were attempts to influence our decision in the coal situation, neither Hodgson nor Rumsfeld ever voiced any "threat" or exerted strong pressure. This proved to be a precedent confirming our relative independence and our policy of refusing to decide price approvals in advance of labor settlements.

Late that first week of the life of the Commission, I was informed by Rumsfeld that the PC had to issue a statement of its policies on or before November 13. However, he said, if the Pay Board was not ready by that date the CLC might simply issue a holding statement continuing the freeze for some defined period.

I closed that first week by asking each of the Commissioners to reflect on our discussions, read stacks of materials, and come back on Wednesday of the next week (November 3) with what he/she would consider to be the "perfect grand strategy." In addition, I asked that Lou and the other staff members develop an interim statement on strategy, one that would stress the key concepts of Phase II as "firm, fair, and flexible." I was hoping they could prepare a statement outlining a program without going into great detail, something that could be issued prior to November 13 so that the public could begin to see the direction in which we were moving.

Also we agreed that we really had three mandates, not just one:

– –Bring the inflation rate down to a level of 2 to 3 percent by the end of 1972;
– –Do not impede the recovery of the economy; and
– –Do not build a control program so tightly that when controls are lifted, a post-control explosion of prices would occur.

The next week, each Commissioner came up with a different program.

Two advocated setting maximum price increases across segments of the economy, with inequities handled by an exceptions procedure. Two wanted only straight cost pass-through with no profit margins added. One recommended that only 80 percent of costs be passed through, but with profit margins added. Several worked on systems to capture "windfall profits"—profits generated simply because of actions of the Stabilization Program.

14

For the most part, however, they agreed on some form of modified cost pass-through, a productivity offset, and varied levels of control on profit margins. *A majority favored prolonging the freeze until some "catch-up" in wage, price, and other inequities had occurred, until November 30 or January 1, or until the Pay Board acted.*

The staff's proposal was that all prices remain frozen until increased operating expenses forced a firm's operating profit margin below some base period.

There we were.

Seven Commissioners and a staff—and eight proposals. Some features were common. We were still far apart, however, in some essential features. There were still the messy administrative and conceptual problems of how to *apply* any program to manufacturers, wholesalers, retailers, services, professions, nonprofit organizations, large and small businesses, international trade, and firms operating in multiple sectors.

The sentiment for postponing the end of the freeze grew. We simply needed more time.

And yet we knew also that we needed action to remove growing anxiety and uncertainty. The stock market fell almost daily. Wilson Newman voiced the general feeling: "Look, about the most important thing we can do is to tell the public and business what we're doing and why. If they understand, they might support what we do." Toward the end, we agreed that any program should have an impact on public attitude and be explained as broadly as possible.

During the middle of this second week we met for dinner with a distinguished group of economists and persons experienced with prior price control programs. Attendees were Arthur Burns, Gardner Ackley, Michael DiSalle, Richard Heflebower, Walter Heller, and Dave Grove.

We asked them, "What do you think we should do?" Their answers were as mixed as their varied philosophical differences: Control profit margins; don't control profit margins; control rents; don't control rents; control wholesalers and retailers; don't control retailers; control manufacturers; control large firms; hire twenty thousand people and get tough. We were also advised to work with the Department of Agriculture on the control of food prices—accurately predicted to be our worst problem ahead.

This meeting, while helpful and interesting, added little that was new. It did, however, provide us with some feeling of confidence that this assemblage of experienced and wise elders didn't have any magic answers either. At least, we felt sure that we hadn't overlooked many possibilities. Now it was a matter of creating the best combinations.

If we had any general consensus among ourselves following all previous discussions and the dinner meeting, it was:

- --The basic control policies would involve some cost pass-through, some cost absorption, and a profit margin control;
- --The freeze would be extended to some future date (probably January 1, 1972), but a "Basic Regulation No. 1" would be issued right away to "normalize" the freeze for gross inequities; and
- --Between November 13 and January 1, we would periodically issue "Basic Regulations No. 2, 3," etc. to cover rent, health, and whatever other issues cropped up.

Just before the end of the second week, we were informed by the CLC that the Pay Board expected to reach their decision and make their announcement by November 9. They wanted our announcement by November 10—two days earlier than we had planned!

We summarized on a blackboard our common points essentially as follows:

Sector	Prenotification	Reporting	Monitor	Portion Exempt
Manufacturing	Yes	Yes	Yes	No
Retail	No	Yes	Yes	Yes
Wholesale	No	Yes	Yes	Yes
Services	Yes	Yes	Yes	Yes
Nonprofits	No	No	Yes	Yes
Universities	No	Yes	Yes	Yes
Rent	No	Yes	Yes	Yes
Health	No	Yes	Yes	Yes
Financial	No	Yes	Yes	Yes

The staff was asked to explore options over the weekend to pull together various ideas into some overall scheme, and to develop a first draft of a general policy statement. We tried, in the last hours of our meeting, to come up with a general preamble to such a statement.

> In applying the rules, the Commission intends to hold price increases to 2–3% in order to achieve the President's goal of reducing the inflation rate to that level by the end of 1972.

Several Commissioners urged that we be much more specific. Others felt that 2.5 percent should be stated simply as a goal, nothing more.

With the first glimmer of hardening positions and a possible deadlock, we closed that second week of deliberations.

Also, for the first time, I began to be really worried about making our deadline—November 10.

Here it was Friday, November 5. We had no public statement, no concurrence of specific policies, and some signs of a few strong basic disagreements. We had no legal regulations. And over the coming weekend we had to move the staff (now grown to about fifty) to a new building at 20th and M. On top of everything else, the deadline had been moved up on us by two days—and we still didn't know what the Pay Board had decided.

Continuation of the freeze in some form seemed the only way.

Then over the weekend, on November 7, something happened that crystallized our policy. Bob Kagan, Lou and I had a meeting with Dale Bowen and Al Bowes, who headed up the CPA study group. It turned out to be a significant meeting because (1) they contended controls could work out at the retail level and would be acceptable to retailers; (2) they suggested a gross percentage markup rule for retailers, applied not to individual items, but to aggregates—departments, lines, whole stores—depending on customary practice (this got away from separate ceilings for each can of peas); (3) for manufacturers, they advised increases only if costs went up, and then they should be limited by (*a*) a "cost justification" formula, (*b*) a net profit margin, and (*c*) a flat percentage maximum (e.g. 2.5 percent).

Starting on November 8 these thoughts became the working hypothesis, and were reflected in varying degrees in the later draft policy statements.

The third week of Commission meetings opened with businessmen, consumer group representatives, and labor leaders.

We began with a high-level group of eight dry goods retailers filing into a barren conference room in our new building at 9 A.M. on Monday morning. in our new building. (Commissioners and businessmen alike had difficulties finding the right room in the building still under construction.) The retailers were told that we were down to the eleventh hour, and that while we had not yet firmed up our policies, we were thinking about a method of controlling markup percentages and overall profit margins. No figures were given, no paper was distributed. We said that we wanted their quick reaction to this general approach. The total time of the meeting was one hour.

Reactions were:

– –"It's too tight. We can't live without getting some price relief for increase in general operating expenses."

– –"We can live with it for a short period of time."

– –"Everybody has to make some sacrifices if this is to work. Go ahead."

– –"Whatever you do, announce it quickly and clearly. We need to know!"

The retailers were followed by nine manufacturers at 10 A.M., and eight food retailers at 11 A.M. In each case, we repeated the same message: "Here is only the barest outline of what we are thinking about, what are your reactions?" The answer from each group was essentially not too different: "It sounds fairly reasonable, but please try to be as fair as possible and get your regulations out as soon as possible."

Some persons have wondered why we didn't have more people at these meetings, (or certain specific people), and public announcements. There simply wasn't time. The Commerce Department had been asked late Friday afternoon to assemble the groups in Washington on Monday morning, and it was surprising that they were able to get the people they did. With few exceptions, all were Presidents or Chairmen of the Boards of their firms.

18

We also met with six representatives of consumer groups and three labor representatives that day and the next.

Consumer representatives urged us to be alert to product deterioration, to avoid rationing and shortages, to launch a public education program, and to be tough with business. While they unanimously agreed that prices should be posted for consumers, they were as uncertain as we were as to *what* price should be posted. Rigid ceiling prices that would be easily understood might lead to shortages and/or the frequent updating of millions of items. Flexible prices would change as often as the market changed, but would be confusing to the public. We shared their dilemma.

The three labor spokesmen urged that coverage of the program be extensive, that posting be made mandatory, that we establish a very large, strong enforcement mechanism, that productivity and volume gains should enable us to hold all price increases in the economy to zero percent, and that profits be limited.

The group meetings with business, consumers, and labor were helpful. But time was running out.

During the Monday morning sessions, Lou slipped me a note: "The Pay Board has reached an agreement. They are going for 5.5% announcement tomorrow!"

Our Monday afternoon and evening sessions with the Commissioners now took on an urgent tone. We simply had to come down on some alternatives and end the debates. Our new timetable was now completion of our basic policy on Wednesday, press conference on Thursday, legal regulations to the Federal Register on Friday.

In the middle of it all, telephone men were making installations, carpets were being laid, furniture and files being moved in, personnel streaming in with no desks, supplies, or even places to sit. One person described it as resembling a "replacement-depot of the French Foreign Legion."

That Monday afternoon and early evening, we hammered out some tentative policies for the manufacturing and retailing sectors.

Manufacturing:

— —Product or product line cost control, not total costs.

– –Full cost pass-through, subject to an upper boundary not
   exceeding base period profit margin.
– –Base period—two out of the last three, four, or five years.
– –Productivity and volume increases, to be deducted from
   labor costs.

Retailing and Wholesaling:

– –Average markup by department or customary business unit.
– –Overall firm profit margin limitation.
– –An individual firm-wide price index system to measure over-
   all firm price changes.

Though not complete yet, these tentative policies did constitute
the basis for the final regulations we later adopted.

The next day, Tuesday, at the request of the CLC, we reconsidered our earlier plan to "extend and normalize" the freeze. It was
pretty obvious that if the Pay Board was going to let wage costs
increase right away, we simply could not let prices remain frozen.

For the remainder of Tuesday, we continued to debate the
manufacturing and retailing policies, deciding that all services
would be limited to a flat percentage increase, tentatively selected
at 2.5 percent. As we did not have recommendations from either
the Rent Advisory Board or the Health Services Industry Committee, we decided to leave both of these sectors frozen for the
time being.

While the division of the economy into tier sizes for prenotification, reporting, and surveillance was the responsibility of CLC,
they asked our opinion of where the cutoff levels should be. The
number of employees would be the criteria for the PB; sales levels
for the PC.

But what level—$100 million? $250 million? $500 million? The
higher the cutoff for Tier I, the less the paperwork for prenotification. But less control. Data for making this decision were far from
complete, and we really did not know whether we could catch the
price leaders in various industries at different overall levels.

Pros and cons were being debated by the Commissioners when
I was called out of the room to take a phone call. Before I left,
I personally argued for a $250 million cutoff. By the time I re-
turned, everyone had agreed to $100 million.

20

I recall that I concurred because it would save further debate and we were already behind schedule. That one decision—moving from $250 million to $100 million for prenotification—was to prove later to triple our workload (from about 500 prenotifying firms with $250 million cutoff to 1,500 firms with the $100 million cutoff). CLC approved the recommendation, and later on chided us whenever we reported an increased workload: "You did it to yourselves!"

As the Commission wearily adjourned on Tuesday night, they instructed the staff to come in Wednesday morning with a summarization of all of the policies tentatively agreed to in the past two days. They also asked that the legal staff report on the status of draft regulations following the broad outline of these tentative policies.

Wednesday morning got off to a bad start.

The majority of the legal staff filed into the meeting and said, "It can't be done!" Up to now they had wanted to extend the freeze, but modify the regulations governing it. Now the whole situation was changed. Now they wanted to simply extend the freeze with few if any modifications. They stated flatly that it was simply not possible to write the public legal regulations in time to make the Federal Register on Friday. Some of the policies had not yet been decided on. Others were so loosely worded that it would be a lawyer's nightmare.

In their opinion, any regulations written in that short a period of time would be so inaccurate or vague as to be uninformative and unenforceable—and dangerous for the nation. Their best estimate was that it would take at least a month to produce regulations that were legally sufficient.

There was no alternative in their opinion but to extend the freeze.

The Commission refused to accept that opinion, and we asked them to leave the room. I was tired. It was one of the few times I blew my cool. I told Lou to "get rid of them." He went out and told our Acting Executive Director Dick Feazle to "send them back to their agencies and get somebody who would do the job."

Don Rumsfeld responded to our request for help and sent over several new lawyers by early afternoon. They were told that they had forty-eight hours to produce regulations. The *New York Times* story of November 12 described what followed:

The regulations are being drafted by a team of nine lawyers, besides Mr. Jones and Mr. Kagan. They scurry around, legal pads flying, or sit, locked in antiseptic white conference rooms, on the seventh floor of a new downtown office building here.

After dark, the building, whose only tenants are the fledgling Pay Board and Price Commission, seems eerie, with its bare walls, minimal furniture, and empty corridors.

It is in this setting that the lawyers will, Mr. Jones said, spend all night. They have been borrowed, helter-skelter, from several agencies.

. . ."I don't even know where some of them come from," Mr. Kagan conceded.

"Thank God for Xerox," Mr. Jones said, "I don't know what we'd do without being able to cut and paste quickly. I don't know what they did in World War II."

The lawyer heading up the staff was Bill Blunt from the Department of Commerce. Together with several of our staff—Carleton Jones and Bob Kagan—and lawyers from the IRS, they met the deadline. Blunt and the group slept only two of the forty-eight hours, but the job was done. . . .

The next Commission agenda item produced as much trouble.

We reviewed the staff product of the night, and immediately hit the manufacturing sector policies which produced sharp disagreement:

Manufacturing

Prices charged by manufacturing companies may not be increased over the freeze levels, except as a result of cost increases incurred after November 13, 1971, reduced to reflect productivity gains, and subject to two limitations:

1. Price increases shall not result in an increase in a firm's pretax profit margin (as a percentage of sales) as established during its base period, and
2. Price increases shall not exceed 2.5% per year.

Wilson Newman *strongly* objected.

He felt that such a reference to a 2.5 percent limit at the

individual *firm* level would create confusion and misunderstanding. He argued that it would be virtually impossible for corporations to meet this rigid requirement, given the diversity of our economy and the need for some prices to be higher and some lower. "A figure for an entire economy cannot be turned into a figure for a single firm," he warned.

There was some sentiment for Newman's position, but others argued just as strongly that the 2.5 percent limit was necessary for a strong program, and that cases of inequity had an escape valve through "exceptions." We went back and forth all morning without resolving the issue.

That afternoon, we were visited by Herb Stein—at our request —to give him a last-minute preview and to ask his opinion on the program. Herb agreed with the basic concepts, but questioned the inclusion of the 2.5 percent manufacturing limitation. He argued, as had Wilson, that some prices needed to exceed 2.5 percent and others to be below. He feared that this might be so restrictive that it would cause discontinuation of products, distortions in investments. His comments, on top of Wilson's, caused a surge of new discussion, with the Commission now about evenly divided on a key issue—*just twelve hours prior to the public announcement.*

The argument went on into the early evening hours, degenerating to a point only slightly above personal insults between Commissioners. People were too tired to reason or be very polite, and positions hardened.

An informal poll showed that we were still about evenly divided. Since I no longer favored a rigid 2.5 percent limit, my vote would be the deciding one if we had to take a formal vote. We had hoped to have a unanimous decision, and we were all disappointed.

I adjourned the meeting at midnight, stating that the staff and I would work through the night to prepare a new draft statement and somehow try to incorporate all viewpoints. We would reconvene at nine the next morning. I delayed the press conference announcing our policies, scheduled for 10:30 A.M. next morning to 1:45 P.M.

Though we were all worn out, Lou, Nona Slutsky, and I settled down in the early hours to give it a try. We were joined by Don

Rumsfeld, together with three members of his staff, Marvin Kosters, Dick Cheney, and Earl Rhode. We took the previous draft and chewed our way through it. By 4 A.M., we had a revised draft. We were all groggy and, at the conclusion, three people were asleep in corners of the office.

The Commissioners filed in the next morning.

It was a weary crew. Bill Coleman had even forgotten to put his socks on! He hurriedly sent a secretary out to get a pair.

The compromise draft was on the table. Everyone read it in silence.

The major change was to place the 2.5 percent figure at the beginning of the preamble, stating that this was the goal across the entire economy by the end of 1972. The specific limitation of 2.5 percent for individual manufacturing firms was removed.

Just to be on the safe side, we had also added a catch-all "basket-clause" at the end of the regulation which permitted us to do anything we wanted to do:

Other Considerations

Notwithstanding the foregoing, in making determinations based on the standards set forth in this statement, the Price Commission will take into account whatever factors it considers relevant to an equitable resolution of that case and considers necessary to achieve the overall goal of holding average price increases across the economy to a rate of no more than 2½% per year.

The conversation was now restrained.

Everyone was too tired to argue. Besides, in a few hours, we were to go before national television cameras to announce our policies. Wilson Newman asked me to personally confirm that no individual firm would be subject to a 2.5 percent limitation. I did.

Several others questioned a slightly revised posting policy, but in the end it also remained unchanged. They all agreed that they would unanimously adopt the entire policy statement.

It was now 11:15.

Legal and public relations staff accelerated their already speeded-up world.

The deadline for the Federal Register was twenty-four hours away. Lawyers had been coming in and out all night with tough specific questions: "Did you really mean this?" . . . "What about this situation?" . . . or "Did you realize that this opens up a big loophole?" In many cases, our thinking had been vague. In others, the policy principle was so broad that the lawyers had difficulty in making it sufficiently specific.

The public relations staff practically ripped the final approved draft (Appendix B of this book) out of our hands, and began typing and reproducing it as a press release for the 1:45 P.M. press conference.

During the several weeks previous, the Director of Public Affairs, Bill Helmantoler, had sat in the meetings, reminding us of our need to secure public support and to be clear and specific, and offering estimates of interpretations that the public and the press would place on proposed actions and/or wording. Now he had the job of handling the upcoming press conference at the Treasury Department.

In the car on the way over, Bill gave me a valuable piece of advice. "Tell them," he said, "that you want the public to be completely informed, and that all of your remarks in or out of press conferences are always on the record. Say that you have charged your Public Affairs Director with the job of helping you to inform the American public." It was excellent advice.

The entire Commission (with the exception of Governor Scranton who had an important prior engagement) entered the room and sat before the bewildering array of television cameras, a hornet's nest of clustered microphones and a room absolutely jammed to overflowing with reporters. *So this is the Washington press corps,* I thought.

I was nervous, but also calm, almost numb with fatigue and an over-caffeined system.

I began . . . "This is like a faculty meeting where we are going to debate the question of tenure."

The press conference went well.

Afterward, the Commissioners returned to their homes. The staff hurried back to get ready for the rush of business when we opened our doors on Monday morning. Press releases, regulations, personnel, forms, and a million other things still needed action.

25

At about 9 P.M. that evening, most of us who had been through the sixteen days were so exhausted, we called it quits.

I had dinner with two staff members at a nearby restaurant, and during the meal, I began to shake violently all over from a deep chill. My heart accelerated alarmingly, and I excused myself to go home to the University Club about five blocks away. I recall walking down the street—teeth chattering, heart racing—positive that I was having a heart attack after the stress of these weeks. On one of the street corners was a newspaper in a coin box—

Price Rise Guideline Set at 2½%

What a helluva time, I thought, for the Chairman of the Price Commission to die on the streets!

The desk clerk at the University Club stared at me, for I must have looked like a walking ghost. I took three aspirin, got two blankets out of the chest of drawers, piled my topcoat on top of them, and dropped off to sleep, thinking: "If I do die, it was the most fantastic sixteen days I've ever spent. It was worth it."

In two minutes, I was asleep.

Part two

The environment

What happened after November 13, 1971 was a sequence of rough periods—opening for business, completing the regulations, sweating through the post freeze price bulge—followed by a summer of relative content, and the final lull in fall 1972 as a prelude to Phase III.

I interrupt the narrative of chronological events that followed the sixteen days to help you understand the environment that surrounded these subsequent events:

- --Going public—our efforts to influence the public and their influence on us.
- --The greatest pickup volleyball team in town—how we got organized.
- --The commissioners—a group portrait of who they were, and what they argued about.
- --Making it work—how and why we operated as we did.
- --We steer our own course—life with the Administration and the bureaucracy.

Part Two presents these factors that influenced our thoughts and actions, and shaped our policies in the months that followed. Part Three will pick up again with the events as they developed sequentially.

2

Going public

September 13, 1972

Dear Mr. Grayson:

We are in receipt of your letter and copy of Federal Register in which we are listed as a Tier II company.

Please send us all information and applications and reporting forms to do with this Economic Stabilization Program, as we are not familiar with this operation.

Yours very truly,

HOLLOWAY CONSTRUCTION CO.

You know what you can do with your Price Commission. . . .

ANONYMOUS LETTER

29

Dear Mr. Grayson:

I appreciate your letter to Lucy [inquiring about the increase in her psychiatric counseling fee]. I am afraid that she is a difficult person with whom to communicate. In fact, I feel sorry for the Government official who will have to confront her in person with his complaint.

Kindest regards,

CHARLES M. SCHULZ

We are committed to cooperate fully in the Government's effort to stop inflation. We intend to maintain current prices until they hurt. We feel that the alternative of continuing acceleration of inflation is not a condition that we, our customers, our employees, or our shareholders want to see happen in this country.

TELEGRAM FROM A CORPORATION
November 1971

Dear President Nixon,

May we raise our school journal from two cents to three cents because we need some more dittos to make our magazine. And if we don't have the money we can't make the magazine.

RYE ELEMENTARY SCHOOL
ROOM 25

When I was flying from Dallas to Washington to become Chairman of the Price Commission, an elderly woman came over to me and said, "Mr. Grayson, I've heard you're going up to Washington to take a job. God bless you. You have my prayers."

Sixteen months later I was giving an address before the New York Society of Security Analysts. Two women stormed the podium, screaming and throwing flour over me and the head table.

"You fraud . . . these flour price increases . . . it's a crime . . . get out . . . go home!"

In between these contrasting episodes, I was called a price czar, St. George, King Canute, a pawn of the Administration, a hero, a tool of the big corporations, a sellout, an errand boy, a price-fighter, and a stupid sonofabitch. The program was called a smashing success, a fraud, a shambles, a travesty, an amazingly effective force against inflation, a joke, a snow job, a winner.

The solution to our "economic" problems, we found, embraced much more than what could be found in a textbook.

Anyone who thinks that controlling prices is simply the application of economic principles has a hard lesson to learn about the human factor. Economics, in the first place, is a social science. And, as such, it reflects the basic needs and wants of people—human animals, subject to hope and despair, trust and suspicion, greed and giving, antagonism and cooperation, and much more. Inflation, an economic problem, is particularly thorny because it involves a great many psychological elements—unspoken or spoken "expectations" of what the future holds.

People act to protect themselves by over-saving, by switching to certain types of investments, by building security provisions into labor contracts, by whatever methods they can think of. And each of these steps tends to feed inflation. Continued long enough, the inflation takes off into "hyper-inflation," as in Germany following World War I.

A price control program, therefore, couldn't ignore these expectations. Such a program would necessarily be intertwined with the workings of politics, power, and people; it would be, as someone said, an exercise in "Political economics"—with a capital "P" and a small "e."

Because if people don't believe in the control system, not only do they fail to support it; they violate it. Voluntary compliance was particularly important to us. Staff for local enforcement, the responsibility of the IRS, was limited. Our PC staff was only 600 people. Compare that to 17,000 in the Korean controls and about 60,000 in World War II. And it was peacetime, not war, so the wartime patriotism motive was missing.

During the deliberations of those sixteen days of designing Phase II, we were always saying:

"How will this affect the public attitude?"
"Will this seem credible?"
"What if they see 20 percent increases?"
"Will business believe us if we do that?"
"How could they support that?"
"They'll never believe it."

Posting prices was one example of our awareness of the importance of public opinion and support. We knew that with flexible markup policies, posting changing prices didn't mean much. But we felt that unless we required *some* form of posting, consumers wouldn't believe that there were *any* controls. So we required that "base prices" (static reference prices from which price increases were computed) be visibly posted or available in a book in the store.

As it turned out, few customers ever consulted these base prices, and the policy was largely unsuccessful, except for one not insignificant value. The mere existence of the large signs, "BASE PRICE INFORMATION IS AVAILABLE. . . ," created a psychological "presence" of controls in the store. Later, when we felt that posting should be abandoned, we kept the requirement because of the negative impact of removing the signs.

Considerations of the impact of policies on the public, labor, businessmen, and Congress influenced our rent discussions, health regulations, the statement about the 2.5 percent average price increase, the speed with which we released information, the timing of our policies, the way we treated particular industry price increases (autos, steel), our penchant for holding public hearings, pretty much our overall attitude.

Sure, we based our policies on economics, accounting, law, finance, and management. But we knew that we must also carry the message to the people:

--What we were trying to do and why
--The methods we were using
--How they could help

Above all we had to listen, listen, listen and take actions that would satisfy the public's expectations.

Our very first press release on October 29, 1971 was based on that kind of reasoning.

> Dean C. Jackson Grayson, Chairman of the Price Commission, announced today that the Commission will continue to maintain close contact with the public to benefit from its ideas and suggestions.
>
> If we are to be effective in our efforts to stabilize prices . . . we must remain in tune with the people . . .
>
> "To establish that relationship," Dean Grayson further stated, "the Price Commission wants to hear in writing from as many people as possible who can contribute ideas as to how price increases can be most effectively controlled."

At first, we heard that six boxcars of mail had been received in response. Then one truckload. Then six mailbags. It turned out to be hundreds of letters, but hardly a flood. There weren't many usable suggestions among them, but people at least noted that we "cared."

Thus, from the beginning, we did our best to keep our "publics" in mind, not only to go to them with our story but also to listen to theirs. In a November 1971 staff memo, I said:

> Let's not forget that we need to design an overall strategy for altering, exciting, notifying the average citizen. We are so close to the problem we forget the majority of the people hardly know a Pay Board and Price Commission exist.
>
> 1. Enlist the aid of high school and college students— Boy Scouts, leadership groups.
> 2. Enlist the aid of the League of Women Voters.
> 3. Plan unusual ways to reach the average citizen. Try to contact them while shopping, paying bills, listening to the disc jockeys, etc.
> 4. Organize Speaker's Bureaus.
> 5. Inform college newspapers, small town newspapers.

On November 27, I sent a telegram to the presidents of fifteen hundred firms in Tier I, that said, in part:

> I need your help. If we are going to stop inflation in this country, your company's active participation is vital.

33

In the newspapers these days we read only of the companies that are requesting price increases. We don't read of those that are holding prices down or of those that are reducing prices.

I asked them to state what efforts they were taking to keep price increases down. (I later learned that I had violated a government regulation by not getting the procedure and message cleared.) Of over a thousand respondents, the majority said that they would do their best to hold price increases to zero, or to very small amounts, as long as they could. It was a heartening response.

An analysis of the replies by industrial leaders, however, should have focused our attention more specifically on those sectors warning that they had to have prices increase substantially:

Percent of Increase

Food packaging and sales 23
Utilities 16
RR/Trucking 11
Agricultural Commodities 8

We were struggling with a residual pressure for price increases that had been building up long before our program got under way—a kind of "bulge" that developed after initial price controls had been applied. Price increases of 8, 15, even 25 percent started coming through in some manufacturing areas. Rents and insurance climbed, sometimes 8 or 12 percent or more. New utility rates took effect.

Our price approval list was full of increases (although many of them were reduced by the staff), with few outright denials. "The whole program leaks like a sieve," said one AFL-CIO official. The number and intensity of "anti-program" letters picked up: The ones concerned with food were the most numerous in the beginning, then utilities, insurance, health, rents, leather, taxes, and lumber. (Rents later became number one.)

In January, I was awarded the Consumer Federation of America's Blackout Award of 1972 for "successfully keeping the consumer in the dark."

The Internal Revenue Service was having difficulty in answering questions clearly and consistently from the public. Senator Humphrey attacked the Price Commission on the floor of Congress for inadequate regulations with too many loopholes and inadequate enforcement.

I wasn't about to panic—we knew the bulge would come through, and we knew people would be mad, doubtful about controls, and screaming for action. But neither was I about to sit there and do nothing.

The first thing I did was to get out of the office—and shop. I wanted to check prices myself, to look at the base price sheets, to listen to people talk. I went shopping in Washington quite often, sometimes with the press tagging behind. On one occasion, I had a full shopping basket, the store manager was anxiously trailing behind me and the press was milling about and snapping pictures —and when I turned around to put an item in my basket, I found the basket gone.

Someone had stolen it!

We also started a systematic program of giving out information, feeling the heat, and listening to suggestions in major cities across the nation. We planned trips with forty to fifty staff members to meet businessmen, to talk to local IRS personnel, to shop, to meet with consumer and labor groups, to spend time with the press and editorial boards—in short, to talk and to listen. The press quickly labeled them "road shows."

We started in Washington.

At the end of January, we met with twelve hundred business executives at the Washington Hilton, in cooperation with the U.S. Chamber of Commerce. After some speeches by Secretary Connally and myself, the group broke into special industry panel sessions where the staff could explain our regulations, defend them, and answer questions as best they could.

Preparation for this meeting was extensive. Our staff teams of lawyers, economists, case analysts, industry specialists, and accountants had to work closely together in an interdisciplinary way to get ready for such meetings—an effort that proved to be a tremendous benefit for us all. Groups of such specialists were formed into teams and drilled with some real and hypothetical questions in advance. Quite often the staff didn't know the answer themselves. Executive Director, Bert Lewis, hearing rambling and

35

hedged responses, said, "You sound like a bunch of bureaucrats. When you don't know, tell 'em. Start over."

The risks were high in "exposing" ourselves so openly, but we felt the dividends would be worth it—and we were right. Not only did the businessmen appreciate and sympathize with our problems, but we got to know what they were up against, too.

This same procedure (expanded to include public hearings, shopping tours, meetings with labor and consumer groups—any occasion for meeting the public) constituted the format of the trips as we swung across the country to Dallas, Chicago, Los Angeles, San Francisco, Boston, and Philadelphia.

A lady walked across the hearing room in San Francisco and offered us miniscule portions of food available to a family with a limited budget. Our hearings were picketed. An elderly couple who had sunk their life savings into a rental apartment house told us our rent regulations had about ruined them. Farmers challenged us to get up at 4 A.M. with them and feed the hogs. A lady shopper waved some carrots under my nose in Los Angeles and said, "You can't tell me there are any price controls!" An elderly man in Boston complained, "You're from where? The Price Commission? Can't you get my Social Security up?"

A reporter from the *New York Times* said we were grandstanding. Some reporters felt the whole thing was rigged, or at best, "press agentry." Consumer and labor groups often received us icily or angrily.

Even the Cost of Living Council complained. They said we should stay at home "minding the store" instead of taking some of the key staff out on a boondoggle. But we kept right on because we believed the effect was beneficial, and by late summer of 1972, the CLC was sending some of its own staff out for similar conferences.

We thought it was worth every minute of it.

Doing anything that exposes you to people and to criticism is too often ducked by Washingtonians. Yes, it's risky and uncomfortable. But you need to be shouted at, to be implored, feel hostility, to know the impact that you are having on people. Hiding behind secretaries, sticking to Washington, dispensing "no comments," or only proceeding when you are absolutely sure, leads to isolation and inability to get feedback, creates bad poli-

36

cies, loses public support, and is just not good government. George Reedy, in *The Twilight of the Presidency,* spoke correctly when he complained about the dangers of isolation of the Presidency. His complaint could also be applied to Washington in general.

There is a scene in Tolstoi's *War and Peace,* in which a general is wearily signing execution orders late in the night. A ragged man bursts into the room and pleads for his name to be taken off the list. He is dragged away: The general sighs, crosses the name off the list, and goes on signing.

After our "road shows" and the end of the bulge, the tempo of criticism decreased. Businessmen and the IRS became more aware of the regulations, and our staff became more experienced. Resources were freed to do some preventive, instead of only reactive, public education.

Brochures, films, newspaper mats, teaching kits, and other educational materials were prepared by our Public Affairs Office and distributed as widely as possible. I made films with shoppers, senior citizens, students, and businessmen discussing inflation and the Stabilization Program. An information service was begun to all firms in Tier I to inform and remind them of new regulations, and to send along speeches and statistics.

Though we used all forms of communication, the most important was the press.

God bless 'em. Curse 'em.

The reporters were there the first day I hit Washington. They were always *there.* They were camping on our doorstep, hiding in the garage, riding in the elevators. Our Public Affairs staff were continually calling: "The press wants to know . . ." They were the last to say goodbye when I left, and they maintained more contact with me after I returned to Dallas than the CLC did.

Much has been written about the value, the dangers, the responsibility of the press, what's wrong with the press, and so on. In my view—*the press is a very healthy influence on the democratic process, and their freedom and right of inquiry must be preserved.* For the news media were our earliest and best communication channels. In the early days of Phase II, regulation distribution often followed press releases by several days. Later in the program, reporters performed a different role: they explored the "why" of everything, they criticized and asked good questions that made us think deeper. Sometimes we had to consider policies quicker, stay a little later, or be more precise because of their inquiries. As with preparation for testimony before Congress, preparation for press conferences kept us on our toes.

From the beginning, therefore, I decided to be open with and available to the press. There were times when this policy created difficulties (premature stories, leaks, word-twisting), times when I disliked the policy myself ("For the hundredth time, I don't know when controls are going to end!"), and times when I just plain got tired of talking to newsmen.

And despite all the good that comes from working closely with the press, you are never completely relaxed with a reporter. One single word, or a slight deviation from the way you said something last time, can make headlines.

Jim Rowe, for example, an excellent reporter with the *Washington Post,* asked me in mid–1971 whether I was "very confident" that we would reach our goal by the year end. That question had been asked of me a hundred times, and I was tired of repeating the same old answer.

"Jim," I said with exasperation, "if you mean by 'very confident,' am I *certain?* No, I am not. If you mean my degree of confidence, then I would have to make a probability statement over the range of outcomes. Achievement of the two-to-three percent goal would be on the high side of the probability distribution."

"That's too academic," he said. "You did say you are not confident."

"Not in the sense that I am certain."

The next day in the *Post:*

Grayson Says He Is Not Confident of Reaching Goal

I should have stuck to the script: "I-am-confident-that-we-will-reach-our-goal,-but-I-will-not-make-a-prediction-as-to-when."

That headline wasn't the only one that rankled either, because the press was not always correct or objective. They printed stories,

38

such as several rent stories, that were absolutely false. They spread rumors that were sometimes harmful. They made innuendos in their stories that were a mixture of fact and supposition. And they printed stories when a little more fact-finding would have made it a non-story.

A common activity by the key PC staff was to gather in my office at 7 A.M. to read the *Post, Times, Wall Street Journal,* and *Journal of Commerce* to see how they each covered a story.

"How did they play it?" "Great." "Oh, no!" "Look, they buried the main point in the third paragraph." "Look at this headline!"

As an example, when we reported a new regulation on loss/low profit firms in March 1971, the *Wall Street Journal* headlined it:

Price Panel Tightens Rules for Firms Having Losses or Low Margins

The *Chicago Tribune* said:

Price Commission Eases Rules

When I gave interviews or held press conferences, I could almost tell by the type of question and/or the tone of the questioner, the kind of attitude he/she had about the program and how the story would be slanted. An interview on exactly the same topic would come out two different ways in the *Wall Street Journal* and the *New York Times:* The *Journal* was generally friendlier; the *Times* more antagonistic. And I am not just talking about the editorial pages. The story would be slanted by the choice of the lead and the adjectives used.

One incident during our food public hearings clearly demonstrated that the press does not always "objectively" cover events.

During George Meany's testimony, all three of the big TV networks were present. Strong TV lights blazed in our eyes, and the room was jammed with reporters. As soon as Meany had finished, William P. Gullander of the National Association of Manufacturers came up to follow him.

Out went the lights. Away went most of the reporters.

There was Gullander and the Commission in the relative darkness. Two hardy reporters stayed. Meany made the evening TV news with his remarks. Gullander did not.

If the hearings were to present the "public" with information to air the issues, then at least something about Gullander's point of view should have been mentioned. I am well aware that the news cannot report all events, and that millions of cases of non-rape do not get reported daily. But seldom have I seen such blatant coverage of sensationalism versus comprehensive reporting.

The fact is that in reaching the people, we had to work through—people. (Businessmen—heed the lesson.)

On a lighter side, during the same testimony, Meany accused the PC of permitting the number of matzoh balls in Mrs. Adler's Matzoh Ball Soup to go from four to three without a corresponding price decrease. Meany appeared on national TV news that evening holding up the one-matzoh-ball-short can.

I ordered an immediate check.

We called the manufacturer of Mrs. Adler's shop. "No," he said, "we still put four matzoh balls in every can. Four, not three."

Our staff went out and bought matzoh ball soup from stores all over Washington. We opened all of the thirty cans we bought. Four matzoh balls were in every can. Four, not three!

Meany is seldom wrong, but he was this time, and I wanted as much national news coverage as he had with his accusation.

Next Sunday, I appeared on "Face the Nation." Unknown to the reporters, I brought along a can of Mrs. Adler's soup. At the right moment, I produced the hidden can and held it up, telling the story and stating that there were four—count 'em, four—matzoh balls still in Mrs. Adler's soup.

* * *

SENATOR PROXMIRE: Mr. Grayson, you are violating the law.
CHAIRMAN GRAYSON: Senator, I disagree.

Senator Proxmire was always critical of the PC, and particularly me, for not holding public hearings. The Senator—along with Ralph Nader—believed that the company data on which we based our decisions should be made public, and he hoped that the hearings process would force such data into public view. In his opinion, the law required the airing of such data, and we were violating the law. He was right insofar as the Economic Stabilization Act did indeed call for public hearings. But it also stated two provisos: (1) that the subject should have significant bearing on the economy; and (2) that hearings be held to the "maximum extent feasible."

Well, in the first place, we did hold general hearings in Washington, Chicago, San Francisco, and Boston. We also held specific hearings on food, cement, automobiles, lumber, rent, and utilities. Secondly, those were about all we could hold with the staff and time available—our "maximum feasible extent."

Therefore, we always had hearings on the *basic* issues of price controls, where they affected the general economy or a particular sector, arguing that, yes, this was a matter for public discussion and comment. But we couldn't say the same for confidential company data. This was our position all through Phase II, largely because of specific language in the Economic Stabilization Act which made it a criminal act for me to release data of a "confidential nature." Of course, the argument then hinges around the definition of "confidential," a question that the federal government, Congress, unions, corporations, and consumer groups have battled over for years: "What can a company truly withhold as confidential data, and what must it make available to the public?" This issue becomes critical anytime the government holds hearings for the purpose of making decisions concerning individual companies. If we had held hearings on a specific company price request, we feared that the confidential cost data would have been forced into the public domain, a possibility which worries businessmen as long as a control program lasts.

And the longer controls last, the greater the danger that the program will be used to invade this area of corporate privacy. In fact, the IRS did have access to our files on matters pertaining to the Stabilization Program, and it was clear that observation of such data could not be cleared from the minds of the IRS agents on tax cases.

The Justice Department was denied access to the records because of the possibilities of using such data for anti-trust purposes. We had to maintain a hard policy on this, for, once breached, any precedent could have become the basis for all other federal agencies to view our files "in the public interest."

The whole "secrecy" issue concerned me.

I did want to protect company cost data. But I did not want "secret dealings" with anyone—a member of the White House, Congress, businessmen, press, associations, anyone.

We were already publishing everything we could: names of companies filing, requested price increases, product lines, minutes of PC meetings. We issued press releases furiously. But after viewing one headline, SECRECY CLOAKS PRICE UNIT, I decided to explore opening up all our correspondence and meeting files—whether with businessmen, associations, consumers, or the Congress—to the general public. I wanted to try keeping a telephone log and a personal visit log of everyone contacting the Commission staff for any reason whatsoever—date, caller, time talked, subject covered.

This threw our organization.

We were a wide-open group, but this was going too far! One big hesitation was the publishing of Congressional letters. That frightened a few—"what might the Congress do?" A few of the staff objected in principle, even though they really wanted openness.

But where it eventually fell down was administrative feasibility. We ran a pilot program for several weeks with some staff keeping contact logs, and we simulated the record keeping of the correspondence files. But people forgot to log all of their calls. They forgot to write down the substance of the call. Staff took calls at someone else's desk and subsequently forgot to record them. The staff found that record keeping took time away from analysis of cases.

And what if they forgot to record a call? That might be viewed later as grounds for suspicion of fraud or material for a court suit. And what about letters with some data confidential, and some not?

After much discussion, I abandoned the idea. I'm not sure even now whether it is practicable or worthwhile. The matter of disclosure in the public interest versus confidentiality in the interest of privacy is a matter which probably should be left to the Congress rather than to the discretion of a regulatory agency.

So we went public at the outset and stayed public to the end.

And, even in the successive control programs (Phase III, Freeze II, Phase IV), the public attitude toward prices and controls continued to be a major influence.

42

One of the reasons for continuing controls into Phase III was the feeling that the public would fear complete abandonment of controls. When Phase III failed to stop rapidly escalating prices, the freeze that followed (Freeze II) was due largely to pressures from the public that influenced Congress and the President.

Then, the last Phase—Phase IV—was gradually wound down, *despite even fantastically higher prices,* due to strong public pressure to get out of controls because of distortions, apparent ineffectiveness, and just plain weariness with controls.

Thus, throughout all the various phases of controls, the public has had, as it should, a strong influence on the direction, shape, and duration of controls. It *is* a political economy, and any control program should have an ongoing process of conscious contact with its publics. And the more frequent, open, and extensive it is, the better.

3

The greatest pickup volleyball team in town

I think of the analogy of surf riding. If you can get on top of the swell as it begins and continue riding the crest, you have much less chance of being "wiped out." If the curl breaks over you, you're deluged.

Now is the time to get on top.

Memo from Grayson to Rumsfeld 12/4/71

"Don't fall behind the power curve," advised Gen. George A. Lincoln, Director of the Office of Emergency Preparedness (OEP), the second day I was in Washington. Though I had never heard the term, I knew instinctively what it meant. I had to set up an effective organization quickly—or be hopelessly swamped.

And organization meant *people* and *systems.*

"How did you get started?" "Where did you get your people?" "Who did you turn to?" "How did you organize?" "How did you get going so quickly?" "How did you create such a competent, enthusiastic organization?"—Questions such as these were asked of me almost as often as those about our control policies. I can say, without much disagreement and with a great pride, that the 600-man Commission was one of the most exciting, hard-working, fun, independent, competent, open, adaptable, client-centered organizations that Washington had seen for many years.

All that just doesn't fall together on its own.

Bob Kagan, of course, was the first assigned. Kagan, in turn, recommended Lou Neeb, who joined us the second day. Neeb, in turn, recommended Carleton Jones, a young government lawyer assigned to OEP during the freeze, and Nona Slutsky, a 22-year old "management intern" whose first government job was at OEP during the freeze. They all seemed bright, energetic, quick, and enthusiastic. "Come aboard," I said within minutes after meeting each of them.

Whether what I was doing was legal or procedurally proper, I had no idea. I did not have time to learn government regulations or procedures, nor time to seek clearance for any personnel or administrative actions. November 14 was too close to worry about such matters. In one of my first conversations with Rumsfeld, I told him that I had to go ahead without worrying about the paperwork, and he said "Go—we'll pick up the pieces later." That was a great thing he did for me—with no idea of a budget, and only a vague prediction that about four hundred fifty people would eventually be needed.

At the very first meeting on October 26, the Commissioners were advised of the important and immediate need for staff. Each was requested to jot down the names of as many good people as he could, whether they were in the government or in the private sector.

Everyone I met I asked to suggest names—not just warm bodies, but hard-hitting, quick-moving, results-oriented people. Arnie Weber, Paul McCracken, Herb Stein, Ed Fiedler, Earl Rhode, General Lincoln—they were all asked the inevitable question.

Lou, Bob, and I pursued leads relentlessly, wherever they came from, and pulled people in left and right from other federal agencies and from private industry. I was worrying much less about organizational structure and protocol than about building an effective team. Interviews were therefore held at all hours of the day and night. No hour was sacred.

I personally concentrated on finding people for the top positions, delegating recruitment responsibilities for other positions to Lou and Bob. (Their only restraint was that we didn't need people next week or next month. We needed them *now*. This afternoon or first thing in the morning.)

Someone told me, for example, that one of the best public

relations men in Washington was not in the federal government, but working for American Airlines. I asked the White House telephone operator to locate American's President, George Spater. He was called at 6 A.M. one Saturday morning and hung up, thinking it was a joke when he heard, "This is the White House calling." When I did reach Spater and told him of my desperate need, he said that he would give Bill Helmantoler an immediate leave of absence from American. Helmantoler was working for us the next day.

I had heard in my few days in Washington that the Office of Management and Budget (OMB) was a source of real management talent—a sort of elite corps. I called Frank Carlucci, the Deputy Director, and asked him to give me someone right away as an Acting Executive Director, someone who got results and knew their way around Washington. The best man, he said, is Dick Feezle, and you can have him for six weeks if you guarantee you won't try to keep him. "A deal," I said.

Feezle walked into my office four hours later, spent fifteen minutes with me, and was on the job within the hour. That night, and in subsequent days, Feezle filled my office with organization charts, flow charts on decision procedures, draft budgets, and personnel statements. A flurry of meetings and telephone calls put them into operation. A real take-charge guy and one of the best administrators I've known.

I also called a number of my good friends in business and in universities—either asking them to join me or asking them for leads. Harvard Business School Professor Bob Anthony responded simply by saying, "I'll be down tomorrow." Another was Ted Mills, then living outside of Nice, France—writing and growing grapes. He said, "I'll catch a plane next week."

And so on.

Though we needed a large number of people, we also recognized that it would be a mistake to hire someone simply to make numbers. We turned down a large number of people, quickly and intuitively. I must have interviewed at least twenty good people for the key Executive Director's job before I found exactly the right man—Bert Lewis. Bert was in the Labor Department in Chicago and highly recommended by Feezle. "Labor Department?" people asked, "for a business Commission?" "Why not?" I answered, "he's far and away the best man." He was.

I interviewed about eight people for my personal secretary, each with a fantastic work record. But none was just right, until the ninth one walked in. After ten minutes, I knew she was *the* one—Carolyn Andrade*—one of the most important and best decisions I made, for, in my opinion, a good secretary can add or take away 10 percent of your personal productivity.

Not all of the people were sought out. Some just walked through the door because they heard about the need and thought it would be an exciting place.

Many of the candidates were bright or had great records or special skills, but I waited and waited to find the right person for each absolutely key position: General Counsel, Policy, Congressional Relations, Exceptions . . .

Many of our top staff were found right in Washington in government.

One was Pete Carpenter, then directing an important program for OMB. He came in one evening in the very first week, introduced himself, walked over to a flip chart and proceeded to tell me—without my asking—how to organize the PC. "What an arrogant SOB," I thought. "Who does he think he is?" But he was quick, aggressive, and he didn't know the meaning of the word impossible. He would cause some troubles, I knew, but he was the kind of person you build organizations with.

Another was Don Wortman, a former Controller at the Office of Economic Opportunity (OEO), who had the experience, the drive, and was a good blend of accountant, administrator, and pragmatist. He said he loved to have a job defined, then given his head to let him figure out how to do it. Music to my ears.

There were problems. This quick recruiting style ran against the grain of Civil Service procedures and defied the political checks of top officials, and we had to battle for it. The labyrinth of recruiting regulations and unformed budgets made it very hard to recruit and set salaries for private sector personnel. CLC efforts at control made it clear that we didn't have exactly a free hand.

* *Editor's note:* Subsequently Secretary to the Senate Select Committee on Watergate.

And since the "right of return" to their home agencies was not guaranteed to people we hired at the new salary levels, some were hesitant to leave their steady progression at their home agencies.

While our main focus was on filling the top positions in those first few days, we also needed the lower and middle organizational level people almost as badly. For these, we relied on "detailees," people temporarily transferred from one government agency to another. CLC arranged for the White House to send out personnel "levies" to various agencies, requiring them to provide lists and biographical sketches for a specified number of people with specified skills who would be available to the Stabilization Program for up to ninety days.

I feared that such a forced draft system would draw in people unwanted by the parent agency, but for the majority of cases, my fears were not justified. In situations where they were, we either sent them back home, or the people changed, and we were glad to keep them. Given new challenges, responsibilities, and expectations, many people "awoke"—exercised unused capabilities, generated a new excitement about work, and discovered newfound pride in themselves.

Other help also arrived on the scene in a few weeks. McKinsey & Co., the management consulting firm, had worked with many start-up agencies in Washington and said they would be glad to help us. There wasn't time to work out the full details of the contract with them, or even to explore detailed assignments with them before we wanted them to start work. On November 8, they assigned eight people full time.

Two CPA firms similarly volunteered manpower. "Just let us know if we can be of help and you can have some of our best people for a few weeks to get you over the hurdle." Business firms also volunteered assistance, but we couldn't use them for fear of a conflict-of-interest situation.

Later, we hired some individual consultants and consulting firms to do specialized or comprehensive tasks. This was one way to get quick talent, and a way around budget limits for high-level personnel that we could not attract under the limits of the pay scales for Federal employees.

48

On November 14 we were open for business to the public.

We had what Arnie Weber, the Executive Director of CLC during the freeze, called his group, "the greatest pickup volleyball team in town." People had come from all sectors of government, some from the private sector. Personnel specialists, borrowed from the Civil Service Commission, were processing people with assembly line speed and dispatching them to the point of greatest need, as in a beachhead command post. Many didn't have desks, a telephone, or a typewriter. People were "passing the hat" for lunch money during the next few months while paychecks caught up with them in their new location.

> The office building in downtown Washington is still unfinished, and the top two floors are a jumble of cardboard file boxes. A staff of experts hastily recruited from a variety of government agencies moves through windowless, white-walled rooms; jangling telephones frequently go unanswered.
>
> *New York Times,* November 21, 1971

But we were in business.

On the very first day of operations, I wrote a memorandum to the key staff. "Here are my thoughts of the objectives we should set for the Commission. Let me know what you think of them." They weren't altered much and guided us during Phase II.

Objectives
1. The Commission will be a results-oriented organization with its employees evaluated and rewarded without regard to age, race, seniority, status, religion, sex, or background.
2. The primary goal of the Price Commission is to hold average price increases across the economy to a rate of no more than 2½% per year by the end of 1972. Once the primary goal is achieved, the economy will be decontrolled so as to return it to normal market operations.
3. The Commission will be operated so that it is an exciting and fun place to work, with an emphasis on individual excellence and responsibility.

49

4. The Commission will be organized so that the American people are considered "clients" of this organization and are to be treated with courtesy, helpfulness, and prompt response.
5. The Commission will seek to accomplish its program largely through voluntary compliance of the American people, and not through a large bureaucratic system built on detailed control procedures.
6. The policies, procedures, and daily operation of the Commission will be designed and implemented to achieve price firmness, public acceptance, and fairness.
7. The Commission will seek to achieve price stability through the control of prices. It is not the responsibility or objective of this Commission to operate the program so as to achieve other social or economic effects (e.g., antitrust, pollution control, balance of payments, etc.).

We knew we needed effective people, and a great number of them, but no one really knew—specifically—how many. No one really knew what the job was at first. The only real guideline that the CLC used in estimating numbers was to heed the President's statement, "Their staffs will be small."

Feezle, Acting Executive Director, prepared a "budget in the blind" on November 6, estimating a need of four hundred fulltime and one hundred fifty parttime persons, with a total budget (including all overhead and contracts) of $13 million. CLC allocated us three hundred sixty positions but did not give us authority to appoint people to these permanent slots.

We were in trouble the first week.

Detailees from other government agencies were arriving at a fast rate, but the price request forms were arriving even faster. We needed to accelerate the system.

Don Wortman hit on the idea of asking the other agencies to provide *teams,* instead of random individuals. Rumsfeld agreed that it was a good idea and a letter went from the White House to the heads of major agencies that were likely to have the skills in which we had the shortest supply. The letter read:

> . . . in order to meet these urgent needs, I would like your organization to provide (x) team of auditors, price ana-

lysts to the Price Commission no later than Tuesday, November 16. Each team should consist of a team leader (GS-15) and six analysts plus two secretaries. These teams will be required for 30–45 days and should report to the Price Commission . . .

The plan worked extremely well. The teams came intact, already knowing each other, complete with secretarial support, and ready to work on the first day.

But an analysis of actual workloads in the next few weeks prompted a December 4 memo to Rumsfeld, urging that the staff level be increased by fifty to four hundred seventeen and that administrative delays be overcome. While we did need additional staff, the main objective of the memo was to tackle a serious problem that had emerged between the CLC and PC concerning the authority for administrative decision making: hiring personnel, purchasing of supplies, letting of contracts, reprogramming of budgets, and the like. Apparently, while the "Meany memo" guaranteed the PC autonomy in *policy* decision making, no such autonomy existed regarding *administrative* control.

CLC clearly intended to keep control of all budgetary matters, and most of us with years of administrative experience know the wisdom of the saying, "He who controls the purse calls the shots." Rumsfeld and his staff assured us that this did not mean control over our actions, and that they would process our administrative requests expeditiously. They also argued that it didn't make sense to duplicate staff functions, and that it was more efficient to maintain central personnel, purchasing, accounting, and other routine procedures.

But it was not turning out that way.

Requests for administrative action were delayed or never heard from. No one was even put on the PC payroll until mid-December. On many occasions, Carpenter, or Feezle, would charge into my office, "Are we an agency or are we not!" (Lou didn't ask because he knew.)

McKinsey's report to me on November 27 stated:

> The single most important problem . . . is a lack of clear distinction in the role, responsiblity, and authority of the Commission in relation to the Cost of Living Council . . .

51

Decisions do not seem to be forthcoming from CLC in regard to staffing, support, and other such problems.

In our view, the problem is either a lack of clear-cut understanding of who is responsible; or if indeed CLC is responsible, then it is not providing the leadership at this crucial time.

. . . It seems to us CLC ought to be giving the Price Commission clear authority to do what it considers essential in the way of designing systems, organizing, submitting and defining budget, making staff appointments, and obtaining support.

I pointed these out to Rumsfeld verbally and then wrote a memorandum on December 4, detailing the problems:

I see increasing signs of frustration that border on despair over some administrative delays.

I am not talking about the desire to behave as an independent unit apart from the U.S. Government—but a desire to get decisions rapidly and to exercise decision-making power within the framework of clearly designated authority and within the policies and procedures of the Government.

The question of administrative relationships between CLC and the Price Commission has probably cost more manhours of frustration, delay, and temper flare-ups than any other single item.

On the one side there is the desire to coordinate, and on the other there is the desire to act with speed and independence. Obviously, there will have to be some tradeoffs . . . Continued delay at this time could prove near fatal for the program if we fall behind . . . the power curve.

The memo requested authority to appoint personnel to permanent slots, to sign requisitions for supplies, to sign contracts, to reprogram budgets after approval, and to obtain security for our building. We were hiring and spending, but with no formal approval of the budget from CLC, OMB, the Congress, or anybody else. After extended discussions, CLC did delegate limited authority on many of these items, except for one—and perhaps the most important one—authority to hire personnel. It was a sore point right to the end.

These internal administrative struggles raised irritation levels between the two staffs that were never completely removed.

CLC felt that we were trying to run a separate uncoordinated unit with complete independence from CLC, and we felt that CLC was hobbling us with administrative glue that prevented us from operating with the speed and authority that we felt was necessary to achieve our objectives. Each point of view gave a little. However these different perceptions and internal administrative disagreements lasted right to the end with deleterious effects. In the last six months, they settled down to a kind of administrative detente that permitted cooperation.

Though CLC did raise our permanent ceiling to four hundred fifty, we later found that this was not going to be sufficient. The backlog was growing, despite the fact that we were supplementing the permanent ceiling figure with over two hundred detailees on temporary assignments.

By mid-December, I could see that our recruiting efforts had to be stepped up. We needed a cross-section of quality personnel with business experience. I had set a goal of having a third of the staff recruited from the private sector. A broad mix of skills was also needed: lawyers, economists, statisticians, accountants, financial analysts, systems experts, public relations specialists. More minority members and women had to be included in the total staff. And time, as always, made the situation more urgent: Only forty-five days remained to complete the staffing, when two hundred temporary employees were scheduled to return to their agencies, necessitating replacement with permanent personnel.

Complicating the problem was the fact that this was a temporary agency (it could go out of existence any day), and no employee would be given career status in the government. All appointments were labeled "emergency indefinite," which meant the employee could be terminated immediately and without cause. We had to be extra careful about conflict of interest appointments. Additionally, money was not an enticement: We could not pay any moving expenses; and salary levels were typically below the private sector.

On the other hand, there was the attractiveness of an exciting challenge, a new agency, and a dynamic group of high achievers.

I decided on an unusual strategy.

Calling a firm known for its excellent recruiting program, I asked for one of their best men for three or four months to organize an intensive recruiting program. The man would have to take a leave of absence from the firm and never discuss price request cases with anyone inside the PC that even remotely related to that firm or that industry. The firm agreed. The man, Frank Breth, was in my office the next afternoon.

Through personal referrals, alumni recommended by universities, association referrals, and government contacts, over eight thousand resumés were accumulated. By March 31, 1972, out of four hundred fifty employees, 180 (40 percent) were from the private sectors. That was quite a feat, considering that on Dec. 16, *the Commission was 94 percent government employees.* Besides that, significant increases had occurred in the women and minority categories, particularly at the professional levels. (After finishing this fantastic effort, Breth decided that he did not wish to rejoin his firm and went into the Marine Corps.)

We needed this kind of intensive effort to help us stay up with the turnover of personnel—inevitable under the detailee system —all through Phase II. Once in late March, all of the Price Commission were assembled for a staff event, and I asked those who had joined the Commission staff since January to raise their hands. The count was well over 50 percent. This turnover cost us. Sometimes a staff member would send out a letter to a firm or develop an understanding on a particular request only to find that either (a) we had to transfer the individual to another area within the Commission, or (b) the individual had gone back to the home agency.

It was clear that we needed a larger and more stable staff. But I wasn't sure how to convince the CLC.

At my request on February 1, a task force under Peter Carpenter reviewed our projected staff needs for normal case processing, profit margin analyses, exceptions, policy regulations, systems development, public affairs, etc. In seventy-two hours, working around the clock, they developed an estimate of what we really thought we needed to do the job thoroughly, and the total came to 1,101 people.

That shocked CLC.

They had assumed we were building an empire, and the whole question of administrative control now became a greater sore point between the PC and CLC. I discussed the problem with the Commissioners and they assured me after hearing the needs that they supported the position. I then went to Shultz (at the time, Director of OMB) to explain the request, as OMB would have to review and approve any supplemental funds, if the request were authorized by CLC. I explained that most of these personnel were needed right away, not later, and that we would wind down the numbers in the latter part of the year. He said his answer depended on Rumsfeld's recommendations.

Rumsfeld gave me an opportunity to present the case for an increased staff to the entire CLC one day. I argued strongly, but sensed that while they were sympathetic to the workload, they were fearful that we were trying to enlarge the program, contrary to the President's wishes, and to build a large bureaucracy.

Our request for eleven hundred was denied.

After much jockeying between the PC staffs of CLC and the PC, the PC staff was brought to a level of approximately six hundred, with IRS supplemented by one hundred fifty personnel.

Who was right?

We were *not* trying to build a bureaucracy. We *did* need the staff. I think the program suffered because we did not get sufficient personnel when we needed them, but it didn't fail.

It is true that the Commission, realizing that we were not going to get the requested staff, decided in March to cut back on the quantity and quality of the screening of price requests and to stop some projects that would have allowed for a better monitoring of the economy and analysis of the data accumulating in our files.

Determining the kinds of personnel we needed was one problem. Getting and keeping them was a tougher one. But perhaps the most difficult and most persistent question was organization. In the very early days, people hardly thought of any organizational affiliation. They did what had to be done. Later, there was specialization, but we resisted such identification when it interfered with task accomplishment.

We had an organization chart, but it was very flexible. Created in the first few days of operation, it set forth the principal functions: General Counsel, Public Affairs, Price Policy, Congressional Relations, Administration, Exceptions, Program Operations (case processing). These were altered only slightly at later stages. The most significant characteristic of our structure was the ability to change organizational lines and to tackle problems quickly, regardless of organizational charts and status.

An example was the establishment of the Activation Task Force in the very beginning as an arm of the Executive Director. It provided a pool of manpower not tied to the organizational structure and available for short-notice assignment to critical start-up projects. Also, whenever there was a problem, a project team was quickly assembled from many organizational units, disbanding after completion of the project. Everytime the Commissioners shifted the regulations, it was back to the drawing boards for shifting the emphasis in organizational design, forms, and timetables. In turn, policies were influenced by organizational or resource constraints.

Probably the single greatest organization problem concerned the placement of the General Counsel's office. I had followed general business organizational practice of having the legal department report on an equal basis with all other departments. Such is not typical governmental organization, I was told. I was requested by Dave Slawson, General Counsel, to have his office report on legal matters to the Executive Director for administrative matters, but to the Chairman.

I acknowledged that legal advice and assistance were extremely important, but no more important than advice and assistance from the policy group, Public Affairs, Program Operations, and so on. I was concerned that if I gave one unit higher organizational status than others, it would damage morale and also undercut the authority of the Executive Director.

The issue was brought up, partly, as some of the lawyers admitted, as a matter of prestige, and partly because they wanted three divisions in the Commission—judicial, executive, and legislative. But we repeatedly said no. They didn't like it, but took it in good spirits and remained completely cooperative throughout the program.

As soon as feasible, I set about using the organization structure to delegate authority.

It was clear that I could not read or even scan the thousands of price increase requests that flooded in, review carefully all of the regulations and rulings that flowed with increasing frequency, review exceptions—among many, many other duties. In the beginning, I did study as many individual price increase requests as possible, particularly the big ones in dollar amounts or percentages. And I did read thoroughly all of the initial regulations and those of major impact. But I soon had to delegate.

Initially, I delegated small-size and low-impact cases to the Program Director, Don Wortman, and reserved large ones for my decision after staff study. As soon as Bert Lewis was firmly in place, I made a fairly broad delegation of case approval power to him, and delegated some regulation-signing power to our General Counsel.

Problems developed with this style of management. There were sometimes overlap in functions, some confusion about general assignments, "fuzzed up" organizational lines, some status problems. But we considered these a good trade for the creativity and results we obtained from a more fluid, task force-type approach.

This approach was something I had more or less had in mind even when I first arrived in Washington. I knew that a traditional, bureaucratic type of organization could never do the job. I jotted down some words on one of those early, sleepless nights, that I wanted to characterize the organization:

dynamic	integral
exciting	tough
fair	open
patriotic	hardworking
apolitical	youthful
competent	aware
energetic	alert
quick	action oriented

It may sound odd, but even the working quarters came to be important to the maintenance of spirit. Buildings, particularly government buildings, are often thought of as cubicles to hold people, files, desks, and telephones. But buildings, if thought of as spaces for human interaction, are much more than that. They are organizational variables that can be motivators or depressants. At least that's the way we regarded our spaces at 2000 M Street in Washington.

In the middle of November, I wrote a memo to Bob Cassidy, then Director of Administration:

> Let's find some way to personalize our spaces.
>
> Could we carpet the offices?
>
> Also, the color of white is deadening. When we next repaint, let's allow people to choose their own colors for their spaces—and the more colorful the better.
>
> Some people would like blackboards in their offices—ask them. Also, how about paintings along the corridors or in the offices, preferably abstracts or colorful.
>
> Finally, how about some plants? Let's make the building alive.
>
> And give me a report on the open office landscaping.

The building burst into colors—red, blue, purple, fuchsia, orange. Carpets were put in as many offices as we could afford. Pictures, cartoons, and planning boards hung on all walls.

The last point in the memo—open office landscaping—was something I had asked Cassidy to explore earlier: removing most of the interior building walls and placing partitions and plants to break up the open spaces. The openness encourages interaction, gives an atmosphere of aliveness, and is easier to remodel as changes in the organization occur. For all of these reasons, I thought the concept would be good for the Commission.

It turned out that, while some recent government offices did use this concept, we were denied it because it was felt that the next tenants might not like the idea. The "temporary" organization label inhibited the innovating.

Another difference in our spaces was the Management Briefing Center, a room designed especially for meetings of the Commission staff and for visitors. The Center contained the latest in facilities for presentation of information through modern media techniques. Our former drab Conference Room was remodeled so that we had facilities for large rear screen display of slides, for taping, for showing of films, and for displaying quantities of economic data on six smaller rear screen displays in the back of the room.

At first I was kidded for creating the "Star Trek" room (Jack Anderson did a small column "exposing" it), because it looked glamorous and was of modern design. But the cost was much lower than most people thought, less than $100,000 as compared to centers in business that sometimes run from about $500,000 to $1 million. When presentations were made to Commissioners for decision, the impact of resulting decisions often had an impact on the economy of hundreds of millions. It seemed a small investment to speed up presentations, to make them more succinct, and to present information for simultaneous viewing and discussing.

Rumsfeld's first comment on seeing the Center was, "Do you think the President could schedule a Conference in here?"

I thought that creative, colorful, individual spaces had an impact on people and their effectiveness. The result was noticed by people who frequently remarked that the building reflected the spirit of the people inside it.

Maybe it was the challenge of running the first price control system in peacetime . . . defeating inflation . . . getting an organization up and running as a crash objective . . . being at the top of the news . . . the degree of independence . . . the organization structure . . . the fun around the place . . . the place itself.

Whatever it was—and it was probably a little of all of these— the PC had a tremendous esprit de corps. It wasn't a rah-rah spirit, no one had time for that. It was a pride, a sense of anticipation, a sense of high purpose, a commitment that caused people to put forth effort they didn't know they had—both physically and emotionally.

Staff members started from the very first day putting in hours that were almost medically unbelievable. Weekends and night work were not regarded as unusual at all, and people never grumbled about the overtime, or even thought about it as being "overtime." It was just a job that had to be done.

Families, exercise programs, and outside interests dropped almost to zero as the workload increased and the staff size couldn't increase as quickly. The extra effort came out of their bodies and minds. And it wasn't just the Price Commission, it was also the

Pay Board staff and CLC. And it went on that way until an incident in February rocked us all.

Earl Rhode, Rumsfeld's Deputy who was the linking pin with the PC, was working as hard as any person in the entire Stabilization Program. Harder, if anything. One night in February his wife took his life and hers. No one knows the reasons, but it was suspected by friends who knew them that she was no longer able to tolerate his work habits and preoccupation. Though it may or may not have been the reason, the story was so widely believed that the shock wave rippled throughout the program—not only because we loved and respected Earl, but because everyone suddenly began to think of what we were doing to ourselves and our families. It was too much. There was a noticeable (and desirable) let-up in the cruel price being paid prior to that incident.

Though there was a lessening of the almost total commitment, people still put in long hours, weekends, and nights. It was common to find people there at seven in the morning and ten at night—Saturdays and Sundays.

As time went on into summer and fall of 1972, that pace did slacken a little. Ed Cowan of the *New York Times* reported it on November 11 as "settling down to a hectic routine."

> After a year of administering this country's first peacetime price controls, the Price Commission's staff finds that life is no longer frenzied. It is merely hectic . . .
>
> Even with a computer and established routines, the commission's senior staff members work long hours. They start at 7 A.M. and rarely quit before 7 P.M.
>
> Mr. Neeb, recalling the 9 and 10 P.M. quitting times that prevailed last winter and spring, says the 12-hour day "is not bad."

Another reflection of the loyalty and pride in the organization was the lack of a single known incident of someone "on the take." Think of it.

Here was a group of people, assembled in a hurry from inside and outside the government, sometimes very young, in control of the prices of giant firms, making decisions (or influencing them) on the order of millions of dollars, and often dealing with Presidents and Chairmen of the Boards. I would have given anyone

60

odds that we would have had several of the staff taking advantage of their power and information for personal gain.

There were only two suspicious instances reported. Each was thoroughly checked out by the FBI and proved groundless. Yes, there *could* have been some instances which were never detected. We'll never know. But I personally don't believe there were *any*. This was due, not to a tight external police-type control system, but to an internalized self-policing control that derived from commitment to the organization.

Honest and resourceful people, all of them, grappling with a quicksilver enemy.

What did I learn about organizations and people? I wrote these notes in October, 1972.

1. New Organizations are much easier to adapt to fast changing circumstances and high task demands because . . .
   a. the new organization does not have a past history of tradition to conquer;
   b. people who enter are not afraid of the unknown whereas a person "in place" will often hate to enter an unknown area;
   c. people who are high achievers are attracted to an obviously demanding task;
   d. the crises atmosphere makes people forget status, seniority, old arguments, roles, etc.
2. People can respond to much higher task demands than most organizations ask for. There is more unused reservoir of energy, innovation, commitment than most organizations demand—and get.
3. Too much is preached about seeking "order" in organizations. Right away people seek to establish rules, regulations, and to decrease random variables from invading set procedures.
   It is true that any organization must seek to establish some routine methods for handling variables. But one must resist too much or too quick an adjustment away from an *ad hoc* or "crises" type organization toward a rigid, orderly, neat mechanism that will tend to resist change. It may function well bureaucratically, but lose its adaptability and take the

heart and fun right out of a spontaneous, task response organization.

4. Jobs can be done in an amazingly shorter period of time than most managers think. People tend to stretch out the task deadlines to weeks, even months, in some organizations (particularly universities). If people are given very high task demands, with very short deadlines that they know are firm—and particularly if they know that they will be evaluated on how they respond—then people can generally "do the impossible."

   All through wars we find examples of people responding to such challenges—"we do the impossible here"—and in peacetime there is no reason we can't do the same.

5. The entropy in organizations, contrary to what most people believe, is not toward disorganization and decay in organizations. It is toward order and hat takes energy.

On November 14, 1972, the PC staff was celebrating their first birthday. I thanked them not only for their long hours, commitment, competency, and everything they had given. I also thanked them for demonstrating that the goals I had envisioned long ago for an ideal organization were not an "impossible dream."

- --To create an organization where the individual is the focus.
- --To live in, to grow in, self-renewing forms of organization, in temporary systems.
- --To be entrepreneurial and achievement-oriented.
- --To be change agents.
- --To focus on results, not procedures.
- --To live with ambiguity and uncertainty.
- --To help people manage their own learning activities.
- --To develop innovation as an organizational norm.
- --To make people aware of their changing assumptions about values, man, and his organization.
- --To direct people's attention more away from yesterday and more toward tomorrow.
- --To have fun in organizations.

They had "made it happen."

4

The Commissioners:
A group portrait

*Each commissioner must have and gets time to com-
ment on issues at hand; disagreements may occur, but they
have never come close to anger or to bruising encounters;
staff members come and go, reporting on price requests
and making recommendations; the austere, windowless
conference room fills with smoke and the U-shaped table
acquires a chain of paper coffee cups; night falls, everyone
aches.*

New York Post *(December 18, 1971)*

For one who never sat in on the Commission meeting, Helen
Dudar of the *New York Post* did a pretty good job of reporting.
That's about how it was.

There were seven of us: Six were part-time, and I was full-time.
Together we constituted a kind of "economic jury," seven
ordinary people pulled from private life to take responsibility for
setting price levels for the major portion of the economy. We were
not "Twelve Angry Men," but "Seven Individuals"—sometimes
scared, often awed, by the enormity of what we were up to, and
frequently surprised by what we hath wrought. But always determined.

It was a balanced group, each member a strong individual,
reflecting (as much as possible) different viewpoints, skills, and
personalities. Only a few of the Commissioners knew each other

63

prior to being named. I knew none of them. The original seven were:

Bill Coleman—a practicing attorney in the Philadelphia law firm of Dilworth, Paxson, Kalish, Levy and Coleman, and President of the NAACP Legal Defense and Educational Fund.

Legal equalizer. Praetor. Social lantern of concern for people, not figures; for justice, not form; for have-nots and haves.

Robert Lanzilotti—Dean of the College of Business and Professor of Economics, University of Florida.

Lover of good questions. Keeper of the Phillips curve. Academic activist. Economic guru. Dart maker. Hit man.

J. Wilson Newman—Chairman of the Finance Committee, Dunn and Bradstreet; Director of the National Bureau of Economic Research.

Gentleman and Virginia ham. Witty, acidic, gracious, independent. Phrase maker and upstager. Candide, indeed. Cyrano of integrity, knight errant.

John Queenan—retired managing partner of the accounting firm of Haskins & Sells; past President of the American Institute of CPAs.

Wise beyond recollection. Practical, human accountant. Book value high. Goodwill undepreciated.

Bill Scranton—former Governor of Pennsylvania, candidate for the Republican nomination for Presidency in 1964, and Chairman of several Presidential Commissions.

Hewer of the golden mean. Lightning rod for angry debate. Wise in the political soup. Fun. Washington-worldly, not weary. Social elasticity advisor. Political consigliori. Conversation oxygenator.

Marina Whitman—Professor of Economics at the University of Pittsburgh.

Searcher for levers. Newspaper devourer. Economic Portia. Full employment of mind.

When we lost Marina Whitman to the Council of Economic Advisors, she was replaced in May by Mary Hamilton.

Mary Hamilton—Professor of Finance, School of Business, Loyola University.

Worldly philosopher. Considered contributor. Economic medicine woman. Merope of the Pleiades. Macro thinker with micro concern.

The other six Commissioners were paid only for the days they worked. All had other jobs and personal financial interests, but under a special provision of the Act passed by Congress, they were not required to divest themselves of these interests. The assumption was that qualified people could not be secured if complete divestiture was required for a part-time activity. Despite this Congressional provision, the Commissioners were extremely sensitive to criticism on possible conflict of interest situations. Several resigned their positions on boards of directors of major corporations, even though they did not have to. Each Commissioner filed a full statement of personal financial interests with the Civil Service Commission and with me. Commissioners did not decide on individual company cases, nor did they intervene during deliberations. Whenever a policy discussion concerned a sector of the economy in which a Commissioner or any family member had any personal connection whatsoever, either I was asked for a ruling on whether that Commissioner should discuss or vote on the issue, or the person declined to participate voluntarily.

Commissioners were, therefore, angered when the press or critics accused them of a "business bias," or charged the Commission with not having a "consumer" point of view. Not only did members feel they had leaned over backward to keep from having a conflict of business interest, but they also were extra cautious about giving business special privileges or considerations above other groups in society. And each felt, like other members of society, that he was also a consumer.

Before our "Star Trek" room had been set up, our meetings were held in a small conference room, described by the press as an "austere, windowless" space. It inspired no one, was bereft of any facilities for audio-visual presentations, and so small that only a few staff could be present. Books, newspapers, stacks of papers, cookies, coffee cups and a paper-hole punch typically covered the top of the U-shaped tables.

Visitors were occasionally invited to the meetings. We invited most of the top CLC officials to spend an hour or so with us to broadly discuss the program—Rumsfeld, Burns, Stein, McCracken, Connally, Shultz, and Butz. In addition, we brought in outside opinion poll experts Lou Harris and Al Sindlinger. Such sessions were purposefully kept general, and never concerned themselves with a specific policy decision before us.

It was in this setting that the policies of the Commission were hammered out in long, often tiring, but never dull sessions. As might be expected in such circumstances, there were periods of personal stress, strain, and even outright hostility.

Tempers sometimes flared. One Commissioner in the heat of an argument said he might have to consider resignation. There were times when one Commissioner came to the defense of another when he had just strongly attacked him on the preceding issue. There was a remarkably high degree of respect for differences of opinion, and a closing of ranks in the face of adversity or crisis. The dynamics of meetings were hardly ever the same. Sometimes we would be harmonious, other days bickering.

In periods of tension and deadlock, Bill Scranton would often come forward as the "honest broker." With his congressional and political experience he had the ability to find a compromise or suggest a way out of the deadlock.

Lou and I purposely altered the seating arrangements for some meetings, rearranging them to cool off some volatile personal relationships, or to have people with differing viewpoints sitting side by side.

By February of 1972, the press was commenting that the Commissioners had divided into two major groups. There was the supposed "softliners," made up of the two members with business-oriented backgrounds, John Queenan and Wilson Newman, augmented on certain issues by Marina Whitman. The "hardliners" were supposedly Bill Coleman and Bob Lanzilotti, plus Bill Scranton on certain issues. I was labeled the swing vote, swinging both hard and soft.

Though the press descriptions were not far off base, they certainly did not fit all situations.

The hardliner and softliner goups did not have consistent membership. For example, on some issues, Wilson Newman would be more of a "hardliner" when he felt that an industry was able to stand some economic pressures; while Bob Lanzilotti felt "softer" in that it was unfair to differentiate between industries on the application of policies. Near the end of the program Lanzilotti ended up in favor of dropping or drastically changing the profit margin rule, while Newman and Queenan argued that this rule was a key to restraint of prices. Bill Coleman might be "hard" in wanting to hold down rent increases, but "soft" when the proposed action might retroactively violate contracts between landlords and tenants. I was in favor of keeping the markup on costs (soft), but strongly in favor of rigid, quarter-by-quarter enforcement of the profit margin rule (hard).

The point is simply that Commissioners did not become trapped in a role perception or a consistent bias when they were shown opposing arguments or when the conditions changed.

Then in February of 1972, Marina Whitman left to join the staff of the Council of Economic Advisors. With her departure, the previously repeated vote of four to three in favor of keeping the cost-plus-profit markup rule, was reduced to an even split. Thus, the issue was deadlocked until the new Commissioner was on board and voted.

A long time elapsed before the appointment was made, the rumor being that the Administration was searching for a person known to be sympathetic to keeping the markups on. I do not know if the rumor was true—I was consulted only at the beginning of the search when I was asked to provide a list of candidates. The final selection, Mary Hamilton, was not on my list. I had never known her.

I informed her immediately of as much background as I could on all of our policies, and particularly on this one particular controversial policy. I asked that she spend time with Bill Coleman and Bob Lanzilotti, and then Wilson Newman and John Queenan to hear the strongest advocates of each position. Then she read all background staff papers and talked to various members of the staff.

At the very first Commission meeting that Mary attended after her confirmation in May, the usual motion was made.

"Mr. Chairman," said Bill Coleman, "I move that we remove the addition of markups to costs as a justification for price increases."

Mary asked to be the last to vote.

We went around the room. The vote was still three to three.

"Mary?" I asked. She paused.

Neither I nor anyone else at the table had any idea of how she would vote. If she said "yes," the whole program would shift drastically.

"No," she said.

I breathed a sigh of relief. It was, in my opinion, a completely independent vote of personal convictions after hearing both sides. It typified the intelligent and conscientious manner in which the Commissioners made their decisions.

5

Making it work

Many a theory and decision model was suggested to us. But when we raised objections about implementation, those making the suggestions would simply respond, "Oh, that's just an operational problem."

Just an operational problem.

I have often asked myself whether we concentrated too much on such problems, whether we might have done better by using management science models. And my honest answer is *no.* At the Price Commission we operated—I think fairly successfully—without getting the data we "should" have had, without using any explicit decision tools, without formally consulting a management scientist, and without building models of our decision-making process. Since I am by vocation an academic, I am not especially proud of these facts. I am a member, and an intellectually loyal member, of ORSA, TIMS, and AIDS.* I believe in the general direction in which these organizations want to go, but at the Commission we faced problems of execution in which hours and sometimes minutes counted.

* Operational Research Society of America, The Institute of Management Science, and American Institute of Decision Sciences.

Using models would have slowed decision making and frustrated most of our personnel. Given the fact that most models omit the factors of time, data, accessibility, people, power, and politics, they simply would not have paid off in proportion to the required input of effort.

Consider the severity of the demands—seemingly impossible tasks and directives:

- --Create and staff a fully competent organization.
- --Work out regulations worthy to bear the force of law.
- --Keep the program consistent with policies established in Phase I and the current state of the economy.
- --Work in conjunction with the Pay Board, the Internal Revenue Service, and the Cost of Living Council.
- --Control the prices of hundreds of millions of articles and commodities in the world's largest economy.
- --Do not inhibit the recovery of the economy.
- --Do not build a post-control bubble.
- --Do all of this with a staff of 600.
- --Have the entire operation functioning in sixteen days.

It would have been easy to say "nuts," for a number of reasons. First of all, nobody could begin to do the job of price control with 600 people, even with 3,000 IRS agents helping out with enforcement. It took 60,000 people to handle the assignment during World War II and 16,000 in the Korean War. Second, doing the right kind of job required a thoroughgoing study of what was involved—the resources and personnel necessary, the most efficient way of actually controlling prices, and the best way of working in concert with other federal agencies, as well as the accumulation of data on the economy and the testing of various models. Finally, the sixteen-day period was too short: It wasn't enough time to even appoint a commission, much less to build, organize, and house the proper staff, promulgate regulations, and get it all working.

But under the circumstances, pointing out what could *not* be done would have served no constructive purpose. My alternative was clear. I started bringing in staff, renting quarters, creating our organization, framing regulations, and developing a modus operandi. Within sixteen days, the staff was at work accepting re-

70

quests for price increases. In some cases they were eight to an office or four to a phone; many put in twenty-hour days. But they were working.

I cite their achievement not to boast. Our record grew not out of extraordinary abilities so much as out of an orientation and inclination toward *action.*

For action—quick response on a very practical level—was our only course. A simple operational policy, by reason of its relative inflexibility, was obviously going to lead to inequities—to complications. Time and time again, the creation and revision of policies were constrained—even prohibited—by administrative, operational, or enforcement limitations. Developing one regulation for the entire economy, beyond a simple freeze order, is extremely difficult. One industry differs from another. One company differs from another. And even within a single company, you cannot duck complications.

Take, for example, just *some* of the accounting problems involved in designing forms, monitoring, and legal enforcement:

Defining sales, costs, product line, or a transaction	By-product costs
	Transfer pricing
	Base period determination
Fifo or Lifo inventory	Cost reach-back date
Seasonal variations	Systems changes in a firm
Mergers/acquisitions	Joint ventures
Divestitures	Treatment of variances
Export sales	Class of purchaser
Promotional allowances	Foreign subsidiaries
Productivity/volume	Customer products
Long-term interest	

It was for these reasons that the Commissioners decided from the beginning to make the program as simple as was feasible, despite the inequities, and to operate as much as possible within existing business records and practices, realizing some firms might "get away" with some things.

Some people may be horrified. But consider the alternatives. To overcome the problem of inequities, we could have created far more complex regulations to treat more specialized and different situations. As it was, the number of pages containing our regulations grew from four at the outset, to over three thousand at the end. Chester Bowles, Administrator of the OPA (Office of Price Administration) program in World War II, wrote that they ended up with six pages of fine legal print for the control of fruitcake prices. And if we had not decided to operate within existing business practices, we would have had to specify standardized bookkeeping systems for whole industries, adding not only to the cost of products but also disrupting many customary practices.

Heavy reliance on voluntary cooperation and customary business practices did *not* mean, however, that we did not monitor and audit firms, nor that there were no mandatory compliance checks and no follow-through.

The IRS did that job for us, becoming the enforcement arm of the Stabilization Program. Making approximately one million compliance checks during the Phase I freeze, they found about a 95 percent voluntary compliance rate. This finding supported the conclusion that they could police Phase II as well. Also, selecting IRS personnel permitted the government to rely on an existing agency for compliance operations, instead of taking on new people. When the program ended, they could go back to their old duties.

The IRS staff was eager to do a good job, and they did. They had difficulty adapting at first, because they were used to a different mode and style of operation that was slower, less flexible, and more detailed. Also, as time went on, they tended to interpret our broad general policies more specifically because they felt that they had to in order to get evidence that would stand up in a court of law.

For instance, one of the regulations stated that a firm could apply its "customary initial percentage markup" on invoice costs to determine selling price. If a grocery store customarily "marked up" peas by 20 percent in the past, then they must mark up peas by 20 percent under controls.

Simple?

It wasn't.

Does the regulation apply on a firm-wide basis (such as, for all Kroger stores or for individual stores)? Does it apply to departments or to individual items within departments (the entire meat section or sirloins, rib eyes, T-bones, and so on)? Does it apply to all products by general categories or by brand (all peas sold, or Del Monte peas, Libby's peas, and others)?

"Whatever your customary business practice was!"

But it still wasn't that easy.

What *was* the customary business practice in the base period? For one thing, the practice might have been changed since the base period. Could we force a firm to go back to a discarded system? Or perhaps the firm has a mixed pricing system—some items are priced on an "aggregate" markup (items grouped together, such as the canned vegetables department), and some are priced on an "item-by-item" basis (such as Del Monte peas). Some food chains, it turned out, don't set prices at all; instead, store managers are given gross margin targets, and there is no control over individual products.

Exasperated IRS agents, under pressure from the public, the CLC, and their bosses, searched for some way to document whatever system was used in the past and then to check in detail against that system. And for the reasons just stated, that wasn't easy. Unless the firm was on a detailed item-by-item pricing system, it was difficult to pinpoint an exact violation. But try, as an agent, to explain this to your superiors and to the complaining public. Toward the end of Phase II, therefore, the IRS tried to push firms more and more toward this kind of pricing system, thus angering businessmen who felt that our "customary business practices" policy was being disregarded.

This is a good illustration of how a control program can gradually remove degrees of freedom in order to achieve standardization and enforcement, thereby altering the normal patterns of business practice. Slowly the economy shapes itself around the convenience of the government rather than the influences of the market. Innovation is naturally suppressed because of its inherent "difference."

Living with this policy also cost us in terms of our credibility with consumer and labor groups. Just before Phase II was launched, the AFL-CIO volunteered a hundred thousand workers to go into the field and check prices for compliance.

Our program completely frustrated them.

How could they check for compliance when the legal price floated with the retailer's invoice cost? If we had adopted "ceiling prices"—fixed prices—they could have done the checking. But under our system the IRS had to do it, and it wasn't easy even for them. I explained this in my press conference on November 11 when Phase II was announced, because we did foresee a problem. Few people heard me, and those who did didn't like what I said.

Sure, some firms did "stretch the rules" for their own benefit. "Generally accepted accounting principles and practices applied consistently" means different things to different people, with or without a control system. And I am sure that there were some outright cheaters. Rules are stretched and broken in our tax system too.

But I believe these unintentional and intentional violations were at a minimum. The intensive compliance checks by the IRS back up this statement; they found a very high degree of compliance, even when they had specific regulations on which there was no room for interpretation.

Looking back at all the problems as they developed, I would still keep the basic notion of "customary business practices" as the underpinning of the program. And I would still rely, most of all, on "voluntary compliance."

Some of the specific regulations, perhaps, could have been designed differently to implement those principles. But to impose stricter external controls on our business system would have been to alter it unfavorably. Besides, such controls would have required a force in Washington and in the field in the tens of thousands. I guess that if we had gone with a rigid, highly enforceable program, we would have needed a hundred thousand people as a minimum. And that figure is probably low.

And then there was the apparently simple matter of the forms.

No matter how quickly the theoretical debate is running along, sooner or later it comes to a skidding halt when it has to be spelled out in a form or in the accompanying instructions.

Should export sales be included in the definition of sales? And which export sales—sales of subsidiaries partly owned, totally owned, or 47.4 percent owned? What about export sales of subsidiaries not located in the U.S., but totally owned, partly owned, or jointly owned? Is the firm-wide profit margin control to apply to profits on just controlled items or to all items?

The forms designers were going through the same unmitigated hell as our lawyers. Just as they thought they had the final design, we altered something. Not surprisingly, the first printing of the forms was wrong: Somewhere in a dusty corner in Washington there are a hundred thousand PC–1 forms (our initial price request form)—with *one* wrong line.

To our surprise, it was also incredibly difficult to create lists of Tier I and Tier II firms. We assumed that all we had to do was ask for a list of such firms and their addresses from an agency of the government or from Wall Street. We should have realized it wouldn't be that easy. And when we finally did obtain and use our lists, we turned up a CIA cover firm!

Even when the form was ready, clearance procedures held us up. Forms clearance in the federal government is handled by the OMB. Any new form has to go through a process involving draft publication, a waiting period, opportunity for written and verbal comment, and final adoption. It was a slow process, but an important one if we were to face up to those nasty accounting questions.

But our very first issuance in November of 1971 was—naturally —in a hurry, and we didn't have time for the usual procedure. After a call to the top, we obtained a pro forma clearance from a worried OMB official in less than fifteen minutes.

No sooner were the forms out, they started flooding back in again. And then there were the nitty-gritty problems of handling the forms as they arrived at the PC.

They had to be legally logged in and classified for routing to the proper unit within the Commission. Different forms sometimes arrived stapled together, and were thus misrouted. Forms were defaced. Forms came in with the wrong data on them. Some had to be returned to the filer for additional data, or because of illegible entries. This cycle sometimes went through two or three loops, stacking up reams and reams of forms and their chasing sheets. This accumulation not only created a decision problem, but also necessitated a filing, tracking, and locating process. In many cases, the anticipated accumulation of paper was enough to preclude further discussion on a proposal. For example, we voted to put a 3 percent ceiling on price increases in the services industry, but we reversed ourselves for two reasons: One, there are millions of service firms, and the IRS said they didn't think they could monitor and enforce the regulation; two, our staff advised us they couldn't create forms to secure the data in the form proper for analysis and decision making. In another case, we recontrolled the lumber industry and moved a large portion of it into Tier I because we suspected violations. Then, because of the paper avalanche, we had to back off.

For a while back in November 1971, we considered operating the entire control program as an exceptions procedure. To illustrate, someone suggested we limit all price increases to 1 percent across the economy and then handle all the inequities and distortions as exceptions. Had we done this, or anything like it, we would have had better than nine out of every ten people on our staff working in the Exceptions Division. And anyone who has ever handled even *one* real exceptions case knows the detail that must be read and the myriad particular circumstances that make a case "different." He must be objective in considering the strong plea for equity and impassive to the pressures from advocates and opponents in Congress and in associations. His is a subjective job, requiring extensive training in analysis and exposing the business system to highly inconsistent actions.

So we *had* to rely on a business-as-usual posture and on the ultimate honesty of the American business man. Thrashing out every alternative, kicking around every proposal, talking until the words ran out—we inevitably came back to the same question: Can we get the cooperation of the public?

I think we did.

How well we curbed inflation, history will have to decide. But we could have done no more without altering the orientation of the economy and in the end being defeated . . . by the public.

6

We steer our own course

Our organization did not exist in a vacuum. Interactions with the people and the press naturally influenced its effectiveness. The same is true of its interactions with other parts of the Stabilization Program.

Much has already been said, for instance, about the relationship between the CLC and the Commission. Our difficulties arose primarily from our divergent perceptions of the PC's authority level. Besides our running battle over administrative matters, there were grating differences in our operating styles. Coming from a variety of career experiences—including newspaper reporting, academic life, and farming—I was more accustomed to openness, independent thought, and quick action. When reporters asked me a question, I answered openly if I possibly could. I was available, and I admitted mistakes or a lack of information. This style tended to permeate the organization. The CLC, on the other hand, was more closed. They were more fearful of quick decisions, of saying too much, of being too open, of being criticized, and of putting anything on paper that didn't have to be written out.

In a nutshell, this contrast characterized the relations between Rumsfeld and me. On a personal level, we got along all during the program, right to the end. He was articulate and personable. He smiled, joked a lot, and helped me in a number of ways. He sincerely wanted to reduce the rate of inflation—a mixture of a genuine desire to help the country and his own career.

But our working relationship was not that of warm colleagues. In the beginning, we talked often, traded information, saw one another socially on occasions, admitted doubts, and so on. As the problems steadily grew, Rumsfeld become more distant. Our contracts decreased in frequency and openness. From his own statements, I got the impression he felt we at the PC were trying to grab for power, to woo the press, to grandstand.

When we discussed problems with the press, he thought of our openness as being destructive to the program or even accusative of him personally. Assuming that we would talk to the press too freely (and he would cite instances where he assumed that some of our people were the source of leaks or unfavorable stories), he gradually began to withhold information about what he or the entire CLC was thinking. When the Commissioners would consider taking drastic action, he was worried that we were overreacting, while we were concerned that CLC was not acting at all.

This increasing distance between us diminished our effectiveness. It was not an overt kind of antagonism, but a kind of irritation and distance that kept us from freely working together. I regret it. But once into it, we remained at the formally polite level until the end of the program. We parted with a cordial note.

The differences were sensed even on the staff level. There was the inevitable friction. The infighting was destructive and full of gamesmanship. We said to ourselves—and I'm sure the CLC did too—"this doesn't make sense for the country." We'd have "peaceful coexistence" talks—and then find ourselves right back in the old rut when the CLC would hold up a personnel appointment over something trivial, or if they felt we "leaked" something to the press.

As time went on, the "independence" of the PC slowly eroded. A couple of incidents caused shifts in our relationships. One was when the CLC staff attempted to get Bert Lewis to change a decision on a stevedoring firm—the first time they ever clearly suggested that they would like a decision to go a certain way. In fact, it was the only time I was ever personally requested by

78

anyone to take any specific action surrounding a decision.

The longshoremen had signed a contract with the stevedoring companies, and the Pay Board had cut the contract. But the remainder was still high, well above 5.5 percent. The stevedoring companies had been allowed to pass through the 5.5 percent increase, plus fringes of 0.7 percent for a total of 6.2 percent. But they wanted to pass through *all* their labor costs. It was the same argument as that of the coal companies: One government agency had "approved" the contract, another should honor it.

Our position was also the same: We would not pass it through.

Rumsfeld and Shultz asked me to breakfast at the White House to see if the Commission couldn't let the industry be an "exception," and pass through more than 5.5 percent. My answer was that we couldn't do it. How could we treat the stevedoring companies differently? Because of their power? Then where were our regulations after that? Who would believe us?

Rumsfeld and Shultz pointed out that this might precipitate a dock strike (the stevedoring companies said that they would shut down rather than reflect only 6.2 percent in their prices), and we had just gotten over a long strike in 1971.

I repeated our position, but said that the only way out was if the CLC decided to take the firms out from under our control by exempting them. The CLC decided to do this, and a specific limited exemption was granted, allowing the stevedoring firms to pass through all labor costs, but otherwise keeping the firms under our control. It was the CLC's perogative, but it was an unusual and potentially dangerous intervention because of the precedent it set.

Another episode occurred in the fall of 1972, when the Commission was considering again whether it would take drastic action on food. Rumsfeld pointed out to me (and he said that Shultz concurred) that the PC did not have the authority to institute a "freeze." But the CLC did. "And if you have any doubts about that, then we'll have the Executive Order rewritten." We did not want to institute a freeze, but such a conversation would not have taken place earlier, particularly when George Meany was still in the program.

For newlyweds, the CLC and the Commission had a short honeymoon and a rough marriage. The PC did enjoy a remarkable amount of independence—a very important asset—but an independence that was being steadily diminished the longer the program continued.

Our dealings with the Pay Board were less stormy.

Actually, the two organizations did not work together as closely as people presumed; this was not because of differences or infighting, but because each of us had a different kind of task, and each was loaded to the hilt with its own work. We scarcely had time to talk to each other in the PC, much less to consult with others. A weak liaison was maintained simply because there was no reason for a stronger one.

The most troublesome policy, because of the separation of the two bodies, was our limitation of labor cost pass-through to 5.5 percent plus fringes. We had the first formal joint meeting between the Pay Board and Price Commission concerning this issue on June 6, 1972. Neither side changed any policy or methods of operations, but we understood one another better and felt a little more kinship after the meeting.

One other such meeting occurred on August 14 when it was nearing time for the Pay Board to reconsider their 5.5 percent standard for the next year. We asked them to consider lowering it, both for psychological impact and for the economic impact on compensation costs. A few Pay Board members expressed sentiment for reducing the standard, but we could sense that the Board as a whole would probably not change its policy. The 5.5 percent, plus fringes, limit was left.

Judge George H. Boldt, Chairman of the Pay Board, was one of the most honest and sincere persons I have ever known. He liked people and he wanted to be liked, but he was cast in an arena for which he was not prepared (few would be), and the Pay Board did not function smoothly in the beginning.

The judge and I talked as often as we could over the phone and in short personal visits. Each of us cooperated in every way with the other, exchanging information, providing comfort, and consulting.

I last saw the judge in Rumsfeld's office on January 10, 1973, at a preview of Phase III. On the way out the door, we put our arms around each other. I never saw the judge again.

At the very first meeting of the PC on October 26, a representative of the IRS, Ed Preston, was present, and he or another IRS officer was present at every meeting. The spirit of cooperation and genuine desire to work together were there for the entire Phase II, but so were the difficulties and tensions.

It was a case of mutual frustration.

The IRS, by background, training and instinct, was not comfortable with the Stabilization Program in the beginning: They liked things codified, stable, enforceable. They were cautious, and liked everything in place before taking action. Accustomed to taking months-long procedures in transforming policies into regulations, they not only had to clear their regulations through the IRS Stabilization Program, but also through their General Counsel's organization—a calm, steady, slow group of lawyers trained in looking for gnat-sized loopholes. And the final regulations were often so complex (the rent regulations, for example) that even our Philadelphia lawyer (Bill Coleman) said he couldn't understand them.

In addition, we often changed the regulations.

Ray Snead, the IRS liason officer to the PC, said:

> Every time the Price Commission meets, they change the rules of the game.
>
> We have a hell of a time keeping our people one jump ahead of the press and keeping them informed on how to answer questions properly. We are very upset when we advise a caller wrongly. We haven't been able to answer questions properly because of the dynamic changing of the rules.
>
> *National Journal* (February 19, 1972)

He was right. At the very first meeting of the PC, the IRS appealed to us to notify them well in advance of our decisions, to work with them to write the regulations, and to give them plenty of time to inform and train their personnel prior to public notification.

We would have liked it that way too, but the name of the game we were in was speed, adaptability, and fast public information.

During considerations of policies, we always turned to Ray and said, "Is this enforceable? Can you handle it? How soon can you be ready?" Nearly always, his advice was to slow down or not to create the policy. But concurrently, with shaking hands and sweat breaking out on his brow, he'd say, "If that's what you want to do, we'll do our best. But don't expect too much."

Out would go the PC press release and the IRS teletype to all of its offices across the nation. Our press release often preceded their field notification, however, because of their delay in getting the information procedures cleared and stated in a form that their agents could enforce. As a result, the public would sometimes call up about "this new rent policy." And the IRS field representative would have to answer plaintively, *What* new policy?"

In March, 1972, for instance, the IRS received the following letter:

> Dear Mr. Grayson:
>
> Enclosed is our last fall's catalog. It cost us $71,125 and has 64 pages. Your Part 300.12a states that we must devote "at least one separate page" providing base price information.
>
> $71,125 divided by 64 pages = $1,115 per page devoted to you. Who pays for this?
>
> What is base price?
>
> Anyhow . . . as to how prices are controlled under the Price Stabilization Program . . . it goes like so . . .
>
> We wrote to the Denver branch of IRS as to whether or not personalized items come under the "Custom merchandise exemption."
>
> Two weeks later, we get a phone call that says "Yes, you are exempt."
>
> "Who is this?" we ask. "My name is Francis," we are told . . . and he hangs up. Later we have a supplier raise his price. Again we call Denver. We are told that we can raise to match . . . as long as it is in the same percentage.
>
> "Who is this?" we ask. "My name is Mary," she says.
>
> Please tell me if this is what you want printed on your $1,115 page? There will be room left over . . . so perhaps you could send us your photo or something to pep up the page.

That was the problem: the public's problem, the IRS' problem, and our problem.

If we had slowed down the system to fit IRS standard operating procedures, the economy wouldn't have moved. Speed did cost us something in credibility, enforcement, and public information—but we knew this and attempted at the same time to improve the process for everyone's benefit. From about midway in the program, it worked well.

In fairness to the IRS, as I've said, they did a fantastic job. Imagine a force of people accustomed to the usual steady and sure pace of tax information and collection, suddenly swamped with the kind of operation the Stabilization Program imposed! In the first six months, they answered over a million inquiries on complex regulations that did not remain in a steady state. Telephone calls around the country averaged 25,000 a day. It was no wonder that there was confusion at the local level, evoking public complaints about unanswered questions as well as misleading and contradictory answers by local agents.

As time went on, our policies settled down, their organization began to set up procedures adapted to our needs, and the people in the field offices assigned to Stabilization actually began to like the new freedom and the publicity attached to price control. It was a welcome change of routine for them.

Soon they began to apply our policies with the usual IRS thoroughness, sometimes interpreting our policies in a way that would be enforceable but a little at odds with our original intent. The retail food industry was an example, when the IRS interpreted one of our regulations concerning the calculation of allowable markup.

Near the end, we were working with the IRS to give them more of the actual case processing and exceptions handling. We selected Texas for a pilot project, delegating to the agents there authority to make case decisions on certain price and exceptions requests. If this worked, we planned to adopt the delegation nationwide.

Such a delegation could not have been done in the beginning when policies were being created and revised, but it was working well when the end of Phase II was announced. I believe that many of the IRS people were disappointed to see Phase II end. They were just beginning to enjoy it.

It may seem odd, but after my arrival in Washington I didn't talk with George Shultz until January 1972—almost two and a half months later. I had been too busy, and George didn't want to intrude.

On that occasion, we had lunch at the White House. George made only two references to the Stabilization Program. One was in reference to some public remarks I had made about food prices and agricultural policy. He said, "If you crawl out on that limb, you may be all alone." The other concerned the 5.5 percent limit we placed on labor cost pass-through for the coal industry. He didn't agree with that decision, but, overall, he thought we were doing a good job.

Many people naturally assumed that Shultz and I would be in frequent contact, and that he might even prevail on me or relay messages from the President concerning policies or the conduct of the program. Yet these two remarks were probably the strongest he ever made concerning the operation of the program. Not once did he ever intervene or offer critical comment to sway the minds of the Commissioners. That was as true when he was Director of the Office of Management and Budget, as it was after he became Secretary of Treasury and Chairman of the Cost of Living Council.

The same was true for John Connally, the Chairman of the CLC during the freeze and the early part of Phase II. I had never known Connally in Texas, nor did he know me. (People presume that everyone in Texas knows each other.) I first met him in Washington when we were introduced at the formal ceremonies in late October.

Our next contact was when he came over in January to visit the PC, at our request. We wanted some feedback as to how he thought we were doing, and to ask if he had any suggestions. Connally said that he felt we were doing very well, and that we should continue about as we were. A question was asked of him as to whether we should take into consideration any of the factors concerning Administration politics. "You just do your job as you see it," he responded. "You call the shots. And you let somebody else worry about the politics."

We never forgot what he said.

Arthur Burns, a valued advisor, took a direct interest in our program from the beginning. Contacts with him, however, consisted of one visit to the PC for an hour's discussion, about five telephone calls to give me his opinion, about five lunches to discuss the progress of the program. He gave his views to me just as he did publicly to the Congress and to the press, but in no way did he exert "pressure" for any particular action.

And then, of course, the President.

I first met the President on October 22 in the White House, together with other members of the PC and Pay Board, when he welcomed us to "this thankless job." Later, right after Phase II was launched, we came back to the White House for another full meeting of the two bodies. Just prior to the meeting, Judge Boldt and I sat down with the President for a light conversation in the Oval Office.

I did not see the President for the rest of Phase II. I heard from him only once, an indirect communication via Rumsfeld when the President wished Secretary Butz and me to "cool off" after I had criticized the Secretary about his remarks on food prices.

The last occasion was in a farewell ceremony in January after Phase III was announced. The President, during the "thank you" ceremony, turned to me and said:

"You did a good job with Phase II. Now we're taking over. Do you think Phase III will work?"

"It has a good chance," I said.

"The Price Commission and the Pay Board deserve credit for getting us this far, and I'll take the flak from here if we drop the ball. You've gotten us close to the goal line, that's all we asked."

He then gave us each a Presidentially engraved ash tray and added, "With due regard for the Cancer Society, it can be used for a candy dish."

I would have liked more contact with the President, not for prestige kicks, but to get some feel for what he really wanted when the tradeoffs had a serious impact upon the national economy. In mid-1972 we wanted to know whether to "crunch" the economy if it appeared that we would not make the goal. But despite my personal request to Erlichman, the direction did not come.

We steered our own course.

Part three

The life span

The sequence of events after November 13, 1971, concluding with the January 11, 1973 birth of Phase III:

--Open for business—precedent setting decisions in the early days.

--The battle of the bulge—living with the post-freeze price bulge.

--Summer of (relative) content—Phase II's success period.

--Decompression—the lull before Phase III and recommendations for Phase III.

7

Open for business

The Controllers must now take up the specific disputes and claims of hardships awaiting them in the most unimaginable numbers and variety. Everything now depends upon the good sense and equity with which they decide the first crucial precedents.

Washington Post *(Nov. 12, 1971)*

On Monday, November 15, we were open for business. And the numbers, varieties, and crucial precedents were waiting for us.

Questions flowed in to the Price Commission and the Internal Revenue Service by the hundreds of thousands from all across the nation. There were nearly four hundred thousand inquiries in the first three weeks of Phase II alone: Are we allowed a markup on costs? . . . Are all costs "allowable"? . . . What if we had a loss in the base period? . . . How far back can we go for costs? . . . How do we calculate productivity? . . . What if we're a new firm and have no base period? . . . Is artificial insemination a service or a manufacturing industry? . . . Is prostitution (legal, but controlled, in Nevada) a service industry or a regulated utility?

The period from November 15 to December 31, roughly forty-five days, was characterized by uncertainty and some confusion, as businessmen, the press, and the public attempted to keep up with policies, rulings, and press releases spewing from the printing presses. Where regulations were not specific, answers were created on the spot, or the questions bucked up to the Commissioners.

Inside the Commission staff, we were still recruiting furiously; inventing decision-making procedures, forms, organization charts; moving in furniture, telephones, filing cabinets; opening up to the press; and establishing relationships with other governmental agencies.

While struggling with these immediate issues, the Commissioners also had to create policies for a major sector of the economy still frozen (rent), as well as for special problems or sectors overlooked or postponed (such as, health, insurance, loss/low profit firms). They also had to handle important precedent-setting cases that were to chart the direction of the PC (autos, coal, and steel).

A day-by-day narrative of those forty-five days would fill whole bookshelves—and bore readers. But there were a few key events that shaped our policies and our lives for the duration of the program.

The development of the 72-hour rule was one such event.

In the week preceding the end of the freeze, the Pay Board decided to waive all wage increase prenotifications between November 14 and January 1, 1972. Anticipating that the PC would therefore do the same for price increases reflecting these added costs, the CLC issued a press release on Friday, November 12, exempting Tier I firms from both pay *and* price prenotification requirements until January 1. The regulation went into the Federal Register the next day.

On Saturday morning, Ford Motor Company raised the price of its Pinto $110, about 6 percent. (It later turned out that Ford was increasing its prices under an interpretation of freeze rules, not under Phase II rules. But the public impression, including ours, was that the price increase was generated by Phase II.)

Anxious calls came in from the Commissioners as they heard the news over the media. Bob Lanzilotti called, "If they can all increase prices right away, we're in trouble."

Bob also pointed out the peculiar circumstances of the auto and steel industries. Both had announced price increases just prior to the freeze, but they were forced to postpone them. The auto industry was facing a wage contract increase on November 23 and another one on December 2. Steel had already incurred a wage increase just prior to the freeze and had implemented only a

90

partial price increase before the freeze hit. The auto increases could have run to 5 percent and more; steel, maybe 7 percent in some product lines.

A terrible way to launch Phase II. Yet both industries were exempted from advance PC approval by the CLC action.

I was ill in bed when notified of the problem on Saturday morning. Lou Leeb told me not to worry: "We'll get together with Earl Rhode [Deputy to Don Rumsfeld] and work something out. Rest."

We agreed that we wanted firms exempted by the CLC regulation to prenotify us in some fashion. But how? We didn't have the administrative machinery in place for processing prenotifications on such a fast schedule, for we had planned on thirty-day advance notifications. Yet, as John Queenan and other Commissioners maintained, many firms were already hurting from not being allowed price increases to reflect higher costs incurred just before the freeze. Any undue delay, therefore, would further penalize these firms.

The CLC also questioned our ability to handle a heavy influx of paperwork in so short a period of time. They argued that if we introduced a lag, even inadvertantly, this would really be a *de facto* extension of the freeze, which was already creating inequities, distortions, and perhaps some unemployment. Expansion of the economy was vital to reducing the unemployment rate—a number-one priority for many Administration officials. In particular, Secretary of Commerce Stans, a member of the CLC, was adamant in opposing any delay in the price increases. Lou was told that Stans' position was nonnegotiable.

Two of the Commissioners were also ready to go to the mat. One of them, Bob Lanzilotti, was so concerned that he boarded a plane for Washington.

In the subsequent discussions with the CLC, Lou offered an initial compromise of "priority" treatment for such firms. That was too uncertain for the CLC. Lou then proposed a one-week processing of notifications. Twenty-four hours, said the CLC, on the assumption that the Commission could challenge the visible price requests and let the remainder go. At that point, Lanzilotti threatened to "go public" with his opposition to the CLC's position, thereby hardening the negotiating.

Late Saturday afternoon—only hours after the Ford Company's increase announcement—agreement was reached that the PC would give firms a *72-hour* turnaround on freeze-related filings submitted up until January 1, 1972. Unless we challenged a request ("stopped the clock") within the 72-hour period, the increase could go into effect automatically.

"Good God!" was all Don Wortman could say when he heard about the agreement. As head of our fledgling Program Operations, *he* was the one under the breaking wave of paperwork.

Hardly anyone went home Saturday night, Sunday, or Sunday night. Press releases were issued Monday, November 15, announcing the switch. The press played it up as a struggle between the CLC and us—and a victory for us. It *was* a test of our independence and strength, but it was not a fight. Earl Rhode and Don Rumsfeld cooperated with us all the way, though I think Rumsfeld felt we were making a mistake.

We'll never know if it was a mistake. There are, however, some certainties. Besides asserting the independence of the PC, this decision created an almost unbelievable work load for the administrative staff, who had to learn and take action as they were organizing. It also accelerated the bulge in prices, gave business confidence that we were trying to act fairly, and helped the economy to recover from the freeze. Most important, it strangely added a boost to staff morale—we had made our presence felt.

Right or wrong, it was done, and the 72-hour filers were on our doorstep Monday morning. During the following week, we were making quick decisions on some of the early requests, meeting with the press, setting up administrative systems, recruiting-recruiting-recruiting, and moving into our newly completed offices. We worked sixteen hours a day for a solid seven days.

The Commissioners did not get back together again until the end of that week. They had already been exhausted by the grueling sixteen days, they needed to get back to their own businesses, and they also wanted some feedback from staff operations and public reactions for that week.

At the end of that first week, a reporter from the *New York Times* visited us and in his story for the November 21 Sunday edition observed:

> Just what decisions will be made in these rooms—just how
> they will affect the wage earner and his family—is uncertain
> . . . there is a vast difference between a rigid but temporary
> holddown on prices and wages supported by public opinion
> and the succeeding phase which began last Sunday, when
> controls and formulas and regulations come into play.

There is no way to describe adequately the variety and sequence
of the Commissioners' deliberations over this 45-day period. Some
of the daily meeting "agendas" until January 1 are reproduced
in Appendix C of this book. The word *agendas* is in quotes because
they often became lists of things we *should* have been working on,
had we more time or fewer emergencies in a day. For example,
both the discussions leading to the steel pricing decisions and the
approval of an average across-the-board price increase for Dow
Chemical were considered in Commission meetings, outside of the
agendas.

Decisions in the key areas, however, make for some interesting
reading.

The auto companies showed up the first morning we were open
for business.

Chrysler was the first to file for the price increases on their 1972
model cars that had been blocked by the freeze. American Motors
and Ford quickly followed.

There was little question of approving American's request.
They asked for 2.5 percent and presented a three-year record of
unit costs, volumes, estimated volumes, profit margins, and other
information. The increase was reasonable and the costs well docu-
mented.

Ford filed for 4.4 percent and Chrysler for 5.9 percent. We
"stopped the clock" for both in order to study their requests
further. We were not satisfied with their documentation, and their
increases were so high they scared us. Because of their size, and
our concern over public reaction, we wanted to make doubly sure
about their requests. Subsequently, we stopped the clock several
times on them, and each time a new 72-hour period would begin
ticking away. GM—filing a week later than the others—came in
with a request for a 2.5 percent increase.

Because of the importance of these cases, I asked several of the Commissioners to assist the staff. They met with company officials to obtain more and different data and provided a brief synopsis of their opinions to the full Commission. We particularly relied on the judgment of Lanzilotti who had studied extensively in the area of auto pricing and industry structure. The Commissioners stated all during this process that the determination of the exact percentage figure of each increase granted was my decision as Chairman, but that the details of this (and a few future individual cases) were being reviewed in order to determine the feasibility and correctness of our policies in actual application examples.

During the discussions, I had to remind the Commission on several occasions that the clock would run out in a few hours. More than once, we barely issued the challenge in time to prevent price increases from going into effect.

First, Chrysler was cut from their requested 5.9 percent to 4.5 percent, largely by substituting our higher estimates of volume for theirs. Our estimates reduced their costs per unit, and thus decreased the amount of their cost-justified price increase to the 4.5 percent level. (The actual sales turned out to be a great deal higher than both estimates.)

That left GM and Ford.

We knew that although we might allow higher price authorizations for other auto companies, they could probably not get much more in the marketplace than what we authorized for GM. It was tempting, therefore, to hold GM down to an extremely low number (a thought tempting to all price controllers). But if we reduced GM any further, by whatever means, we might have brought about a price level that only GM could live with, possibly bankrupting the other auto companies. Also, if we cut GM any lower, we would have had to set aside our own regulations and invoke the so-called "basket clause" (technically labeled "Other Considerations" in the regulations—created late in the afternoon on November 10 just before we announced our final policies). Using the basket clause in GM's case would have been a sign of toughness to the public. And, since GM could influence the general price level in their industry, it would have helped us with the problem of price "bulges" we expected in the future.

94

Though the staff and several Commissioners extracted every ounce of data from GM and subjected it to all kinds of widely ranging estimates of volume and productivity, we could not—under normal regulations—reduce GM's cost justification below the requested 2.5 percent. They submitted convincing documentation that their actual costs would justify a 4.5 percent price increase, but in the interest of cooperating with the Stabilization Program, they had filed for only 2.5 percent.

Lou even tried to get me to "jawbone" them by calling Jim Roche, Chairman of GM, to ask him to reduce their request to 1.9 percent. But I didn't go along with jawboning then, though I later approved it on a low-key basis for selected industries.

The Commission unanimously decided not to invoke the basket clause at that time. Business could not trust us in the future to apply the rules consistently, and we might have ended up with nothing more than a series of subjective case-by-case decisions. Our General Counsel also reminded us that if we chose that route too frequently, the courts might decide that we were acting in an arbitrary and capricious manner and override us. Finally, it was just not equitable to force more cost absorption on the companies. If we hit profits too hard, this might further erode a shaken business confidence, hinder economic recovery, and hurt employment.

We approved GM's request for a 2.5 percent increase, and cut Ford from 4.4 to 2.9 percent by substituting our productivity and volume estimates. As it turned out, most companies hovered around the approved GM figure of 2.5 percent.

We also had an informal understanding with the auto companies that, unless something drastic occurred, they would not return for any further price increases during the 1972 model year, except for federally mandated safety equipment on a direct dollar pass-through basis.

Expecting they would be back for increases for model year 1973, we set up a small unit inside the PC to follow the industry closely.

Like autos, steel walked in the door right away. They too had been trapped with announced price increases that had to be postponed because of the freeze.

But steel presented a more difficult problem. Steel was acknowledged in business and government circles as a relatively sick industry, urgently in need of increased earnings.

U.S. Steel filed for a 7 percent increase on selected product lines. The staff, and even several of the Commissioners, gave their price application a thorough going-over. We wanted to make absolutely sure that the price increase was necessary, because any increase in steel has a significant ripple effect in the economy (and in the press). In one of the Commission meetings, we expressed hope to the analysts that the total price increase could be held to an average of 2.5 percent across the industry.

But it was not possible.

No matter how we adjusted for volume, productivity, or overhead, their cost increases were substantial. Not only did they have increased costs from their 1971 labor settlement, they faced another labor increase early in 1972. They would be back again soon requesting another price increase.

We finally decided to grant a weighted averaged price approval across *all* their products, in which we included approval of some anticipated costs to be incurred early in 1972. In that way, we tried to avoid two things: (1) approving a figure of 7 percent, and (2) *two* early announcements of increases.

The approved increase was for 3.6 percent.

What we failed to do, however, was to restrict them in the size of an increase in any *one* product line. As a result, U.S. Steel implemented a more than 7 percent increase in tin plate products, the very type of thing we wanted to prevent. We learned from this experience. In the future we placed a maximum increase (a "cap") on individual product lines.

Thus the conflict between control criteria and marketplace decisions. The tin plate increase may very well have been justified in the marketplace, but it ran counter to the psychology we wanted to create. Later, the increase would also be reflected in cans—which, in turn, would affect rising food prices.

We were fortunate, though, for the remainder of Phase II with steel. For, contrary to everyone's expectations, they did not come back for price increases despite some additional cost increases beyond the first labor costs in 1972. This luck was due to a combination of competition from imported steel, some self-restraint on their part, and some staff level jawboning, including calls to the auto companies encouraging them to resist steel price increases where they could.

Virgil Day referred to these early cases on the pay side as "letting the last cows out of the gate." We on the price side were hoping that few others would be coming through after autos and steel.

The coal decision was, in the words of Arthur Burns, "our finest hour." In the eyes of the coal industry, it was our blackest.

It was another early decision that set a policy tone and attitude for the future. I personally think that it was the single most important decision the PC ever made.

As related before, the coal industry had sought the PC's assurance before the freeze ended that they could pass through the full cost of whatever wage increases they settled for. We had refused to give an advance decision. As it turned out, the industry and the United Mine Workers settled for an estimated 16.8 percent increase in average hourly compensation on the night of November 13, reportedly just minutes before the midnight ending the freeze.

The problem was first in the lap of the Pay Board. Would they pass it through or cut it back? Rumors flowed to our staff all that first week that the members of the PB were moving in the direction of full approval.

One evening I received a call from Kermit Gordon, a public member of the Board, asking if Lou and I could come up for a brief meeting with the PB's public members. At that meeting, they informed us that a vote was coming up soon. They were discouraged because it appeared almost certain that the business members of the Board were siding with labor and that the full amount would be passed through. They also felt that the business members were yielding to pressure from labor, some perhaps even fearing retaliation against their own firms if they did not vote with labor (there were such rumored threats). Labor-business self-interest coalitions had destroyed previous control systems involving tripartite boards, and it looked like a similar fate might be developing for the PB.

I told Chairman Boldt that we were of a mind to stand tough

97

on high labor cost pass-throughs, and that they could use that information as they saw fit. In fact, I told them, I was going to be on the NBC "Today Show" the next morning, and that I would indicate our attitude, if asked. We adjourned the meeting on a note of pessimism about the coal decision and perhaps the future of the Pay Board.

The next morning Bill Monroe of the "Today Show" did ask me a question about the pending decision of the Pay Board, and I strongly stated our views. Hoping that this publicity might influence their decision, I had a press release prepared immediately following the show and hand-delivered to the PB:

> Price Commission Chairman, C. Jackson Grayson, today indicated on the NBC "Today Show" that the Price Commission would not necessarily automatically grant price increases reflecting the full amount of labor costs which could be considered inflationary.
>
> In particular reference to the coal settlement, Chairman Grayson stated: "If the labor increase is as high as the reported 15–17 percent, the Commission will examine these labor costs very closely to determine whether companies will be allowed to increase prices proportionately."

Either it didn't reach the Pay Board in time, or it didn't cut any ice.

The Pay Board approved the contract, substantially as written. Management and labor voted for approval, and public members voted to cut the contract. The coal companies, of course, rushed to file with the Price Commission for full pass-through of the "approved" labor costs. The issue was now in our laps.

As the *Washington Post* said on November 24:

> Ironically, any hope that is left of getting a reasonably effective wage policy, now that the Pay Board has approved a coal miners' increase three times the 5.5 per cent "guideline," rests with the Price Commission.
>
> If the Price Commission passes the cost of this wage increase right on to the consumers in the form of a soft coal price increase of 8 to 9 per cent—as asked by the coal opera-

tors—there won't be much left of the whole Phase II operation.

After many staff studies and discussions stretching across four meetings (November 22, 23, 29, 30), we decided to hold the coal industry—and all other industries in the future—to a maximum allowable labor cost increase of 5.5 percent plus fringes of 0.7 percent for labor costs agreed to after November 8, 1971, *regardless of what the Pay Board approved.*

Our stated position was that everyone had knowledge of the 5.5 percent guideline as of that date, the day the Pay Board announced their policies. Also, we felt that this ruling was consistent with our general goal of getting the inflation rate down to 2.5 percent: If wage increases were held to an average 5.5 percent, and if productivity increases ran at the average historical rate of about 3 percent, the overall price increase would be roughly 2.5 percent. The use of the term "allowable" costs in our regulations permitted us to decide which costs (or which levels of costs) could be used to justify price increases.

Applying this policy to the coal industry led to substantial reductions in their requested price increases. The first case decision was the Old Ben Coal Company, a subsidiary of Standard Oil of Ohio. They sought a 16.71 percent price increase, reflecting the full labor cost pass-through, with no profit markup added. They were cut to 3.78 percent.

Coal companies called it unfair.

Some companies told our staff privately that some unnamed Administration officials had assured them prior to the settlement that the Price Commission would approve whatever the Pay Board approved. Also, some said they would shut down marginal mines, cut down on investment in future mining, and reduce supplies of coal to heat homes and operate utility plants.

A number of Administration officials were reportedly certain that this would be the doom of the coal industry, perhaps of the economic expansion. Lou was told that several members of CLC were furious, but in light of the Meany memo they felt they could do nothing. Though Rumsfeld never officially commented, I sensed that he cheered the decision. Lou said Rumsfeld had supported us at CLC meetings, while others on the CLC were objecting to our policy on limited labor cost pass-through.

The general reception by the press, the public, and even some businessmen was good: They all felt it was the right step. Some businessmen were also pleased in that it gave them an opportunity now to bargain harder at negotiations time: "Look, you may want more than 5.5 percent. The Pay Board may approve more than 5.5 percent. But we can't *pay* more than 5.5 percent. We can't get it back in prices and therefore we can't operate with it."

But not all businessmen were pleased. Our decision now raised the specter of a profit squeeze, caused by pay increases passed by the Pay Board at a higher level than the Price Commission would approve. There was also some resentment over the fact that one government agency had refused to "honor" what another government agency had approved. We were accused of trying to do the Pay Board's work.

These arguments kept coming up over and over again as the 5.5 percent bit into other industries. And my answer consistently was, "You didn't have to give increases over 5.5 percent. And if you did, you must have thought you would get higher productivity than 3 percent, or the results would be inflationary." It may not have been perfectly good economics, but it did make broad logical sense. And it was a clear stand.

Our credibility was considerably strengthened, and I think this policy was one of our most effective in holding down prices.

Our rent program, on the other hand, was a disaster at least in one sense. It consumed a fantastic amount of physical, financial, and emotional resources, both on the part of the PC and the IRS. And it also generated a large credibility gap for us.

But it was also a tremendous success. Residential rent increases were held to only 3.4 percent all during the Phase II period, as compared to a rise of 4.3 percent in the eight months prior to the program.

When we arrived in Washington to design Phase II, the decision to control rents had already been made. The CLC really didn't want controls. Neither did the economic advisors who gathered that evening during the design of Phase II see their worth. The PC didn't want them either.

But we were stuck with them.

I was told informally—but never officially—that labor had demanded controls on either interest rates or rents as a condition for participation. Labor felt that wage controls could hardly be defended to the rank and file if one of these two areas were not controlled. The Administration opted for rents as the area least likely to suffer severe distortion from controls (there were many geographic areas with high vacancy rates).

Our first decision in the PC was to do nothing about rent policies until we had the recommendations of the Rent Advisory Board (RAB), a board designed to propose policies to the PC. The tripartite membership of the RAB—five members from industry, five from consumer groups, and five from the public sector—was not decided until November 16, and the official appointment wasn't made by the President until November 23. Though they met the same day as their appointment, it was still ten days after the end of the freeze.

Meanwhile in the PC's first post-freeze meeting, the Commissioners were faced with the need to make an immediate rent decision.

New York City still had local rent controls lingering on since World War II. Over this thirty-year period, the suppression of rents far below market values caused increasing abandonments of unprofitable units—at a rate estimated to be over fifty thousand a year in 1971.

There were also numerous distortions and administrative problems. In a single building in New York, there were identical units renting for 200 to 300 percent differences in rent. And New York City had to employ over ten thousand people for the administration of rent controls.

New York, after many years of bitter struggle between tenant and landlord groups, finally decided to move *toward* equalizing rent controlled prices with market values. The adjustment process was scheduled to occur over a ten-year period—the annual average adjustment to be about 7.5 percent in increases. All of this was set to begin on January 1, 1972.

With the freeze and the creation of the Price Commission, the tenant groups were hopeful that we would reduce the 7.5 percent figure or postpone any increase at all. New York City officials and landlord groups protested that if we did not permit that program to go into effect on January 1, we would increase the rate of abandonments and destroy a program that had taken years to be accepted by the legislature.

We decided (after several stormy staff meetings with New York tenant groups and landlords) to let rent increases occur, where permitted by rent-control authorities "authorized by State and local rent control agencies." We made it clear that this ruling applied only to private rentals governed by local rent control authorities *in existence* prior to November 14, 1971. We did not want any new local rent authorities to be created as a way of getting out from under controls.

The announcement was generally publicized negatively in New York City—not exactly an auspicious beginning for our rental program from the public's point of view.

The RAB conducted meetings from late November through early December. The IRS was urging speed on us to adopt some clear-cut rental policies (their heaviest work load was already in rents); and we therefore hurried the RAB, also charging them to think decontrol while they were creating control policies.

The RAB recommendations were presented to the PC in the middle of December, and we approved them almost verbatim, with two exceptions. First, we decided to reduce their proposed annual rental increase from 3 percent to 2.5 percent—a figure that would fit in with our overall goal. The PC vote was four-to-three in favor, with Newman, Whitman, and Queenan dissenting because they felt we should fully support the RAB. The second, by a unanimous vote, was the deletion of an 8 percent cap on composite rental adjustments in any one year.

The RAB recommended this cap because they did not want outsized rental increases of 15, 20 percent, and up. We rejected this because we felt that the public might misinterpret the 8 percent as the allowable limit, and also because 8 percent might not be enough in some local situations where increases were badly needed to prevent abandonments.

In retrospect, I think that the removal of the 8 percent cap was a mistake. While it made good economic sense, it cost us a lot of public credibility when selected increases of 15 percent, or even 50 percent, were announced in early 1972. And a lack of an explicit cap complicated the IRS' job of enforcing the regulations. It later proved to generate so much pressure (particularly in New York and New Jersey), that we essentially reinstated the cap. But by that time, it was too late to correct the negative public image and to roll back increases already in effect.

The rent regulations were hammered out in long sessions by the RAB, and the members did an amazing job of trying to balance the equities. But the results were a tremendously complex set of rules and policies, which the lawyers in the PC and the IRS found difficult to write. We also found them difficult to explain, and the general public couldn't understand them. The IRS estimated that about 50 percent of their time in Phase II was spent in enforcing and explaining rent regulations. We tried revision after revision to clarify and simplify them, but each time we seemed only to generate more confusion.

Had I the benefit of foreseeing later developments, my recommendation would have been to exempt rents and leave them for local controls. Rents are only 5 percent of the Consumer Price Index (CPI). Rent controls intrude on an intensely personal relationship between tenant and landlord—a battle that has raged for centuries and one of the most complex areas of law in the nation. For that reason and because of the diversity in local conditions around the nation and the widely varying rental controls, any attempts at writing a national rent code becomes unbelievably complicated. Equity entails complexity in this area. Complexity means difficulty of enforcement and widespread misunderstanding, and people generally won't support what they don't understand.

But, whatever the reasons, overall rental increases behaved very well in the CPI during Phase II. Maybe it was our rental program. Maybe not. I only hope the program did some good, for it surely was a huge allocation of resources by *all* the agencies involved.

Health care costs had been exploding in recent years. Hospital costs had been rising at an annual rate of 12.6 percent and doctors' fees at about 5 to 6 percent a year.

We knew we had to bite into these numbers, but how? And how much?

Since a Health Services Industry Committee (HSIC) was just being created in late October, again we decided to wait for recommendations. For the beginning of Phase II, we simply announced that health care, for the time being, was included in the general "Services" sector of regulations.

When the recommendations did come in, their central feature was appealingly simple—cut the allowable rates of increase by half, to about 6 percent. Why not 2.5 percent, we asked? They felt that to cut that deeply might severely damage the quantity and quality of health care in the nation. But why 6 percent then? Why not 5 or 8 percent—or some other number? They replied frankly that they had no models, no prediction of whether this number was correct or exactly what it would do to health care. But, after much debate among the members of the Committee (doctors, nurses, health insurers, health administrators), they arrived at an acceptable compromise of 6 percent for institutional health providers, such as hospitals. This 50 percent cut seemed "about right."

I was amazed that the degree of knowledge about the structure of the industry and about health care statistics did not permit a more refined analysis. But there was no time for more homework, and the Committee seemed to represent the best judgment of those familiar with the field.

Though the 6 percent figure was not one we liked, we concurred that it might be dangerous to reduce it further. Besides, there were two other features of the Committee's recommendations that interested us: The first we knew would have favorable public impact—a ceiling of 2.5 percent on the fees of doctors, dentists, and other professionals. The second was to create State Advisory Boards in every state, appointed by the governor, for the purpose of screening exceptions requests. This system would lighten our work load considerably. We knew that to crack down on health care so hard would generate hardship cases, and that these cases would be numerous and heartrending. A heavy case load would drown us administratively, and we also didn't have the expertise to sort out true hardship from loss of luxury. There was no legal authority for what we did, but we had to try. As it turned out, forty-nine states created such boards; Montana was the exception, simply because of funding problems.

All together, the recommendations made a sensible package. We adopted them on December 13.

The last major policy announcement—on insurance—was made together with rent on December 22.

Our policy on insurance was generated without a formal advisory board, as in rent and health, but we did draw heavily on people from the Federal Insurance Administration, Blue Cross, experts from the insurance industry, and from state insurance administrators.

The main control valve was the insurance rate premium, constructed both by looking backward at experience and forward with guesses. Using past experience, we limited the components of anticipated costs that make up the rate, holding operating expenses to no greater than a 2.5 percent increase and limiting the anticipated "inflation trend factor" to about half of what it would have been. The first test in insurance came, however, even before these policies were announced.

It was known as the "Blue Cross decision." Employees of the federal government may select their health and accident insurance from several insurance programs including a combination of Blue Cross organizations throughout the nation. They pool the risk, so to speak. Blue Cross federal insurance claimed that 1971 had been a financial disaster and that they expected to lose about $200 million in 1972. The reason: The rates had been set too low, not anticipating the huge increase in use of one of the popular features —outpatient X-ray—and not covering the large increase in operating costs due to inflation. The Civil Service Commission, which audits Blue Cross' books and rates for the federal government, had tentatively approved an increase of 34.1 percent for 1972 to recover past losses.

Since these rates were now subject to review by the Price Commission, our phone began ringing off the wall with calls from Congress, the Federal Insurance Administrator, the press, and the general public. Letters poured in from federal employees all over the country—"Not 34 percent!"

The 1971 losses suffered by Blue Cross were for real. If rates did not rise, Blue Cross would not only fail to recover those past losses, they would incur another large loss in 1972.

But would they? Policies regarding the use of the costly outpatient X-ray feature had been tightened. And operating costs might not rise as rapidly if our health policies reduced costs.

Just prior to the decision, Blue Cross officials flew in for a late night meeting with several of us on the staff. They stated that they could not stand any more heavy losses, and that they might have to withdraw the insurance coverage altogether. Some of their state Blue Cross organizations were already on the verge of bankruptcy, and a heavy allocation of losses might just put them under. When we asked them if they would accept a lower figure than a 34 percent increase, they said that they could consider it, but they didn't think that they could live with it. Coverage would probably have to be withdrawn.

Dilemma: If we did not cut the increase, we'd have a large credibility gap—with the public, the press, federal employees, and our own staff. If we did cut it, then Blue Cross might withdraw the coverage. This would be a major inconvenience to federal employees, and a hiatus could occur while a search for other insurance companies was made. (And other companies had already shown us their heavy losses in health insurance in recent years.)

I decided to apply our proposed policy, which I thought would cut the percentage a bit. The results were that we could approve anywhere between 16 and 27.8 percent. This was the best our analysts could do, given the limited data and our then limited staff.

Following the evening meeting with Blue Cross, I asked each of the three staff members present to write down on a piece of paper what they would recommend. The slips read 28, 17, and 20 percent. The next morning I made up my mind—22 percent.

Why 22 percent? Taking a lesson from the HSIC, I judged it to be "about right" given all the information and tradeoffs. Besides, it was the midpoint of the staff's recommendations.

Announcing the decision to the press, we also said we would monitor the results throughout the year and consider adjustments if it appeared heavy losses might be sustained. (We knew, however, that an adjustment at any in-between point in the policy year would be almost impossible since the "use factors" are valid only for an entire year.)

Later that day, Blue Cross decided to accept the risk.

Some hailed the transaction as a victory—"34 percent rate hike cut to 22 percent." Others screamed, "Giveaway!" Some subsequent letters argued, "How can you let insurance rates go up by 22 percent when my wages are held to a 5.5 percent increase?"

The decision was a gamble. But we were fortunate, because utilization rates did drop. Cost increases moderated. Blue Cross even generated a small surplus. But the multimillion dollar loss from 1971 was still on their books, and it eventually would have to be paid by the users in the future.

All we did was shove the problem off for a few years.

Lou closed the door to my office and smiled.

"Guess what," he said.

"The President just announced Phase II is over."

"Nope. Dow Chemical's in my office right now. They're willing to settle for a 2.5 percent increase across their entire product line, and they won't come back to us for a year—no matter what happens to their costs."

"Are they willing to put that in writing?"

"Yep."

"How much can they justify from increased costs that we know about?"

"Well over that. About four percent."

There has to be some catch, I thought.

"Then why are they willing to settle for 2.5 percent?"

"They get the flexibility to put their price increases where the market dictates instead of where their costs are. Second, they can plan ahead for the next year. Third, if they have to come in to prenotify for every one of their products, they estimate they will file as many as a hundred thousand applications."

"Go back and tell 'em we're interested."

Not knowing exactly what to do with the unusual request and being embroiled at the same time with steel, autos, and coal, we could only briefly review the Dow proposal at our December 7 meeting.

Coleman suggested that Lou go back to Dow and ask them if they would agree to a 2 percent increase instead of 2.5. One reason was that the Commission had to hold increases down to lower than 2.5 percent in the higher productivity industries in order to offset the larger increases in lower productivity industries. Also, the Commission frankly wanted a low number to compensate for some of the publicity the higher increases had been getting.

Lou's call to Dow sent their Board of Directors into an immediate meeting. Word soon came back that they could accept the lower limit.

So the new baby was christened: "Term Limit Pricing (TLP)." It was first dubbed "Term Average Pricing," but the word "limit" sounded more control-oriented.

Eventually about 185 major firms, with over $200 billion in sales, accepted TLPs of various limits—at or below 2 percent. For us it meant that instead of dealing with multitudes of prenotification requests per year for each of the large firms, we had to deal with only one request per year for each—about 185 filings. Without TLPs, I don't believe our staff could have administered all the prenotifications.

It took months of tough work to develop effective statistical methods for monitoring price actions by TLP firms; and many, many hours were spent negotiating the specifics of each agreement. But the time and effort were good investments.

Economically, TLPs were a mixed bag. Some firms had base prices well below the 2 percent limit, so the upper boundary never restricted them. Others used the TLP's flexibility to price where they had the greatest market power and opportunity. Later analysis of results in 1972 showed that many other firms were well below their TLP limit, not because of the PC, but because of competitive market conditions which would not allow them to use up their authorized increases. TLPs, therefore, permitted the economy to move more as the market system really operates, thereby decreasing the dangers of distortion. Businesses also absorbed more in way of increased costs—sometimes as much as 3 percent—because we demanded it as a condition for the greater flexibility.

As always, we were racing the clock to complete *all* our policy decisions by the end of 1971. Finally, the policy rudders were in place, and we were ready to steer an anti-inflationary course. The November Consumer Price Index had just been announced in late

December and showed a moderate 2.4 percent increase. A robust economy was in the making.

But were the policies correct?

Were they strong enough? Were they too strong?

Would they inhibit recovery and add to unemployment?

Or would there be a bubble? If so, when? How strong? How long?

Already a few harbingers had darkened our skies. Food prices were rising, particularly lettuce (69¢ a head!) and meat. Lumber prices had shot up. Cattle hides were escalating.

But never mind, we felt good. Autos . . . steel . . . coal . . . the big ones were behind us now. Our press was generally good, including a surprising editorial comment from the *New York Times* of December 15:

> . . . it is time for organized labor to resume its proper role of cooperation in making the Pay Board work.
>
> This is especially true since the Price Commission has been doing an outstanding job on its half of the anti-inflation program.

Writers of *Time* even composed some "economic carols," the most memorable of which is as follows:

God Rest Ye, Jackson Grayson
(God Rest Ye Merry, Gentlemen)

God rest ye, Jackson Grayson
GM did you dismay
They asked for five, you gave them three,
Stand up to coal that way
And save us from the Pa-ay Board's
In-fla-tion-ary sway.
We will think you direct from heaven sent
Hea-eaven sent,
If-f you can hold the li-ine on our rent!

The PC offices broke out into Christmas parties. The Commissioners went back to their offices and homes. Some of the staff even got to see their families for a few days.

A sign in the corridors reflected the hope:

Happy 1972½!

8

The battle of the bulge

Chairman Grayson: There will certainly be some price increases, obviously. We can expect these, but a big surge in the inflationary rate? No. I don't think so.
Member of the Press: A small surge?
Chairman Grayson: A small surge? Perhaps.

Transcript of a Press Conference
November 11, 1971

The holiday mood was short-lived. On January 2, Dan Rather of CBS News asked the President about a statement by departing Council of Economic Advisors Chairman Paul McCracken that controls would be needed "well beyond" this year's Presidential election. The President replied that he "saw decontrol coming perhaps at a faster pace."

Then on January 9, an interview of Herb Stein was reported in the *Washington Post.*

Stein Sees '72 Phaseout of Controls

The Nixon administration will follow a process of "selective decontrol" of its wage-price machinery over the next several months and there is "a possibility that the controls will go (completely) before the election," according to Herbert Stein, the President's chief economic adviser.

This interview was followed by statements by several other government officials hinting at an early decontrol, albeit contin-

110

gent upon the achievement of a lower inflation rate. These statements, technically, were not incorrect. The President had always stated that controls would be ended when the goals were achieved. But such statements were being widely interpreted by business and by the public as hints of decontrol "around the corner."

I was disturbed that such talk might lead people not to comply with a short-lived program or to withhold supplies in the hope of an early decontrol and increased prices.

During an interview on January 14 with Phil Shabaecoff of the *New York Times,* I was asked: "Do you agree with the comments by the President, George Shultz, and Herb Stein about ending controls as soon as possible?"

"Yes. But I think such statements are premature. They could distort the whole control mechanism."

"Do you think it might be damaging?"

"Yes."

The story was headlines in the *New York Times* the next day:

Grayson Chides Officials for Talking of Decontrol

While the story was correct, I did not like the headlined verb "chides." My academic background tolerated open disagreement without having such comments regarded as chastisement. I had not realized how rare it was for one official in the administration to express public disagreement with the actions of another.

I called Secretary Connally to explain the story, and he said "Don't worry." He also agreed that further talk about decontrol would be harmful, and said that he would see it was stopped.

Public speculation by anyone in the administration was quieted for a long time. But the end of controls was a continual subject of speculation by the press throughout the entire control program.

From January to the middle of April 1972 reports of escalating Consumer Price Index and Wholesale Price Index figures made headlines. Heavy increases in rents, food, and utility prices occurred all across the nation. Public support declined drastically. Major overhauls were considered for the program, and there was even some talk of scrapping it altogether.

Coming off a freeze, avoiding *some* surge in prices is impossible. The delicate trick is to provide some price relief for accumulated cost pressures and inequities, keep these increases as small as possible, and maintain public support during this "blowing-off" process.

We called it the "Battle of the Bulge."

It occurred in many sectors of the economy, but the first and most visible increases were in a sector that plagued us all during Phase II—and that endured as a problem through Phases III and IV—*food.*

It began with increases in meat prices in December, but the worst single item was lettuce. The lettuce crop in California had suffered from bad weather, and prices ballooned to 40¢, 50¢, even 69¢ a head in some parts of the country. I'll never look at a head of lettuce again without recalling housewives shouting at meetings about 200 or 300 percent increases in lettuce prices, or waving a head of lettuce angrily in front of me in a supermarket and complaining, "*What* price controls?"

But the biggest blow came in January 15 with the announcement of the WPI for December—a 0.8 percent increase! This monthly rate was immediately annualized as a 9.6 percent inflation rate, and it confirmed suspicions of some people that "wages were going to be controlled, but not prices." Fifty percent of the increase was in food.

At the same time, thawed rent controls permitted immediate rent increases to begin on January 1, some in the 5 to 25 percent range. A postal rate increase of 23.9 percent was approved by the Cost of Living Council in early January. Freeze-delayed utility rate increases began to be announced for telephone, railroad, subway, gas, electric, water, and other services. Small businesses of less than a hundred thousand dollars were exempted in late January. The press reported increases all over the economy.

From this first wave of reaction, we learned that, to the public, price controls mean no price increases at all, or practically none. We had not done a good enough job of getting across the idea that we were only trying to reduce the *average* rate of increase, and not stop *all* increases. People judged the program by a few price increases, particularly if it directly affected them. And we were getting some large increases in the most sensitive areas directly affecting the public—food, rent, and utilities.

112

No one, it seemed, understood the nature of the battle. If an item went up more than 2.5 percent, we heard about it with bitter complaints from consumers, labor, and members of Congress. Of course, the high percentage increases were headlined, while those that held steady or declined were not reported. This lack of public understanding of an "average" is a problem for all price control programs, and it tends to push controllers into taking more drastic or faster action than might, perhaps, warranted by the longer-run average.

But there was no mistaking the public mood. It was turning against us. Stories were being written in the press with headlines such as:

Phase II Honeymoon Is Over

Public Disillusionment Sets In

Key Control Policies Under Attack

What Price Controls?

Storm Signals for Phase II

A Gallup poll released on January 30 reported that 55 percent of persons interviewed were dissatisfied with the way wage-price controls were working. The *Kiplinger Washington Letter* of February 4 stated:

> *You, too, may be wondering whether gov't controls are working.* Many people are . . . Food costs more, especially meat and uncontrolled fruits and vegetables. More and more exemptions for these-&-those . . . All that employers can see is that wages are allowed to go up. All that consumers can see is that prices are rising. . . . They want the gov't to be really tough, tougher than the gov't wants to be. *A widespread freeze psychology* probably is at the bottom of it. Public seems to think controls are supposed to stop all wage-price rises.

A Lou Harris poll reported on February 14 that 56 percent of the public felt that the PC was doing a "Fair to Poor" job. "Clearly," said Lou Harris, "it is a case of a public verdict that both bodies [the Pay Board and the Price Commission] set 'fair and reasonable' guidelines in the first place, but have fallen down on the job of making them stick."

A one sentence postcard sent to me summed it up:

"WE'VE HAD IT!"

The Commissioners naturally were concerned.

Though we knew that many increases had to be above 2.5 percent, and believed that our policies were set about right, we couldn't ignore the public voice and felt an increasing loss of confidence in the program. We were not about to abandon any of our basic policies until we knew whether the increases were a normal result of coming off a freeze, or whether the policies were set too loosely to stop the inflation rate. No model existed that could answer that question. And we knew that we could defend the bulge increases for only so long.

Against this setting, the first real disagreement occurred in the Commission in early January.

Peter Flanagan stopped me in the White House right after Phase II was announced in November.

"Are markups allowed on costs for price increases?" he asked me.

"Of course. Why do you ask?"

"I just wondered—I wasn't sure."

I dismissed the question quickly, assuming that he simply hadn't read the regulations.

I shouldn't have.

Lanzilotti called me in late December. "We aren't allowing markups on costs, are we?"

"Sure."

"But we didn't agree to that. We said only costs could be passed through. No markups."

"No we didn't."

"Yes we did."

"No we didn't."

"Yes we did."

114

Incredible as it seemed, we had agreed "unanimously," but not on the same price increase policy!

The disagreement was aired at our first January meeting. We went around the room.

Queenan, Newman, Whitman, and I were positive that we had agreed to a policy of granting price increases that included normal markups. Lanzilotti, Coleman, and Scranton were just as positive that we had meant *costs only.*

"Allowable costs means *costs* only. That's very clear from a reading of the regulation."

"No. Not true. The regulation says that allowable costs will serve *as a basis* for price adjustment. If we had meant only cost pass-through, we would have said price increases 'should not exceed' costs."

"But companies can increase profits merely by having an increase in costs. It will encourage cost increases."

"No—there is still something called a market that will prevent that. Also, if we take away margins, many businesses can't survive. Would you invest in a firm that operated only to pass along costs?"

"But the economy is recovering and firms can increase profits by increased volume and efficiencies."

"We could stop the recovery in its tracks if we don't allow normal profit markups."

"You sure won't stop inflation in its tracks if you permit margins."

"You knew about it when we passed around examples of margin maintenance during the last week of November. Also, when we approved the price request forms, they had a margin built in."

"But those forms were passed by us so fast we never really studied them. And if we had, I never would have agreed to them. Allowing profit margins simply runs counter to the goal we have set of reducing inflation."

And so it went. Around the room. Back and forth.

And the more we discussed the issue, the more each felt he was right—not only in memory, but in principle as well.

We took a vote: Coleman, Lanzilotti, and Scranton voted for cost pass-through only. Newman, Whitman, Queenan, and I voted to keep the profit margins on.

Lanzilotti prepared a written dissent for the meeting on January 8, and Bill Coleman decided to join him. It concluded:

> We regret the necessity of this dissent, but the issue at stake in what may be considered simply a *minor* procedural ruling of the Commission is instead so *fundamental* to the achievement of price stabilization that we believe it should receive wide attention.

The positions were now firmly fixed.

The question then became, what should be done with the dissenting memorandum? The majority felt that public disclosure might have been harmful to the program at that time. For one thing, the vote was not going to change. The public lacked a detailed knowledge of the Stabilization Program, but knew the PC was a solid working unit. Public confidence was already waning, and airing of this disagreement might have diminished our effectiveness. Besides, business confidence needed a boost. An indication of even the possibility of removal of margins might have increased uncertainty in the capital markets.

Although the debate had been extended, including some heated exchanges, the Commissioners never really lost sight of the goal or of the fact that we were still a team. Neither Lanzilotti, Coleman, nor Scranton wanted to do anything to harm the program. Though they definitely wanted to change the decision, public airing of the issue was less important. They wanted the dissent filed as a matter of record, at least; but if it were made a formal part of the minutes of the meeting, the issue would be aired.

Finally, the issue was temporarily shelved when Coleman and Lanzilotti agreed—with Scranton's gentle persuasion—to a compromise: We recorded the dissent with a letter from me to them, dated February 16, stating that the dissenting memorandum was in the official records of the Commission, as a background discussion paper, and that anytime they wanted to make the dissent public, it would be done.

The dissent was becoming public by this time anyway. The *Wall Street Journal* of February 14 ran the following story:

Price Unit, Facing Criticism,
Inner Split, Appears Headed For Fights
on Key Policies

The Price Commission, faced with mounting criticism from the outside and a widening philosophical split among its own members, appears headed from some major battles over its most important policies.

Currently, fights are brewing over several key issues:

--The commission's "Term Limit Pricing" policy . . .

--Its limited disclosure of information and the lack of public participation in its rulings . . .

--Its practice of permitting companies to pass on additional cost increases on a percentage basis rather than dollar for dollar.

Discussion continued on this "margin" issue in many subsequent meetings, but the vote remained the same.

Meanwhile, we were still trying to defend bulge increases to a public that was coming to believe the PC was too divided to be "with it" any longer. The same *Wall Street Journal* article reported examples of large price increases and mounting criticism from labor: "Organized labor also plans to hit the panel hard. 'They aren't a container of prices, but are turning into a sieve,' charged Leo Perlis, the AFL-CIO official in charge of the federation's price monitoring operation." Symbolically, in the column next to this article was a report that the railroads were going to seek rate increases ranging up to 10 percent.

The release of the January price indicators in February did little to help our cause. The WPI was 0.5 percent, annualized in the press to be a 6 percent inflation rate. Farm products and processed foods remained high at a 0.9 percent rise. But most disturbing to us, and to professional economists, was the sharp increase in one of the important components of the WPI—"industrial commodities." The January rise was 0.4 percent, double the December rate. Though the CPI was no greater than December (0.3 percent), one of the components—services, about 60 percent of the GNP—jumped to a 16 percent rate. Again, that was double the December rate. We felt that this was potentially one of the most explosive and most difficult of sectors to control because of the diversity, large labor content, and small size of many firms.

Suddenly, we were falling behind the power curve. Sample agendas for January and February are reproduced in Appendix D, for anyone interested in the variety of problems that were cropping up.

The agenda for February 8, for instance, was a particularly critical one. Lou had scheduled a review of our policies on utilities for that day, in light of some frightening developments in that sector. Already from early filings, we could see increases of 5 to 20 percent in the offing. Coleman and Scranton, in particular, kept warning us to expect hot public reaction.

The staff paper for that meeting presented the following major options:

1. Ask CLC to exempt public utilities.
2. Delegate all authority to regulatory bodies.
3. Continue with PC control.

Early in the design of Phase II, we had wanted to leave public utilities in the hands of existing regulatory bodies, as was done during the Korean War and World War II. But the CLC decided after a lengthy internal debate not to exempt them in order to maintain comprehensive coverage across the nation.

We then decided to leave the establishing of primary rates in the hands of the federal and state regulatory bodies, but to require that all of the major rate increases above a certain size be forwarded to the PC for final review. This had the effect of making us the court of last resort for all those who fought utility rates —average consumer, business, and Congress. We had, in effect, asked for all of the "hot potato" rate increases in the nation. The biggest of these cases was a mammoth one for the New York Telephone Company.

New York Telephone had already put into effect $190 million in rate increases in July, 1971, and now planned to go ahead with another state-approved $160 million—a rate rise of almost 30 percent in less than a year.

Typical of the complaining letters was one from a widow in Glen Head, Long Island, living on a pension:

> How can you in all conscience allow the frightening increases of the N.Y. Telephone Company rates. What are you going to do about this? I shall have to have my phone taken out. I can't afford it.

Another from Oceanside, New York:

> It's high time the Price Commission Office gets on the ball and works for the consumer. . . . We urge you to roll back the increase and *NOT GRANT* the Phone Company a rate increase . . . The entire increase is ridiculous.

Most of these rate cases, such as New York Telephone, had been going on for years in regulatory hearings, accumulating hundreds, even thousands, of pages of testimony and complicated exhibits. Emotions usually commingled with the documentation of arguments from both points of view: On one side, the utility companies are gouging the public and still not giving good service! On the other, if we don't get some price increases, we cannot give good service—or any service at all!

We could see—from various protest groups arriving on our doorstep, from hot mail, and from telephone calls from some Congressmen—that we were going to be in perpetual hot water with our policy. Our staff of utility "experts" consisted of about ten people, as compared to the estimated twenty thousand "plus" people in the local state and federal regulatory systems.

The staff option paper on this issue said that if we continued with PC control, we had two basic options:

A. Soft Line: Automatically accept certification
   Pro
   1. Eliminates necessity of PC coming into conflict with state and federal agencies.
   2. Reduces demands on staff time.
   3. Does not require PC to make subjective judgments.
   Con
   1. Leaves the PC vulnerable to adverse publicity.
   2. Exposes PC to credibility gap.

3. Loss of public confidence.
4. Ignores our regulations.
5. Does nothing to reduce inflation.

B. Hard Line: Review cases with goal of limiting increases to a minimum, including tighter guidelines.
Pro
1. Removes a possible credibility gap.
2. Improves likelihood of public acceptance.
3. Effectuates our regulations.
4. Controls inflation.
Con
1. Requires subjective decision-making on the part of the PC.
2. Administrative burden.
3. Involves PC in constant controversies.

Recommendations
Do not exempt. Take hard line. Have consultants develop criteria to reduce subjective element to lowest factor possible. Tighten up our guidelines to public utility commissions.

The PC debated the paper all that morning of the eighth.

The pros and cons had been accurately stated by the staff, but it still was not clear what we could or should do, particularly given our staff size and competence in this area.

We took a noon break, and at lunch, Lou and I came up with an alternative that hadn't been considered: *Suspend all price increases filed with us, or about to be filed with us, for thirty days, call public hearings, and then announce new regulations.*

It would buy time to get more expert opinion and make a better decision, delay price increases for thirty days, and respond to an increasing criticism that the PC was not holding "public hearings" as mentioned in the Stabilization Act.

The Commissioners agreed.

Immediately following the meeting, I called Secretary Connally and Rumsfeld to tell them of the decision before it hit the press.

"What!" was Connally's response, "You did *what!*"

"We froze utility rates for thirty days."

"You better have a damn good reason."

"We do. Let me tell you . . ."

When I finished, Connally said it made sense, "but just be sure you get the decision made by that time and don't extend the freeze."

Rumsfeld had essentially the same reaction.

Hearings on public utilities were held on February 22–26. Out of days of testimony and bulky exhibits, the Commissioners formed several opinions:

1. Tremendous inefficiencies exist in the regulatory process.
2. Competition is severely limited by the regulatory process, leading to protection of inefficient firms and practices.
3. The regulatory lag introduced by long hearings and regulatory delays had caused regulated firms to suffer in recent years from rapidly increased costs without compensatory price increases.
4. The quality of presentations of the utility, consumer, or regulatory agency point of view was generally not good.
5. A lot of pent-up price increase requests were on the way.

Our decision was to regulate largely through the state and federal agencies, but *only* after they had formally written into their regulations stabilization criteria that embodied our general control policies—cost-justified price increases, productivity offsets, and return on investment checks against a base period. Until these agencies adopted the regulations and had them formally approved by the PC, we retained a final review. As an incentive to get their regulations approved quickly, we extended our rate increase review period to sixty working days. Also, we stated that this authority delegated by the PC was temporary, subject to revocation at any time.

Given the size of our staff and its relative expertise in utilities, this was our best move. The decision did allow some large rate increases, but we were satisfied that they were at least justified on account of the screening process we had established.

The decision taught us something else too. Utility price increases are never popular, but they very often *are* necessary. Getting the public to understand this was a job by itself—the utilities decision became part of our larger problem of convincing people we were not looking to keep *all* price increases to zero.

The battle of the bulge, we saw, was not going to be won with barrages of policy statements, press releases, and answers to letters. Up to this point, we had been pinned down to our Washington offices, fighting the deadlines and the mail.

We had to get out of Washington, move the attack out across the country. I had to make myself—me, personally—visible to businessmen, workers, consumers. The PC needed their support, and we therefore needed to know how they felt.

First, we held a conference right in Washington for businessmen, a program sponsored by the U.S. Chamber of Commerce to outline the tier structure, to answer questions about the regulations, and to explain the philosophy behind what we were doing. Then, we planned a trip to six cities over the next few months: Dallas, Chicago, Los Angeles, San Francisco, Boston, and Philadelphia. In each city, we met with the press, consumer groups, citizens at large, businessmen, labor, and the people on the enforcement firing line—the IRS. Going public, I knew, would not necessarily win the battle of the bulge, but it would help us fight a better fight.

One of the most significant outcomes of our going public was our gaining of new insight into the "loss and low profit" firms.

Some firms are hurt by setting a limit for their profit margins for many reasons—the base period was a cyclical low period, it was a new firm in the base period, or the base period was poor because of just plain bad management at the time. If we held such firms to this period as a ceiling, they could not improve, even if they had the opportunity to do so. Clearly, we did not want to freeze firms at a loss or at an unreasonably low-profit position. But how could we create a regulation that would allow them price increases outside of the general rules, but still have some control?

The main difficulty was that every time we tried to create such a special rule we found ourselves referring to some reference criterion—how high could their profit positions climb before they, too, should be subject to the general regulations?

Inevitably, the answer kept coming back to "Return on Investment" (ROI). And every time it did, several of the Commissioners, particularly Newman and Queenan, registered violent objections to the use of an ROI criterion. They felt that such a criterion anywhere in our regulations gave rise to a real danger that we might shift to ROI as a general method of regulation. They insisted that the resulting loss-low profit rule be cast in the same general framework as the other regulations—profit margin and base period control.

Bob Anthony worked very hard with us to create a workable and equitable rule. He kept urging us to use some ROI reference rule. When this was rejected, he tried to create some alternate base period reference periods, such as the best two out of five years, three, four, or five out of five. But every time one base period seemed acceptable to help some loss-low profit industries, it hurt or opened the barn door wide for others.

Time and time again the item appeared on the agenda.

Time and time again, the answer eluded us. We debated this issue for ten meetings over two and a half months!

Lou finally came up with an acceptable compromise. He took a reference ROI of 10 percent and translated it into equivalent capital turnovers and profit margins. Thus, a loss-low profit firm could enter the table with its capital turnover, derive an equivalent allowable profit margin, and end up with a "profit margin control," not an ROI control. Yet behind the table was an implicit 10 percent ROI—which fooled no one, but which gave the objecting Commissioners what they wanted to see—a profit margin control.

The resulting rule, however, really satisfied nobody since it, too, had inequities. Try as we might, we could come up with no better rule. Though everybody despaired of doing anything further, the rule came back again and again to plague us. As bad as it was, the rule was carried over into Phases III and IV.

March brought no let-up.

The first PC meeting in March had on the agenda a tightening action suggested by the staff. Not only were the Commissioners feeling the pressure of the bulge, so were the staff.

After negotiating Term Limit Pricing (TLP) contracts with firms, staff members observed that many of the firms, when using the permissible pricing flexibility, were putting into effect increases of high percentages on some product lines—sometimes 15 or 20 percent. Such increases were perfectly legal under the TLP concept, but the publicity, as well as the economic impact, was hurting the program.

A recommendation was introduced by the staff to go back to the TLP firms, now 120 in number, and ask them to place maximum limit increases on key product lines. The suggested upper limit was 8 percent, a procedure that we generally were following with non-TLP firms to minimize the appearance of high numbers.

The Commissioners liked the general idea, but did not like going back to the firms to violate the TLP "contract." No maximum had been placed on them in the signed agreement. It didn't seem quite fair to change our minds, and so soon.

Finally, we agreed that all firms would be contacted and urged to come to the Commission to renegotiate maximums, but that no firms would be absolutely required to do so. As it turned out most firms did agree to institute 8 percent or lower maximums for most product lines. Some told me later that they felt that they had no choice if they wanted to "keep on the good side of us." As a matter of fact, they did have a choice. But it illustrates the power that a regulatory agency has to even "suggest" behavior.

During the discussion of the TLP maximums, Coleman suggested that, at the same time, we lower the future TLP maximum level from 2 percent to some lower number. It would lower the permissible price level, and it could be regarded by onlookers as a sign of strength. Discussion then centered on what number—1.5, 1.9, or even 1 percent?

If the new number was set too low, we would merely get no future takers of TLPs. They would ignore TLP and come in for regular prenotification, product line by product line, and our administrative burden would collapse us. If we lowered it by only one tenth of one percent, it didn't seem worth while.

We picked 1.8 percent.

This was strictly a guess at about what the market would bear in return for the TLP flexibility advantage. We agreed, however, that we would not go back to present TLP firms and ask them to renegotiate their 2 percent numbers to 1.8 percent, since firms had already made year-long plans and had established market prices with the earlier 2 percent limit. We also feared that if we changed our mind on such a key issue so soon, we might not find businesses trusting us in the future and giving us the voluntary support that we felt was still there.

The news of the lower 1.8 percent limit for future TLPs, and maximums of 8 percent, was hailed in the press as a significant tightening step by the Commission. It was welcome publicity.

Indeed, it was many times welcome, because of the bad February WPI (announced in the beginning of March). Actually it wasn't bad, it was terrible. It was 0.7 percent (8.4 percent annualized).

The key Industrial Commodities Index did not decline at all from the previous month. It was still 0.4 percent. But the worst part was the agricultural sector—a 1.2 percent increase! Food again, particularly *meat*.

During all of the public clamor about rising food prices in the previous few months, Secretary of Agriculture Earl Butz, had been going around the nation defending the rise in farm prices. Secretary Butz sensed the rising consumer agitation for increased price control over agriculture, but he said, "I intend to fight against it like a wounded steer."

Frankly perplexed and frustrated about what to do, we invited Secretary Butz to visit the Commission and discuss the problem with us. This he did on February 23.

Secretary Butz, as usual, presented his case very well. He argued very persuasively that higher prices would bring forth greater supplies. And, in the long run, this was the only answer to secure lower prices. He pointed out the food bargain that the American consumer still enjoyed compared to the rest of the world, and urged that we take no drastic action.

The Commissioners reminded him of our responsibility, and asked his advice as to what we could do.

"Nothing," he said, "unless you want shortages, black markets, and rationing."

"Then, at least, Mr. Secretary," I said, "could you lower your voice a little when you say that high prices are good. It isn't making our job any easier."

He said that the President had charged him with the responsibility of representing American farmers. High prices were good for them, and eventually, good for the consumer. We reminded him that we had the responsibility of lower prices—and now. We parted amicably.

To make the dilemma even more paradoxical the President said to Marina Whitman in her swearing-in ceremony as a new member of the Council of Economic Advisors, "Now, get those food prices down!"

On Friday, March 17, I was due at a press conference to announce our new utility regulations ending the suspension. When I read my newspapers that morning, they were full of stories about Secretary Butz again championing higher food prices.

It got to me.

I wheeled around to my typewriter and typed out a statement that criticized the statements of Secretary Butz. I knew there would be questions on food price increases at the press conference, and I intended to make my views public. I read my statement:

> The statements being made by the Secretary of Agriculture Butz concerning the necessity and desirability of increasing agricultural prices are damaging to the Stabilization Program.
>
> I realize the Secretary is speaking in behalf of his constituency, but if the leader of every sector of the economy did that, the efforts to achieve price stability would be wrecked.
>
> It is no different than a labor leader claiming that a particular set of workers needs more than the wage guidelines to permit them to "catch up," or a business leader saying that his firm needs more than the price rules to permit them to "catch up."
>
> The name of the "catch up" game is inflation.
>
> Farmers stand to lose by inflation just as all other groups in the nation. And, we will never achieve our goal if each group in the country—labor, business, government, and farmers—insist that they deserve special increases because of past inequities on either the wage or price side.
>
> The success of the President's program to stabilize prices requires that everyone work to hold prices down, not to push

126

prices up, as Secretary Butz is advocating. What the Secretary is really advocating is a larger share of the national income for farmers as a special group—and a smaller share of the personal sacrifice which is an essential ingredient in any stabilization program. If the labor and business leaders were to demand and secure higher prices for labor and business respectively, then we would have no program at all. The success of this program requires voluntary compliance from all sectors of this nation to hold down prices. And this includes farmers.

I am not predicting any action that the Price Commission will take. However, we are disturbed by the rise in the prices of some raw agricultural products, and if the rising trend continues, then we will recommend action to the Cost of Living Council or take action ourselves.

There was amazement at the press conference, "Did you clear this with the President?"

"No."

"With anyone?"

"No."

Reaction inside and out of government was one of surprise and some humor. One part of the Administration was fighting the other.

A telegram from Dalhart, Texas said:

It does not make sense to single out farmers and ranchers and criticize Secretary of Agriculture and the same day a Congressional Committee advocates raising minimum wage to $2.00.

The National Livestock Feeders Association angrily attacked:

Your threat to take restraining action against food prices and your criticism of Secretary of Agriculture Earl L. Butz for his position are grossly inconsistent and inequitable.

On the other side, letters and telegrams poured in: "It's about time someone stood up for the consumer." And "Thank God somebody spoke out."

But many just asked for help in the food price squeeze: "I live on a fixed income. I don't care who is to blame—food prices are too high."

The Commissioners were all supportive. I did not hear one word of criticism, or praise, from any member of the Administration. Just silence.

Having said that we might take action if food price rises continued (and we believed that rises would continue), we informally ran over our options that next week inside the staff. They all looked bad. Yet we felt that we just couldn't sit by and do nothing.

Then we had an idea. Just as we had used the public utility hearings to air the issues on the problems of price increases in the utility industry, maybe we could serve the same functions with food hearings:

1. Obtain different viewpoints and perhaps some new solutions;
2. Educate the public about the complexities of the food industry, and the pros and cons of various alternative control devices;
3. Add another notch in our record of public hearings to satisfy some of our critics (Senator Proxmire and Ralph Nader in particular).

We knew that the CPI would be announced on March 23, the day that I would be in Chicago holding one of our "road shows." We also suspected that it would be a bad CPI, particularly for food. So we decided to announce the food hearings during my scheduled morning press conference in Chicago.

We were right. The February CPI was bad. Very bad.

The increase was 0.5 percent (annual 6 percent) for the overall CPI, almost double the rate for the past two months. And the food component was 1.7 percent, the biggest one-month food price increase in fourteen years! Food was responsible for about 75 percent of the price rise of the entire CPI.

Just as I was about to go for my press conference, I received a phone call in my hotel room from Rumsfeld in Washington. He briefed me on the steps being taken to reconstitute the Pay Board following the resignations of four of the five labor leaders. Then he paused near the end of the conversation.

"The President says that he hopes that you and Secretary Butz will tone down your remarks. You both have made your points, and there doesn't seem to be much purpose in starting a debate."

I agreed. "However, if the Secretary starts in again praising food price increases after this CPI, I don't see how I can remain silent."

We left it at that. I went downstairs to face the reporters, all armed with the latest CPI figures.

In response to intense press questions about the rate of increase and what this foreshadowed for the future, I was very glad to be able to announce the food public hearings in Washington on April 12.

One reporter asked me whether the program was working and how long this supposed "bulge" would last.

"I think we are at the tail end of the bulge now." I had no idea whether that was true. It was more a statement of hope.

"Furthermore," I said, somewhat to my own surprise, "The price indicators for March, that will be out in mid-April, will be the most significant since the freeze ended in determining whether prices have stabilized."

Having crawled this far out on the limb, I went on, "If they do not show improvement, we face serious questions as to whether to revise our basic policies."

Looking back, I guess that was really not the best answer I could have given. It was an impulsive statement and based on no economic analysis. I just felt that it was about time for a bulge, if it was really a bulge, to end. We couldn't keep saying over and over, "It's just the bulge." I think I was about right in reflecting the average person's feelings. But as a controller, I think it was a mistake to promise any course of action based on some specific future event, particularly monthly price indicators. But it was time for a showdown on our policies. We had to act or stop talking about it.

When I got back to Washington there was more bad news. Our own staff of internal economists had been asked to make a forecast for 1972. Their report concluded in part:

Measured by the CPI, the rate of inflation is likely to pick up considerably in the second quarter (to an annual rate approaching 4 percent) due to significantly large advances in the WPI (the bulge) during Phase II and the introduction of new spring automobile models . . .

At the Commission meeting on March 30, we decided to devote the entire meeting of April 11 to consideration of a major overhaul of the entire program. We also agreed that we might do nothing, or that we might take drastic steps. But we must seriously consider all options, regardless of how unattractive they might seem. We requested the staff to come up with basic "packages" of options, ranging from major administrative and organizational changes for streamlining purposes, to drastic overhauls of basic policies in every sector. Further, we decided to request some outside economists to give the program a "quick study" and write recommendations for us to consider in time for the April 11 meeting.

I scheduled appointments with leading Stabilization and Administration officials—Shultz, Rumsfeld, Stein, Burns, Connally, and Erlichman—to give them our assessment of the danger ahead, the alternatives that we might be considering, and to request their advice.

We were moving (at last, I thought) on a course of action. The bulge was getting to all of us.

I scribbled a short note to Lou late that evening: "Are we still on the track?"

Lou couldn't answer. No one could.

Doubts had crept into my mind as to whether our policies were really strong enough to do the job. I had already decided that if the indicators did not show a drop in the next month, I was going to switch my vote and remove markups from price increases.

I wrote a memo to the top staff on March 31, the next day, listing all of the major options that might be considered for altering the program at the April 11 meeting:

1. Take off markups on costs.
2. Put a 3 percent ceiling on all the "service" sector.
3. Eliminate posting, or post differently.
4. Change "markup" rules to tighten.
5. Make selective use of the "basket clause" to reduce prices in firms or industries arbitrarily.
6. Organize selective jawboning.

7. Exempt more small firms.
8. Control raw agricultural products (authority required from CLC).
9. Revoke all TLPs.
10. Remove the May 25, 1970 base date.
11. Shift all of Tier I and II to IRS.

Clearly, this was not an exhaustive list.

There were other more stringent options—we could hold all firms to a 0 or a 1 percent price increase, shift to Return on Investment control, go to ceiling prices, or to item-by-item controls, among many other things. But my list represented a zone of real feasibility.

In addition, I asked a staff member, Nona Slutsky, to prepare a short list of "structural" causes of inflation (such as restrictive agricultural production regulations, import quotas, tariffs, Jones Act, minimum price regulations, and so on). This list was for information only, not action, so we could examine whether we should make some structural recommendations for the CLC or for other parts of government.

Finally, I asked that the resulting options and staff papers be bundled together into at least three major "decision packages" —A, B, or C—so that the Commission might adopt a consistent action set. These options were to be immediately distributed to the key Stabilization officials so that they could see what we were thinking about.

Most of those in the Administration argued against hasty action. They were careful not to veto any policy shifts, but they were obviously fearful that we might move too strongly and precipitously.

Typical were some of the reactions of Herb Stein, excerpted from his memo to me of April 8:

1. Change in the rules and procedures is *per se* undesirable. . . . This means not that change should be banned but that it should be economized.

* * *

5. On the basis of all present information it would not be wise to take any radical step to tighten the system at

131

this time, . . . both because we don't want to use up ammunition that we may need if things become clearly bad.

* * *

8. It seems to me that a strong line against further price increases, or requiring price reductions, by firms whose reports show excessive profit margins, would be beneficial. . . .

9. I don't think that the Price Commission should change its rules about pass-through of pay increases. I didn't think in the first place that any limitation by the Price Commission of the inclusion of pay increases approved by the Pay Board was appropriate.

10. I don't see much merit in the idea of a cap on the increase of service prices.

11. The dollar-and-cents pass-through seems to me the big issue. . . . It seems to me that the percentage pass-through, with the profit margin limitations . . . will achieve the desired reduction of inflation. I can conceive of the possibility that at some later date inability to control costs, and continuing excessive price increases might argue for tightening even at the expense of equity and production.

* * *

14. The "basket clause" issue divides into two parts in my mind. One is the possibility of implementing the "windfall profit" principle. I think this should be done. . . . The other aspect of the basket clause seems to be the "selective" application of regulations or jawboning. Since no clue is given to the principles of selection I am unable to comment on that.

15. In short, I think the Commission's best step now would be to try to implement its present standards . . . rather than try to devise new, tighter, but less logical standards.

This memo was included in the Commissioners books for the April 11 meeting.

Also in the books were the quick-and-dirty recommendations

of the outside economists invited to comment on our options. Lou prepared a summary of the recommendations of the five economists (see accompanying table). The responses ranged from almost standing pat to a hard crunch, even a total freeze.

Economists' Recommendations

		Authors				
Options		*Bosworth*	*Fiedler*	*Kendrick*	*Sansom*	*Woodworth*
1.	Current PC Rules and Regulations Encourage Cost-Push Inflation and Price Increases	Yes	No	nc	Yes	Yes
2.	Induce Lower Prices By:					
	a. Rigorous Application of PC Supplied Industry Productivity Figures	Yes	Yes	Yes	Yes	Yes
	b. Retro-Active Application	No	Yes	nc	No	No
	c. Strict Rules to Induce Reduction in Overhead Costs	Yes	nc	nc	nc	Yes
	d. Squeeze Short-Run Corporate Profit Margin by Percentage Cut-Off on Allowable Costs	No	No	No	*	Yes
3.	Substantial Modification of Cost-Pass Thru Concept	Yes	No	nc	Yes	Yes
4.	Re-Activate a Temporary Across-The-Board Freeze (Excluding Rent)	No	No	No	No	Yes
5.	Re-Activate a Temporary Selective Freeze	No	No	No	Yes	No
6.	Eliminate Posting Requirements for Retail Trade	Yes	Yes	Yes	Yes	nc
7.	a. Price Increase "Cap for Tier III Service Firms"	Yes	No	Yes	Yes	Yes
	b. "Cap for Other Industries"	Yes	No	No	No	Yes
8.	Consider Suspension of Import Quotas and Trade Restrictions on Agriculture Products	Yes	No	nc	Yes	Yes
9.	Eliminate "Term Limited Pricing"	No	No	No	Yes	No
10.	Concentrate on Industry and Industrial Commodity Markets Rather than Company Controls	Yes	*	Yes	Yes	Yes

* Qualified

The April 11 meeting was shaping up as a major turning point. I thought the President should know this, and scheduled a meeting with Erlichman; he listened attentively as I went over the following outline:

1. Some fundamental beliefs:
    a. If wages cannot be held to approximately 5.5 percent including fringes, there is little the Price Commission can do to stop the inflation.
    b. If food prices are not held down by controls or some other means, then the Stabilization Program will not succeed. (Labor will not abide by the 5.5 percent if food goes out of sight.)
    c. The Pay Board and Price Commission should be kept apart so long as the Pay Board is not holding to its guidelines. When this is so, then the two could be merged.
    d. The Program is understaffed and underfinanced. Even with drastic cuts in coverage and operating procedures, the Program is starved. An effort to avoid a bureaucracy/low profile has gone too far, and now endangers the program because of inability to be responsive to the various publics—business, consumers, Congress.
2. Status
    a. Present and future indicators are not encouraging:
       C.P.I. First Quarter —3.7%
               Second Quarter—3.9%
               Third Quarter —3.2%
               Fourth Quarter—3.4%
    b. Consumer (labor) support wavering. President's election may be influenced. (Check this with IRS and field offices—not just in Washington.)
    c. Pay Board approvals likely to rise, not fall.
    d. Opportune time now to take bold action:
       —Tighten screws on wages and prices
       —Educate consumers
       —More compliance checks and prosecutions

3. Need to Know:
   a. Is the President really aware of the true status? Is he being shielded?
   b. How strong is the President's feelings on increasing the resources to some extent (*not* a mammoth bureaucracy).
   c. How free are we to start some real tightening down? (Food, jawboning. . .) Is the White House ready to back us when we hold "tough"?
4. Suggestion:
   a. Call an International Conference on Inflation for early 1973.

Yes, Erlichman replied, the President was generally aware of how the program was going, but he didn't know the specifics. Yes, the President disliked a large bureaucracy for price controls, but he felt sure the President wasn't wedded to a set number.

"And I don't know how tough the President wants to be if the numbers don't come down. That's why you were created."

"But would he really want us to take whatever steps we felt necessary—even drastic ones—if we felt that the goal of two to three percent could not be achieved by the end of this year?"

"I don't know," Erlichman replied. "It seems to me that only the President can really answer that question. He's in Moscow right now. As soon as he gets back, I'll mention our conversation to him. And it may be that he will want to get together and talk about it."

I don't know if that conversation ever took place.

In any event, I never did hear from Erlichman or the President further about our policies, and we proceeded to follow our own course as we saw best.

In fact, I saw Erlichman on only three occasions all during Phase II. In each instance, I gave him a general briefing, he thanked me for keeping him informed, congratulated us on doing a good job, and asked only that he or a member of his staff be informed—even if only minutes ahead—on any major decision before we announced it, not for the purpose of approval or veto, but so that they could be informed when their phones started ringing. (I did set up a staff contact arrangement between Lou and Ken Cole on Erlichman's staff.)

Meanwhile, speculation was increasing in the press that the PC was about to crack down.

But What If Prices Don't Turn Down?
Purchasing Week, April 10

Price Control Rules Likely to Change
Columbus Dispatch, April 9

Board Fails to Cut Inflation
Denver Post, April 5

When the Commission met on April 11, the option papers, economists' views, and Administration feedback were on the table.

But several things caused the Commission not to take any drastic action.

First, the Wholesale Price Index for the month of March had been released the first week of April. It showed a dramatic drop to 0.1 percent, after three successive months of 0.6, 0.5, and 0.5 percent. Within the WPI, the Industrial Commodities component declined to 0.3 percent, and best of all, the farm products component showed a −0.3 percent! The Market Basket report released early in April by the Agriculture Department also showed a decline. Live cattle prices had declined in early March, and given the processing and pricing cycle, we knew that meat prices, in particular, should drop. In fact, when Secretary Connally called the major food chains to Washington for the public "jawboning" session, it was clear that the momentum was going in the right direction.

Given these recent encouraging notes, the fact that we were having food hearings the next day (April 12), the desire to wait for the Consumer Price Index to be out in the latter part of April, and the fact that there was no clear-cut consensus about what should be done either by the economists, the staff, or the Commissioners, we decided to postpone any major action.

"But how long do we wait?" complained one Commissioner, "What does it take to change our mind?" No one had the answer to his question, but no one wanted to move drastically—not quite yet.

We agreed, however, that we should take every possible opportunity to tighten administrative procedures, continue to explore some less drastic tightening options, and stay loose for possible activation of all, or part, of the action "packages." The usual percentage margin versus dollar pass-through controversial motion came up again, and as usual, didn't pass. No one had changed his mind. The vote was now three to three (Mary Hamilton, Whitman's replacement, had not yet been confirmed by the Senate).

It was only three days later, on April 15, that we had an opportunity to take some tightening action—the first profit margin violations.

Two firms had clearly exceeded their base period profit margins, as determined from an examination of some of the early quarterly profit margin reports. Though the excesses were not huge, they *were* violations. We decided that this—our "second line of defense"—had to hold firm, and that we had to take action against any and all violators.

But what action? If we waited for the courts to act, this could take months, perhaps even years. We wanted faster action than that.

We could ask the IRS to take over, but we had all the data in our PC files to determine whether there was a violation and how much. As we had already learned, it took time for the IRS to train people in its system, and they were too literal and procedural for such an emerging, judgmental, unprecedented area.

We could assess a fine and put the money in the U.S. Treasury, but it wasn't clear how much fine to assess since the Stabilization Act read "$2,500 per violation." Was there only one violation?

While discussing the matter with Dave Slawson, our General Counsel, I had the idea of using the "treble damages" provision written in the Act, which was intended to compensate consumers with triple the "damages" caused them from illegal over-pricing. It seemed a roughhewn kind of justice to assess the firm triple damages for the amount of the excess. Further, the President had called for price reductions in the market, not fines in the U.S. Treasury. So we invented the rule of ordering the firm to reduce its prices by three times the excess. In a sense, they would be repaying the market as intended by the Act. If there were identifiable consumers, a direct refund would be made. If there were unidentifiable customers, as in a grocery store, the firm would make general price reductions, on any items, until the firm had "repaid" the market triple damages.

For these two firms, the "damages" of $120,000 and $75,000 were ordered as price reductions, and a new regulation was issued accordingly.

I was able to report this tightening action to the Joint Economic Council when I went before them the next week, on April 18. In addition, I reported that many of the nation's firms had not filed quarterly profit margin reports, as required, by the deadline date, and that there were also apparently some violators, against whom we were planning to act. On food prices I stated that we would take more drastic control action in the future if these prices were to rise as much again. "It is a very delicate thing to move into food price controls, and we would do it only as a last resort . . . but we would act if necessary."

Though friendly and often complimentary, Senator Proxmire gave us his usual lambasting for operating a program that was weak, a fraud, a shambles, a travesty! He raked me over the coals for not being tougher, for not cracking down faster, for not holding public hearings, for acting like a "czar."

All in all, however, our recent actions seemed to be interpreted as a more activist Commission, one that was getting tougher and ready to crack down severely if necessary. Actually, we had changed nothing and were just enforcing regulations that had just taken effect.

When the March CPI came out later that week on April 21, the news was almost too good to believe: *0 percent increase!* It was the first such stability since November, 1966. Food prices rose only .2 percent, a dramatic drop from last month's 1.8 percent rise.

I leaped out of my chair and gave a very undignified cheer, when Lou rushed into my office with the news. I think I may also have gone out and consumed several martinis.

138

"It is much too early to claim a victory over inflation. I do not," I said very soberly in my press release. "Price indicators will continue to fluctuate up and down, but I feel that the March indicators are encouraging and offer a hopeful sign that we are moving toward our goal."

It *was* a nice number!

As I told Lou, "We moan when the bad numbers come out. Let's at least cheer a little—secretly—when we get a good one."

Somehow I felt that this really might be, at long last, the end of the "Battle of the Bulge."

Maybe the enemy was at last in retreat.

9

Summer of (relative) content

One stockbroker approached another after a recent rise in the market. "How do you feel about the future?"
"Optimistic."
"Then why do you look so gloomy?"
"I'm not sure my optimism is justified."

Our mood was shifting from anxiety and need for immediate action, to a more relaxed but guarded optimism.

The March and April Wholesale and Consumer Price Indexes had been good, but there was still plenty that could go wrong: Food was likely to take off again . . . demand was picking up . . . the services sector could explode . . . the public still was not convinced controls were working . . . and many of our policies still needed completing or overhauling.

Several of the Commissioners felt that perhaps we weren't being hardnosed enough, while most felt that our tempered approach was about right and we should "stand pat" for a while. We were, therefore, streamlining procedures, making studies for possible policy revisions *either* way, and handling the increasing complexity of effects of our regulations.

Though it was a summer of relative content, it was a nervous contentment. We now had a little more breathing room to think and plan ahead, but we were also facing more complicated problems in food, construction, rent, health, cattle-hides, lumber, autos, petroleum—you name it. Case backlogs, while still manageable, were growing and kept under control only by long staff hours.

Also, we had to move ahead strongly with enforcement of regulations already on the books, particularly the profit margin rule and the filing of quarterly profit margin reports.

Rumsfeld urged us to spend more time on administering the policies we had created, rather than "messing around." Shultz and Stein agreed: They feared that we might become nervous and overreact. "You never know what that Price Commission will do next," said one member of CLC. Connally was pleased with the recovery of the economy, but concerned (as we were) that rapidly rising profits might trigger increased labor demands and erode public support. "If profits stay high," Connally said, "it might well be that there would be justification for further reductions." [*Newsweek,* May 1, 1972]

Partly to calm everyone's fears, I wrote a letter to Connally on May 4. "The press over the last few weeks," it said, among other things, "has given a lot of coverage to activity by the Price Commission and some remarks of mine . . . and I just want to set the record straight." I then emphasized three things: First, that controls would not be lifted at the end of the year, as reported, but only when they were no longer needed; second, that the recently ordered price reductions weren't a "new, tougher policy," but only an enforcement of an earlier ruling; finally, that controls *should* be lifted as soon as possible, because—by their nature—they are abnormal constraints on the market.

I also distributed a priority memo to Lou and two other top PC staff people—Lewis and Carpenter—at the end of April. It summarized my forecasts and the Commission's priorities for the rest of the year. In my scenario-to-be, I predicted an inflationary rate of 3.3 to 3.5 percent by the end of 1972. I also thought the President would dismantle some of the Phase II apparatus, leaving the Commission in charge mainly of Tier I and general policy-making. The program would probably come under heavy pressure from Democratic candidates, Congress, and labor. Food would explode; and the public would become more and more sensitive to bad news, possibly giving rise to demonstrations, boycotts, and mail barrages. The priorities outlined in the memo dealt mainly with the plannings of alternative Phase IIIs, morale in the Commission, more open public relations, emergency operations, and better internal procedures.

The others generally agreed, but Lou penciled in a few observations to the effect that: There is a lack of desire in our society to correct the problems that impede effective competition. For this reason, he said, we will probably never again accept a free market in this country because we now feel that a free market is not effective; government, because of its responsibility for the economy, will continue to play more and more of a controlling role in our society—the instant solution will always be necessary.

Ironically, whether or not we intended to do so, we were assuming more and more of a "tough" image as we slipped into summer. One incident that enhanced this impression was the publication of the list of nonfilers.

On April 15, we had acted on the two firms that had violated the profit margin rule. When I asked Wortman, Director of our Program Operation, how many firms were in violation of that rule in Tier I, he replied, "I don't know. We're checking now to see how many have filed, and how many report that they are over. But I can tell you from those we've seen—it's a mess! Half of them are incomplete or inaccurate." By the end of that month, we had issued price reduction orders for several clear violators, and we had a count of about how many had not even filed.

At the May 3 press conference, I announced that about a thousand large firms apparently had not filed the required profit margin reports, that we were suspending all of their pending price increase requests immediately, and that we would not receive any future requests from them until their reports were in. I added that we would give these firms five days to get their reports in. "If they don't, we will take further action. Price reductions will be ordered. The Justice Department will be requested to seek civil penalties."

Dan Schorr, of CBS News, asked if the nonfiler list could be published. The request seemed reasonable—the firms were in violation. I looked at Lou. He shrugged his shoulders, "Why not?"

"Okay." I said, "You'll have it in a few days."

Lewis, Carpenter, and Wortman—our top staff—rushed up after the press conference, slightly shocked. "What have you done! The list isn't in good shape." Then they smiled. "But don't worry. We'll get 'er out."

And they did. The staff worked almost around the clock, and the list was published on May 7.

Within the next five-day period, the action was hot and heavy. Some firms protested that they had filed, and they were right. Their reports had been filed at the last minute, misfiled, or were incorrectly clipped to other firms' applications (about 10 percent of the total). They were angry that their names appeared on the nonfiler list, and I didn't blame them. I not only wrote apologetic letters, but also published a retraction press release.

But the list also had positive effects. Within the same period, we received over eight hundred reports!

Another so-called "tough" line was our enforcement of the profit margin regulation.

I was scheduled for a speech on Monday, April 24, before the annual meeting of the Associated Press in New York. Since the profit margin rule had attracted some interest and was apparently new to many people, I decided to focus the speech on this topic.

I asked Ted Mills, a member of our staff, to draw up a draft for the speech, since I was getting ready for the testimony before the Joint Economic Committee (JEC) of Congress and making decisions on the first set of violators. Ted—a friend for many years, and a creative thinker and writer—had joined the staff in the early days, and had helped me with public affairs and some speeches. After a lengthy discussion, he prepared a draft which was altered and redrafted several times before finally putting it to bed late Saturday afternoon, April 22.

John Adams, our Public Affairs Director, came to my office just as I was going home that night. "Say, I just saw the speech. Right in the beginning, you say, 'We've inaugurated a series of major actions on the profit margin rule which will result in hundreds of millions of dollars of price reductions.' Are you sure you want to say that? How do we know there will be *hundreds* of millions?"

"Hundreds? Really? I didn't see that. There surely will be millions. But hundreds of millions? I don't know. Let's take it out."

In New York on Sunday, I tuned in the news: "Hundreds of millions of dollars of price reductions are on the way, Price Commission Chairman Grayson will announce tomorrow . . ."

My heart almost stopped.

Apparently, we had deleted the "hundreds" reference in only one part of the speech—neglecting to take it out of another part.

Anyway, it was in there, and the news was full of it that night and the next morning. My stomach wouldn't even let me eat breakfast, but I figured I had to go through with it—and who knows—there *might* be hundreds of millions!

The speech went well, and it made news throughout the nation, largely favorable. Headlines were three inches high in the *New York Post:*

Millions in Price Rollbacks Coming

Editorial comment reflected a common opinion, "Finally, they're cracking down." That day the Dow-Jones industrial average slumped. What would this do to profits? Most businessmen told me later that while this announcement frightened them, they were also relieved to see a firm hand in the control system. This would help to hold the labor line, if labor could see that business was also being held to the mark.

One word did almost all of that!

Reporters, particularly Jim Rowe of the *Washington Post,* kidded me for the next three or four months about the "hundreds of millions." Where were they? I said that I had meant both reductions done voluntarily *and* those we ordered. If they were totaled, hundreds of millions would be achieved. And that was true—that total did reach well over $500 million by the end of the summer.

About this same time, we were also issuing revised regulations concerning productivity offsets against costs. And, of course, our "tough" image grew.

Our first regulations required firms to offset increased labor costs with the individual firms' gains in productivity. But, firms had great difficulties in coming up with good productivity numbers. Not only were we spending an inordinate amount of staff time arguing about the numbers, we suspected we were getting unreliable numbers, probably low.

So we switched in May to using industry productivity numbers, requiring each firm in that particular industry to use the industry average as its productivity offset. We estimated that this might result in a 1 percent increase in productivity offsets across all of Tier I—a considerable reduction.

Our working theory could be summed up in a simple equation:

$$5.5\% - 3.0\% = 2.5\%$$

Wages were not supposed to increase more than 5.5 percent (the wage guideline). And the corresponding increase in productivity we assumed to be 3.0 percent (the long-term average). The increase in wages, therefore, minus the increase in productivity equals the increase in price.

The purpose, of course, was to allow prices to increase by no more than 2.5 percent, right in the middle of the President's goal of 2 to 3 percent by the end of 1972. So even if a business allowed more than a 5.5 percent wage increase, we limited the labor cost pass-through to that amount. Plainly stated, business would either have to keep wage increases to 5.5 percent, or "eat" the excess. However, we knew full well that (1) we couldn't hold either increase exactly to the desired amount, (2) we had no control over about 20 percent of the economy, and (3) the formula was only a rough approximation to what really happens. But it was a useful conceptual tool, good for keeping us in roughly the right direction.

The biggest problem, perhaps, was in quantifying productivity.

It seemed reasonable to require firms to subtract from their labor cost increases the amount of their productivity gains. But most firms in the U.S. didn't know what their productivity was: that is, they could not come up with an accurate number that quantified what their productivity change was from one year to the next. We had expected some difficulty with the smaller firms in Tier II or those at the bottom of Tier I, but we were shocked to find that even the largest firms could not provide an estimate that was reliable. And they were the first to admit it.

Our analysts worked with their staffs to use some approximate figures, but they knew—and we knew—that the numbers were unreliable and probably on the low side. Almost half of our staff's early time was spent with the firms discussing the proper number.

Our first regulations governing productivity were therefore ineffective.

After about six months, we switched to industrywide productivity figures. Working with the Bureau of Labor Statistics, Federal Reserve Board, other federal agencies, and consultants, our staff came up with long-term productivity figures, based on industry-wide averages over a ten-year period. From then on, firms were required to use these numbers instead of their own individual company figures. About 450 industry figures at the four-digit Standard Industrial Code (SIC) level were released, the first time that such a list had ever been compiled and published by the government.

This helped in several ways. First, time was not wasted arguing over company figures. We did have arguments as to whether the industry amount was valid, but such disputes were few. Second, we found that productivity gains offset wage increases in a greater number of cases, thereby lowering our price increase requests.

The industry figures also acted in two ways as an incentive for firms to raise their productivity levels. Those firms with productivity gains above the industry-wide average only had to deduct the lowest figure, thus encouraging above-average gains. Those with gains below the industry average were encouraged to increase productivity because higher figures were being subtracted from their costs. All firms were also required to take a deduction for the amount of productivity increases obtained from volume increases. The total of these two deductions prompted firms to share their long-term productivity gains and their increases due to increased cyclical volume with the consumer.

There was another added benefit to our entire productivity program: These requirements of the Commission helped to increase the productivity *consciousness* of business. Many firms reported that they had formed task forces to measure and to stimulate productivity. Articles were written in many journals on the importance of productivity as a weapon against inflation and as a deterrent to foreign competition.

The nonfiling announcement, the enforcement of the profit margin rule, and the productivity offset rule all got press play as a new, tough line.

Actually, though they were perhaps tough, they weren't new. It was true, however, that we had decided to enforce these rules strictly and swiftly, and that we were probably influenced by the persistence of the bulge.

All of these actions were having some impact at the CLC and the White House. The reactions ranged from surprise to fright

146

to irritation over the "independent" actions of the PC. A story in the May 10 *Christian Science Monitor* probably accurately summed up the feeling:

> High Nixon administration officials, who never liked the idea of wage and price controls to begin with, now are becoming disenchanted with their chief price controller, Price Commission Chairman C. Jackson Grayson, Jr.
>
> The Price Commission Chairman . . . is coming under criticism for acting—or at least sounding—too tough.
>
> Some officials believe that the commission is cracking down too hard on business, and that its sudden strict enforcement of its profit guidelines will not permit business enough profit growth to keep the economic expansion growing.
>
> Others are mostly worried about appearances . . . If business fears a heavy handed cutback of profits, and responds by entrenching, the results could be devastating to Mr. Nixon's hopes of slashing unemployment by election time.
>
> As Mr. Stein cracked: "We did build a certain independence into the system. The Cost of Living Council has no control over these rules, and the Price Commission has shown no particular concern with our election."

The article also cited an incident which increased the concern and irritability between the staffs of CLC and the PC—the small business exemption.

The PC had recommended early in the designing stage of Phase II that small businesses be exempted from the program. The CLC did not agree for fear that the program would not be regarded as comprehensive. In January, we recommended (and the CLC concurred) that firms with less than $100,000 in sales be exempted.

In April, the CLC asked us for our opinion concerning increased exemptions for small firms. We agreed that it still made economic and administrative sense, but stated that we believed it would be a bad psychological move at this particular time. The bulge was still there, and polls continued to report that the public's estimation of the effectiveness or fairness of controls was low. Our recommendation, by a vote of six to nothing, was to postpone the exemption. My subsequent letter to Rumsfeld stated that while this was our position, we would certainly implement any final decision they made.

We received word shortly afterward that the CLC had decided to exempt all firms from the program that had sixty or fewer employees. I called the Commissioners so that they would not be taken by surprise; and Coleman and Scranton, in particular, felt that our views should not be hidden when asked by the press. It would be worse, they argued, to deny the disagreement and have it emerge later.

Though I had told Rumsfeld that this was our intention, I called his office on Monday morning (May 1) to be sure he knew. He was not in, but I reiterated to his top assistant, Dick Cheney, that we would say the action was not our recommendation but that our disagreement was regarding the timing of the decision, not the substance.

Right after the CLC announcement, the reporters came to me for comment. I stated our position, and within minutes it was on the wire service.

Rumsfeld called immediately. "What the hell is going on!" (I had never heard him so mad.) "What are you trying to do?"

"What do you mean?"

"Saying you disagreed with us. We checked this with you weeks ago, and now you say you aren't supporting the decision. You seemed so cooperative when I talked to you and then you do something like this." (He was almost yelling.) "The White House is hopping mad. My phone is ringing off the hook—what the hell is Grayson doing?" He went on . . .

I was furious. I had told him what I was going to say and why. I had told the truth—we *did* disagree.

"Are you finished?" I said after a few minutes.

"For now."

"Then you listen. I did tell you. I told you with the letter. . ." And I went on to enumerate the steps I had taken to explain why we would honestly state our recommendation. I did not feel that it was destructive, for I had said that we would certainly move to carry out the decision and we recognized that this was the CLC's perogative.

My own guess is that Rumsfeld was reflecting the increasing concern among the top White House staff over our independence.

148

The press report got a bigger play than he had suspected, and he would have preferred a "no comment" or a "fuzzed up" remark on the disagreement. And, apparently, the White House staff did not like *any* sign of disagreement in the Administration.

That was the point at which my personal relations with Rumsfeld were strained. Though we were in the future cordial, there was a noticeable beginning of exclusion from forward planning and thinking of the CLC.

This was even reflected at the internal staff level. The CLC staff began to look over our shoulder and introduce more checkpoints, causing even more irritation between the two units and some bureaucratic haggling and in-fighting. A top CLC staffer told Bert Lewis, "We've set up a zone defense on you."

Another incident that strained our relationships with the CLC occurred around several meetings in June concerning the renewed take-off in food prices.

In May, we stressed that while recent food price news was good and we would not take any tightening steps at that time, we knew that the problem was still there. At the May 3 press Conference, I said that we would set up a "food watch unit" to monitor the demand/supply situation, ask IRS to monitor compliance by retailers and wholesalers more closely, and conduct periodic meetings with the food industry to work for solutions. But by the middle of June, we were in trouble again, particularly from beef and pork prices. We set aside part of our June 21 PC meeting to discuss the situation. A staff paper reported:

Beef: The price of ready-to-slaughter cattle has surpassed the February 1971 level and has now reached a 21-year high. . . The basis for rising prices continues to be one of demand-pull, while the consumer, although complaining, continues to pay the price.

The same kind of report was given for pork, fruits, and vegetables. Predictions were that prices would continue near present levels, or go even higher.

The staff prepared a list of seventeen alternatives that the Commission might consider to mitigate expected food price increases. They started with moral suasion and increased in severity to con-

149

trolling raw agricultural products, and even to a freeze. Pros and cons were given for each of the options.

After extended discussion, we decided that the basic problem was really supply, and that actions on the price side would be taken reluctantly if we saw nothing being done on the supply side in the Administration. But we had not seen any disposition to action on that end. We then agreed unanimously to write an open letter to the CLC, and to meet again in four days, on Sunday, June 25, for an all-day meeting on this single topic. By that time, we hoped for a reply from the CLC. Frankly, we also hoped that this letter would not only put some pressure on the CLC to act but also give them more incentive to take some action because of "pressure" from the Price Commission.

I called Rumsfeld immediately after the meeting to tell him of the decision and the letter he would be receiving. Rumsfeld was out. Jamie McClane, his deputy, said, "Could you possibly hold up releasing the letter to the press until we read it and have a chance to react?" We had agreed unanimously to make it a public letter. But it did seem a reasonable request. "I don't know. The Commissioners have left and are on the way to the airport."

"Could you check?"

Several of the Commissioners were still in the building. But others had left some time ago, headed for the airport in my car. I called on the car phone, and because they were delayed by heavy traffic, we intercepted them just before the airport. They reassembled, and agreed to delay release of the letter to the press, but directed that it be sent that night to Rumsfeld.

In part, the letter said:

> While the [food price] problem has been caused by the natural forces of supply and demand, the Commission feels that immediate action must be taken to prevent further prices increases. We, therefore, are recommending that the Cost of Living Council place raw agricultural products under control so that the Commission may adopt measures to control food prices at each level of the production and distribution process. It is also recommended that appropriate action be taken by the Council to alleviate the shortage of supply.

150

We closed by asking that an answer be given before the Sunday, June 25 meeting.

John Adams told the press that the PC had decided to take no action at this time. Our prepared statement expressed "increased concern" and said that "various measures are currently under active consideration."

The press was angry.

"I was faced with approximately a dozen top reporters," John Adams said later. "They had already been kept waiting for more than two hours. They were all up against a tight deadline and in no mood to be trifled with. In view of this, the statement we provided obviously could not satisfy them. Further, several of them already had a sense of the story. I learned later that Irving R. Levine had broadcast the guts of it in the six-thirty newscast."

Although we had decided not to release the letter until the CLC had a chance to study it, word about the existence of the letter had gotten out, and reporters laid siege to the CLC's offices. The Council responded that they had received a letter from the PC and were studying it.

The President told reporters at an impromptu news conference in his Oval Office on Thursday (June 22) that he had directed the CLC "to see what further action can be taken to deal specifically with food prices, but particularly with meat prices." He further added that action on the meat side "doesn't rule out, also, the possibility of moving on the control side."

On Friday, Rumsfeld released our letter to the press, labeling it a "modest little missive." It wasn't news any more, for its contents were already known and reported.

On Saturday, Rumsfeld called me to say, in confidence, that the President had decided to open up the meat import quotas, to be announced by the President on Monday, and that the Council was studying other ways to increase supplies. Taking us into confidence in advance of the announcement was undoubtedly designed to influence our Commission meeting on Sunday. And it did.

Our meeting that Sunday was pro forma. Given the impending announcement, we could see little reason to act, particularly since that we didn't want to take drastic control steps anyway. But we had made our point, and action would be taken.

The reporters were assembled again, awaiting the end of the Sunday meeting. They came up to my office as a group, and all I could tell them was that I had "no comment" about our meeting. I could not tell them about the President's announcement the next day, and I couldn't just say we weren't going to do anything, for after our strong letter, they would want to know why.

To repeated questions, I replied, "No comment."

I'll never forget Phil Shabacoff of the *New York Times* angrily stalking out of the room, grumbling, "So this is the day that the Price Commission learned no comment."

The press played up the President's announcement the next day as a response to PC pressure. Though the CLC had undoubtedly discussed such actions before, and probably had studies under way, they had not informed us. Though I do not know for sure, I believe that our action served as a precipitating event. But it also cost us in our relationships with Rumsfeld, and probably further antagonized relations with other CLC officials and White House staff over our "independence."

Before we adjourned that Sunday, we directed the staff to take another extensive review of "where we were, what policies needed modifying or changing, what was likely to happen in the months ahead, and what our options would be to tighten if need be."

We agreed to meet again in a month, on August 1 and 2, to see what should be done, if anything.

I was leaving for Europe in a few days for a vacation and to teach at the European Institute of Business Administration, in Fontainbleau, France. Prior to leaving, I prepared a memo for our staff and for the Commissioners to set down my views:

Recommendations of the Chairman
(June 22, 1972)

A. *Central Recommendation*
   1. Do nothing substantial now.
   2. Write a letter to President stating problems in areas outside of controls, state possibility that we will not make goal (possible 3.5) and include a list of contemplated

actions by Price Commission if things do get worse in the next few months.

3. Prepare a battle plan that will be enacted if we get sufficiently bad (____%) WPI and (____%) CPI. Work with Pay Board to develop a joint plan. Bring completed staff work on a joint plan back to the Price Commission for its August meeting.

4. Grayson to have continuing personal meetings with Stein, Shultz, Erlichman, Burns, Rumsfeld to inform them and get their attitudes.

B. *Primary Reasons for Recommendation*
1. Except for food (and a few other non-controlled items), the record has not been too bad. May CPI on *controlled* items was only an increase of .1%.

2. It would be better to move in concert with the Pay Board so that it doesn't appear that business is suffering all of the burden of tightening, particularly because these will be drastic measures.

3. To move too prematurely (if you believe that the record is not too bad so far) is not only incorrect if future indicators in fact turn out not to be too bad, it also makes the Commission look bad when actions will have to be rescinded.

4. If, in fact, the record *does* turn out to be bad in the future, the Commission can still act. Elections, do not have anything to do with *our* power or ability to act. Even if we were to act "too late" for the year end goal, the real goal is getting the inflation rate down, even if it is in the first quarter of 1973.

5. It will take at least a month to have a sufficiently detailed plan if policies are to be changed.

6. We already have some pretty tough policies that are limiting price increases, and often to the point of jeopardizing the existence of the institutions: the 5.5% labor limitation, the profit margin ceiling, industry average productivity, the 6% cap on hospitals, and the 3% cap on services.

7. Many of the prime causes of large increases are beyond

the control of the Commission, and it is very unfair to cause the controlled sectors to bear the full burden of a tightening.

C. *Administration Views*

1. George Shultz wants things to continue as they are, no change. A 3.5% rate would probably satisfy him. Meat does concern him. He would not like a toughening of controls.

2. Herb Stein would be almost the same as George Shultz. He also recognizes the arithmetic, economic and political impossibility of the trend in food prices.

3. John Ehrlichman doesn't really follow the program much. His main concern is the political repercussions of any move. He wants to be informed in advance of any actions so that his office can be prepared for reactions from any quarter.

4. Don Rumsfeld thinks things are going along pretty well, and would prefer no drastic ship-rocking. However, if things got pretty bad in the indicators (or in food), he is supportive of tougher measures. Would prefer that we wait longer to see more data of a convincing nature.

5. Ed Fiedler thinks that the goal is feasible, and that there is more reason to hope that we will be successful, judging from the way he reads the data. He would prefer a period of stability in the policies so that we can see what's happening—and so that business can plan. He believes that the recovery is not yet so strong that we couldn't stop it with some rough measures. He would be satisfied with a 3.5% rate at the end of the year.

6. Arthur Burns thinks the recovery is going well, and is concerned about the rate of inflation. He is still fearful that we might hurt the strong recovery with some drastic measures, but he also knows that continuing high rates of inflation will only accelerate labor demands. He also knows that continuing high profits will increase labor's demands, and he wonders if we might not have to "hurt" profits a little for the overall good of the long run stabili-

zation effort. He basically believes that the trouble rests with the Pay Board who are still pushing through higher wage levels than can be consistent with the overall goal. He thinks that they are too concerned with peacemaking, and not enough with price stability.

D. *Alternative Policies*
1. Relax profit margin ceilings for selected firms which are willing to make price reductions and/or who demonstrate increased productivity.
2. No new Term Limit Pricing (TLP) agreements (unless the firm is "giving up" an X% of allowable costs in return for the 1.8% TLP price increase).
3. Establish some reductions in the amount of price increases. For example:
    a. Establish a ceiling price for price increases on the products of some basic industries. In the paper by Al-Samarrie of June 15, he suggested a 2% ceiling for 32 basic industries where they have a high inflationary impact, degree of product homogeneity, degree of concentration, and ability to absorb cost increases in past inflationary periods.

    or

    b. Remove margins. Grant price increases by product line on cost increases as long as the cumulative price increase since January 1, 1972 has not exceeded 1.8%. Over 1.8%, limit the amount of such costs that will be allowed as price increases. The limits would vary depending on the nature of the cost increases, the financial situation of the firm, the specific situation in the market, etc.
4. Reduction of Pay Board guideline to X% (say 4.5%).

The memo, in its entirety, conveyed my feelings and those of others at this midpoint in the control program; we were still riding the knife-edge between under and overcontrolling. It also reflects our continuing review of our policies, and our willingness to take drastic action if necessary.

Also very important, the memo illustrates something known

mostly by those who follow the Washington economic scene closely: that is, economic policy making is a compromise—and often a heated one—of various points of view, many times with a paucity of data, gun slinging, interpersonal bickering, and widely differing recommendations. It's the democratic process, populated by imperfect people with the emotional and ego needs we all have. But I had assumed—and I think it's true of the average citizen—that wise, gray-headed economic elders, assembled around a polished mahogany table, would lead the way to truth via factual logic and calm discussion, applauded and supported by all. Of course, it doesn't happen that way.

My view was admittedly naive, but I think I was no different in my perceptions (or hopes) from millions of people. There is in everyone a persistence of the child's beliefs, or hopes, that his parents are all-wise, consistent, and right.

In July 1972, just before one of my lectures at the European Institute, I received a phone call from Bert Lewis in Washington.

"Are you sitting down?"

I couldn't tell from his voice whether the news was good or bad.

"The CPI and GNP are just out."

"And . . .?"

I walked afterwards into the classroom and wrote on the blackboard:

CPI	0.1
GNP Deflator	2.1

There was a cheer. The class, mostly all international managers, were following the wage-price control program with great interest. Most knew more about the program than many Americans. They were particularly interested, because most of their countries had tried some form of income policies ever since World War II, with mixed results, mostly bad. When the U.S. embarked on its first peacetime wage-price control program, the world received the news with the same amount of surprise as most Americans, and with a certain amount of sorrow. Now, the champion of free enterprise in the world was embarking on a strong program of government intervention in the economy. They, as did many others, had much skepticism that it would work. But they were

156

surprised and pleased with the latest results, and they wanted to know all the details.

Also while at the European Institute I was visited by a group of French government and industry officials who wanted to know the specifics about our program; and I made a trip to England to spend a day with British officials from the Treasury and the Confederation of British Industries. Though many of the details of our policies—economic, political, and administrative—were not applicable to other countries, the French and English were intrigued and wanted to see what could be adapted to their economies. What amazed them most was that our system was apparently working.

The news of the recent price indicators made my European trip even nicer . . . 2.1 percent.

Wow!

Returning to the States in late July, I found that much work had been done in preparation for the August PC meeting.

Wortman, author of the periodic "View from the Pit" memos, had operational summaries ready:

- –Incoming Tier I price requests are running at 25 a day (who made that lousy estimate of 80?)
- –Rapidly becoming a lawyer's paradise. Full bloom of regulatory process in remedial orders vastly exceeds my expectations and temperament.
- –Average approvals continue at 3.2% of applicable sales, and 1.6% of total revenues.
- –Of the 182 TLPs, monitoring plans are in from 169 and 68 have been approved.
- –Biggest push is on base period profit margin reports. 1830 received, 1394 reviewed, but 49% required resubmission or further documentation from company.
- –Major problem right now with five meat packers who did not get individual company volatility orders . . . We could wipe 'em out.
- –Bert has asked that we start thinking about second round TLPs.
- –Time to take stock of our zealous pursuit of violations. I'm

convinced, from my meetings with companies, that many have been conscientious in support of program and feel that zapping we give publicly is not justified.

--Need to cut down paper flow in this place. Staff spending too much time chasing it all and segregating it accurately.

His report concluded with:

--I've purposefully left out the hot ones on autos, can companies, textiles, and apparel that are coming up. Bert will cover these with you.

There was greater detail to the report, but this much of it, at least, reflects the tremendous administrative detail and paper burden that most people overlook when focusing on more dramatic events and policy decisions.

The staff had also sampled the Commissioners' views on the program to date and their requirements in the way of policy studies and data prior to the August meeting. Reading these reports, I was concerned that the August meeting was shaping up as a "summit" meeting, at which we might feel compelled to take action simply because we had so often decided not to.

Lou summed up what he felt were the Commissioners' views as of July 10:

Coleman: Does not feel the program is going as well as it might be. Discouraged with food prices and the difficulties in handling demand-pull inflation.

Hamilton: Program going well, except for demand-pull areas.

Lanzillotti: Doesn't feel we will reach the three percent target, but will be between 3.0 and 3.5%. Feels inflation might have been 6.0% without controls, but that demand-pull will be beyond our control. He opposes profit margin control, wants more emphasis on price control.

Newman: Working well, but needs more policing of rules. Inflationary psychology still with us. Need major tax revisions. Feels CLC not keeping us as informed as they should be.

Queenan: Not doing badly. Concerned over demand-pull. Fears over-controlling manufacturing sector because of problems with food.

Scranton: Assumes we won't reach 2–3% goal, but will hit 3.6%. Action must be taken by Sept. 15 to have any impact on goal. Doesn't think CLC will take necessary actions to check demand-pull, and will overrule any radical actions we take.

In summary, they feel we have been successful on the cost-push side, but that we lack the necessary tools to meet demand-pull inflation.

The Commissioners, perhaps a bit restless to know what more could be done, asked for additional work in preparation for the August meeting. Among their requests were (1) a package designed to achieve the 2.5 percent annual rate if the aim is to do so at all costs, (2) a package to meet the problems, distortions, and hardships created by existing rules, and (3) a package to tighten the program now, while at the same time limiting the post-control bubble. They also sought papers on the relationship of the WPI to the CPI, on upcoming and past wage contract settlements and their effects on tightening up on the industrial sector, and on the use of TLPs or other tradeoffs with business for guaranteed limitations on future price increases. More data was brought in at their behest: The latest Wharton projections on the economy, and projections by the Federal Reserve Board and other recognized sources; a status report on profit margins for the second quarter and the results of the analysis of Tier II reports; and a detailed study of price approvals by four-digit Standard Industrial Code (SIC) code, with the month of effective price increase date matched to the monthly Wholesale Price Index, unadjusted. Perhaps most significantly, they wanted a paper on redefining our goal in view of the limitation to restrict activities to cost-push areas, the possible effects of pending minimum wage bills, and currency devaluation.

Curt Jones, Director of Price Policy, opened the August Commission meeting with the presentation of a "policy matrix" reproduced on the following pages. The matrix presented eleven basic tightening policy options arrayed against eight sets of inflationary assumptions. It illustrates two things: first, the range of options that controllers scan; and second, the complexity of applying policies under varying assumptions about the type of inflation, the rate of increase of the major indicators, the life of the program,

Policy Action	Strong demand pull inflation. CPI, WPI rise; predict over 3% inflation by year end.[1][3]	Strong demand pull. CPI, WPI continue to rise.[2][3]	Strong demand pull. CPI, WPI continue to rise.[2][4]
Price Reductions			
1. Order price reduction	X	X	
2. Exchange for partial profit margin relief	X	X	X
3. Make reductions in (2) optional	X	X	X
4. No profit margin for firms who have not mixed prices or rolled back with restitution			
Collective Case Processing			
1. Change from individual to collective processing on a monthly basis	X	X	X
2. Change to collective processing on quarterly basis			
3. No change			
Allowable Costs			
1. Dollar for dollar pass-thru			
a. Full			
b. Partial	X	X	
2. Percentage of cost justification			
a. Straight percent	X	X	
b. Percent of justification above a certain price increase percent		X	X
3. Limit indirect costs			
a. Allow direct costs only	X		
b. Direct costs +5.5%; "other" labor and 2.5% remaining "other"		X	
c. Direct + govt. mandated costs (health and safety taxes, etc.)			
4. Cap or ceiling on costs	X		
5. Continue present policy reducing cost justification			

[1]Program ends April 30, 1973.
[2]Program extended beyond April 30, 1973.
[3]Goal of 3 percent rate of inflation by December 31, 1972.
[4]Goal of 3 percent rate of inflation by March 31, 1973.
[5]Goal of 3 percent rate of inflation by end of program.
[6]Program ends April 30, 1972.
[7]Goal of 2.5 percent rate of increase by December 31, 1972.

Little demand pull. CPI, WPI continue to rise.[1][5]	Little demand pull. CPI, WPI continue to rise.[2][3]	Little demand pull. CPI, WPI continue to rise.[2][4]	Little demand pull. CPI, WPI stabilize; projections indicate 3% by end of year.[2][3]	Strong demand pull. CPI, WPI continue to rise; predict inflation over 3% by year end.[6][7]
				X
	X			
X	X	X		
			X	
X	X	X	X	
				X
			X	
X	X			X
	X			X
X		X		X
				X
X				
				X
			X	

Policy Action	Strong demand pull inflation. CPI, WPI rise; predict over 3% inflation by year end. [1] [3]	Strong demand pull. CPI, WPI continue to rise. [2] [3]	Strong demand pull. CPI, WPI continue to rise. [2] [4]
Profit Margin Rules			
1. Freeze current profit margins	X		
2. Cut base period margin by 25%		X	X
3. Average of 3 out of 3			X
4. Roll base period forward		X	X
5. Present policy			
Time Limit Pricing (TLP)			
1. Abrogate all existing TLPs	X	X	
2. Tighten existing TLP agreements			X
3. No new agreements			
4. Continue TLP			
Averaging of Price Increases Granted			
1. Cost justification is the maximum	X	X	X
2. Present policy			
Other Agencies			
Coordinate with listed agencies	X	X	X
Revised Coverage and Classification			
1. Realignment of the tier structure			
2. No change	X	X	X
Recontrol			
1. Recontrol and extend	X	X	
2. Recontrol		X	X
3. Partial recontrol			X
4. No change			
Processing Delay			
1. Delay indefinitely			
2. Change processing time from 30 to 90 days		X	X
3. Selective delay	X	X	
4. No change			
Price Freeze			
1. General freeze			
2. Selective freeze	X	X	
3. No freeze			X

[1] Program ends April 30, 1973.
[2] Program extended beyond April 30, 1973.
[3] Goal of 3 percent rate of inflation by December 31, 1972.
[4] Goal of 3 percent rate of inflation by March 31, 1973.
[5] Goal of 3 percent rate of inflation by end of program.
[6] Program ends April 30, 1972.
[7] Goal of 2.5 percent rate of increase by December 31, 1972.

Little demand pull. CPI, WPI continue to rise.[1][5]	Little demand pull. CPI, WPI continue to rise.[2][3]	Little demand pull. CPI, WPI continue to rise.[2][4]	Little demand pull. CPI, WPI stabilize; projections indicate 3% by end of year.[2][3]	Strong demand pull. CPI, WPI continue to rise; predict inflation over 3% by year end.[6][7]
X	X	X		
	X	X		
				X
			X	
	X			X
X				
		X		
			X	
X	X	X		X
			X	
X	X	X	X	X
			X	
X	X	X		X
				X
	X	X	X	
X				
	X	X	X	
				X
X	X	X	X	

and the level of the goal. Even this fairly exhaustive matrix does not include all possibilities or economic conditions.

The options were arranged, in the opinion of the Policy group, in the order of "administrative and political feasibility and reasonableness." Some policies could be imposed alternatively, in many cases, concurrently. The Policy group remained neutral in its recommendations (though I believe that the staff always wanted to be a little tougher than the Commissioners).

I gave my recommendation first: that is, we should for the most part stand pat. We should continue strict enforcement of all our policies, standing ready to implement some of the more severe options if the situation worsened. We could move fast because all the options we could think of at the time were before us. As we went around the room, though there were discussions of ways to improve our policies (particularly to modify the profit margin rule to give more incentives for price reductions), almost everyone agreed with the status quo.

Again, we had rejected drastic changes in the program, not because of any pressure from the CLC or the White House, but simply because we collectively thought that the rudders were set about right. Affecting the discussion were the recent excellent CPI and GNP Price Deflator figures. It hardly seemed appropriate to crack down when the indicators were behaving so well.

This is not to say that there were not difficult trouble areas in the economy, nor that we felt that inflation had been conquered. Lumber and cattle hides, for example, were trouble spots all during Phase II, and they had not calmed down.

In the case of lumber, we had made study after study to determine what could be done about phenomenal price rises. All of our investigations showed that the principal cause of higher prices was the general building boom, particularly residential housing starts.

We sent IRS teams to the lumber industry and they found some, but relatively few, violators. Small lumber operators with sixty or fewer employees were exempted on May 1, but were recontrolled by the CLC on July 17 when prices shot out of sight. Lumber hearings were held in various cities across the country. The Forest Service was requested to try to increase the timber cut

164

from federal lands. The Department of Transportation was requested to try to increase freight car availability. Japanese lumber importers were urged to reduce their purchases in the U.S.

But lumber prices kept rising.

Cattle hides presented a similar problem. Prices shot out of sight to a point more than double their historic highs. Argentina and Brazil had terminated their exports of hides, thereby decreasing world supplies and increasing world prices. Domestic and foreign demand was increasing rapidly. Hide exports were increasing. U.S. shoe manufacturers could not get enough of increasingly scarce cattle hides.

In desperation, I wrote a memo to Lou on June 14: "Lou—what *are* we going to do about the cattle hide prices? It seems to me that we can't keep 'waiting' for others to do something if they don't act!" On July 18, the Secretary of Commerce did act. Lou, working with the CLC, had persuaded the Commerce Department that export controls should be imposed. Export controls went on, and four weeks later, Congress passed a bill taking them off. All that work went to no avail.

We just gave up trying to do anything more about cattle hides.

Both lumber and cattle hides illustrate the problem of trying to contain prices by price controls when products reach a demand state, and particularly when there are world markets higher than domestic markets.

Administrators of both Phase III and IV fell heir to similar demand situations, except in greater number, and they felt, I'm sure, the same degree of frustration and impotence that we did. Complete price suppression leads to distortions in the domestic market and to the subsequent cry for export controls if the world price is higher. *Little can be done with price controls in demand inflation.*

Other problem areas arose.

The construction industry said they simply could not live with our 5.5 percent labor cost pass-through. Longshoremen said the same. Petroleum, zinc, sugar, silver, wheat, fish, poultry, cement, coffee, milk, and others all presented situations begging for special attention. The number of exception cases increased by orders of magnitude, as firms tried to get relief from regulations that were increasingly burdensome, or were squeezed by the impact of our regulations.

Profits were rising rapidly, as were Wall Street stock averages—good news for the recovery. But high profits were also partly bad news: Labor and the public couldn't understand how profits could increase by such large percentages (10, 15, even 40 percent when wages were held down to 5.5 percent—that is, if price controls were *really* effective.) Explanation of the fact that profits were almost at an all-time low had little impact. With controls, increased profits seemed suspect.

In fact, during one trip to Harvard in the late spring, I gathered together about ten economists from Harvard College and the Harvard Business School, and their advice was to crack down harder on profits—not necessarily because they wanted to hurt business, but because they felt it was essential to keep public support, to hold labor to their 5.5 percent, and to hold down prices. "Spill a little capitalists' blood," one recommended. One of the most dispiriting events of that summer was the return of the auto industry for more price increases.

It seemed like a rerun of an old movie.

We had maintained contact with the industry during the spring and summer of 1972 as they planned their 1973 model year. Lou indicated to them that we hoped that they would file for no more than a dollar pass-through (no margins) of the cost of installing government mandated safety and emission equipment directly on the vehicles.

We made it clear that if they filed for more than that, we felt that we would have to hold public hearings. The CLC was kept informed of the discussions, for they indicated that they wished to track the situation closely in the event that they might want to intervene.

In late June, both American Motors and Chrysler filed for more increases than what we had hoped for. But their filings were perfectly legal and their price increase requests were cost justified. Given that they clearly had no profit margin problem, our regulations would permit them to receive the increase unless we intervened. The only way to stop them would be to invoke the "basket clause."

We ordered a detailed IRS audit to make certain of the submit-

166

ted facts and to buy time. The industry had had an exceptionally good sales and profit year, with volumes that exceeded forecasts made by them, or by us, in late 1971.

Both GM and Ford then filed, also for more than we had hoped. They asked for both dollar pass-through of federally mandated costs directly on the vehicle, and also cost pass-through on product improvements and plant safety and emission costs. These were certainly all legitimate costs that justified price increases under our regulations. But unlike Chrysler and American, both GM and Ford were much closer to their profit margin ceilings.

At this point, Rumsfeld decided to try publicly to get the auto companies to reduce their price requests, or to request none at all. Leaders of the industry were called to the White House for a jawboning session. It was our hope that Rumsfeld would meet with success, for if he did, the problem would leave our doorstep.

He was partially successful.

Ford and GM reduced their requests to a straight dollar pass-through of federally mandated costs directly on the vehicle. Chrysler had already cut its request prior to the White House session (after some jawboning by Lou), and refused to cut any lower. American also refused to cut.

During this process, Ralph Nader filed suit against the PC for not holding public hearings on the automobile price increases. We had not intended to hold hearings if the companies originally had come in for the lower amounts, for it was clear that they had greater legitimate costs, and the lower amounts would represent quite a reduction in a major economic sector. But the companies did file for the higher amounts, and we did schedule the hearings. Nader's suit was thrown out of court when we announced the hearings.

Shortly after the hearings were announced, we had finished our analysis of the profit margin positions of all of the automobile companies. Ford would be over their profit margin limit, by our estimates, if we granted them the increase. GM was not as close as Ford to their limit, but under one set of calculations, they could go over their margin if we granted the increase.

I decided to deny Ford and GM for three reasons: First, they were near their margin ceiling; second, the ripple effect of this major industry on the economy could be great; and third, the denial would have a favorable impact on public inflationary psychology. I do not know whether we would have invoked the "basket clause" if the profit margin rule had not been usable, but I suspect the vote would have been close in the Commission.

An hour before the announcement, I called Rumsfeld, who was pleased at the outcome. When I called Shultz, he was silent for a second. "That's a big one. Are you sure?"

"Yes."

"Thanks for letting me know."

The announcement received very favorable public reaction. Who doesn't like lower car prices? Ford and GM, of course, were not very happy. But after one immediate public blast from Henry Ford, both companies refrained from further public comment and were cooperative.

We said—and meant—that we would review the decision after the next quarter's results showing us their latest profit margins. There was immediate speculation that we had become an arm of the White House in making this decision—that we had become "politicized." Not true. At no time did Rumsfeld, Shultz, or anyone else ask us to do one single thing regarding the auto companies. The decision was strictly ours. Credence was lent to the speculation, however, when Lou walked into my office the afternoon of the Ford and GM announcement and threw a piece of paper onto my desk: "Call this number."

It was the telephone number of the Committee to Re-elect the President (CREEP). A recorded message said: "The following is a recorded message of Price Commission Chairman Grayson at a Press Conference today in Washington, D.C." Then I heard my voice saying: "Today we are denying price increases to General Motors and Ford . . ."

I had not known that my press conference was being recorded by CREEP, nor had I been asked whether I would object to it being played by them. But I was sure of one thing, it would surely lend believability to suspicions that the whole scenario was arranged by the White House.

I requested that it be removed immediately, and it was.

The auto hearings were held on September 12 and 13. Some felt that they were anticlimactic after the earlier denials of Ford and GM. But these companies would be coming back some day after their profit margin problems disappeared, so their testimony was just as pertinent. All four companies participated in the hearings, and over two thousand pages of testimony were accumulated.

Shortly after the hearings, we analyzed the data and the testimonies, then made our decision. Chrysler and American would be given price increases, but at levels below what they had requested. Those who believed that we had been politicized were surprised, for they believed that we would also deny Chrysler and American this close to election day. Even the automobile companies seemed a little surprised after the Ford and GM decision.

Despite the speculations (and I can understand why they occurred), I can state without equivocation that at no time during the entire automobile price considerations was there indirect or direct pressure from the White House or Rumsfeld to have our decision in the PC affected in any way.

With the auto requests behind us, the summer of relative content was drawing to a close. Autumn and elections were on the way. Those of us at the top level of the Commission figured discussions would begin soon about what to do next April 30, 1973, when the Stabilization Act expired. Extend or decontrol?

A rough guess at the timetable projected that the President had to give some signal to Congress much earlier than April, probably in January. And if such an announcement were made in January, then discussions had to begin in late fall.

We—Lou, Bert Lewis, Pete Carpenter, and I—decided that before things began to heat up again (economically and politically), we should get off by ourselves and think over what to recommend, when and if asked.

September was a good time to do it, for a number of reasons.

For one, the revised figures for the second quarter of the economy were released in the middle of August, and they were even better than the preliminary figures. Real growth hit an astounding 9.4 percent, the highest since 1959. But the most welcome figure from our standpoint was the revised GNP Price Deflator. It was reduced from an already low 2.1 percent to an unbelievable 1.8 percent. Given these good figures (and a good announcement in September of the August CPI of 0.2 percent), the Commissioners were not likely to alter the program in the near future. They had already indicated that in the meeting of August 1.

Besides, the major automobile decision was taken care of. Enforcement of the profit margin rule was now working more smoothly. For better or worse, we had finally settled the nasty recurring issues of the loss/low profit rule, long-term interest, and long-term contracts. We had decided not to go through major revisions of the rent or health regulations. It was a period of wait and see, albeit a short period, we knew.

Finally, those experienced in Washington election behavior knew that for the month preceding the election, most of the senior Administration officials are out on the election circuit and largely unavailable. Also, their political instincts tell them to keep their heads low. One senior government official (now a Cabinet member) says his motto is "Run silent, run deep." Then, right after the election, everyone lets down and gets away. In addition, much of the government machinery is paralyzed for at least a month and a half following the election, as the game of musical chairs takes place, with dismissals, promotions, and new hirings. Decisions are delayed until the new chiefs are named, in place, and issuing orders. All together then, the processes of government are terribly slowed for the months preceding and immediately following the election.

We picked the weekend of September 30 and drove to nearby Charlottesville, Virginia. The subject of our retreat was so sensitive, both inside and outside the Commission, that we did not dare tell anyone what we were up to. We took our wives with us, partly as a "cover," and partly to have a chance to spend a little time with our families.

We spent the entire weekend on a topic of increasing speculation—"What next?"

10

Decompression

Assuming you like controls, I have some good news and some bad news. The good news is that I have just moved my family to Washington and rented a house. The bad news is that it is rented for one year and the lease has an escape clause in it.

Jack Grayson
November 1972

The news in the fall of 1972 was good or bad, depending on how you viewed it.

The economy and profits were soaring. Labor compensation increases were climbing at a tolerable clip. Business, labor, and public support for continuance of controls was growing. Price indicators fluctuated, but were still in a range to carry us toward a reasonable shot at the 3.0 to 3.5 percent goal for the entire year. Food was taking off again.

Speculation and rumors steadily increased about the probable date and method of extending controls or decontrolling. Those who wanted out of controls viewed the oncoming decision as perhaps one of the last opportunities to get out. Those who wanted to continue controls for a "little longer"—and there was an increasing number of them—argued against "premature decontrol."

The September Charlottesville meeting of the top staff had produced a "get out" recommendation. We did not reach a genuine consensus, for each of us had forecast a slightly different set of economic and political conditions for 1973. But our basic beliefs were similar.

After returning to Washington, I wrote up my own personal recommendations to give to top Administration officials and to the President—even though they had not really asked for them.

Recommendation

It is my recommendation that wage-price controls be ended early in 1973.

I recommend that the President make a statement in early January (January 1 or January 20) which contains the following elements:

1. Wage-price controls are ended as of this date.
2. Legislation will be requested for a 5-year extension of the Economic Stabilization Act (with some modifications).
3. The Cost of Living Council, Price Commission, and Pay Board are to be dissolved. In their stead is to be created a single new agency called the "Economic Stabilization Agency." It will require reports from firms, analyze price/wage changes, and perform as a monitoring, stand-by stabilization agency, which could act with mandatory authority, if needed. . . .

Reasons

The list of the reasons for recommending the above actions are outlined below:

1. *Wage-price controls are ended as of this date.*
   A. The Program has largely achieved its goals:
      1. The rate of inflation is in the 3% range (statistics currently support this).
      2. The economy has exhibited a strong recovery and promises to continue.
      3. Unemployment is trending downward.
      4. Balance of payments and strength of the dollar has improved.
   B. The frequency of demand-pull wage and price increases will increase in 1973. Controls are not suitable to handle such situations. Continuance of controls in the face of such problems will reduce labor-business

172

support and will require more stringent control measures that could lead to shortages, black markets, and rationing.

C.   All controls tend to distort free markets and collective bargaining. To date, there is little distortion. The longer controls are in effect, the greater the distortion.

D.   There is presently little pent-up wage/price pressure. If controls are lifted now, there is little danger of an "explosion." The longer controls are retained, the greater will be that danger, and thus, the greater the arguments for retaining controls.

E.   The fears of large wage settlements in 1973 if controls are lifted may be exaggerated. (Arguments can be presented both pro and con on this issue—the outlook is inconclusive.) Anyway, the proposed new Stabilization Agency with stand-by authority to impose mandatory controls will be an effective deterrent.

F.   The longer controls exist, the more dependency is created on controls to "save us" from inflation rather than tackling underlying causes.

G.   It is better to quit while we're ahead than to get into trouble and not be able to quit. Ending controls after they have been successful will provide a good model for the rest of the world. . . .

The four-page memorandum continued with supporting reasons for each of the main recommendations.

I feared that if an "Economic Stabilization Agency" existed, pressure would be brought on it to act as soon as inflation increased by even small amounts. But I ended up recommending it for two reasons: First, the new monitoring agency might be politically necessary in order to get Congress to agree to dropping controls at that time when Phase II was generally popular. Second, such an agency could serve as a transitional organization to gradually work into a new Department of Economic Affairs, as proposed in President Nixon's Reorganization Plan, an idea which I supported.

Suggestions were also made in the memorandum to work on economic "structural" problems feeding inflation—artifical restrictions on supply, removal of laws that push up prices, uncoordinated and overextended governmental spending, manpower blocks, and so on. I also suggested a national "call to arms" for increased American productivity to keep inflation from resurging and to stay competitive in the world economic race, calling on the President to:

- –Move the National Commission on Productivity to the new Stabilization Agency and increase funding,
- –Convene an International Conference on Productivity, Unemployment, and Inflation for April 1973,
- –Call on a national "will to achieve," and
- –Announce programs to improve the "Quality of Work" to tackle the declining work ethic and increasing worker alientation.

I closed the memorandum with a statement that *if* the decision were made to keep some sectors under control, then Health and Construction should be considered.

Why did I recommend decontrol?

When President Nixon announced Phase II on October 7, 1971, he not only announced a goal of getting inflation down to 2 to 3 percent, he also stated that he did not want to make controls a permanent feature of American life: "When they are no longer needed we will get rid of them."

From the beginning, we in the Price Commission felt we not only had to get the inflation rate down, but also to encourage the recovery of the economy and to avoid a postcontrol bubble. Thus, even when we were creating our Phase II policies during those sixteen days, we also had decontrol in mind. True, making controls work was our number-one goal. But as I stated at my first press conference on November 11, 1971:

> Our desire is to achieve the goal, but we would like to return to a free economy and deemphasize the control mechanism as rapidly as possible, consistent with the overall goals.

To illustrate, when we gave initial instructions to the Rent

174

Advisory Board, we asked them to think of ways to decontrol, as well as ways to control. Our limited cost pass-through (plus markups) policy was created partly because we did not want to inhibit the recovery too much, and partly to minimize the danger of a postcontrol bubble. The profit margin rule was designed to provide a degree of restraint without being so restrictive as to create strong underlying pressures.

But neither did we want people to think about decontrol.

In an interview with *U.S. News & World Report* on January 24, 1972, I stated:

> My main job is not to focus on some calendar date for decontrol—it is to reduce the rate of inflation . . . If everyone begins to plan for decontrol, controls will not taken as seriously. Also firms and individuals will be planning strategies to take care of themselves.
>
> *Q.* Does this mean that you aren't doing any planning for decontrol?
> *A.* No. We are. . . . [But]. . . . we must win this battle first.
> *Q.* Are you going to keep on with this gradual decontrol process?
> *A.* Yes. We have just started a detailed study on what trigger points or indicators to look for in determining when to make changes in controls.

In a *New York Times* interview, published on January 30, 1972, in their *Magazine,* I stated: "We're here to reach our goal of price stability. I believe we'll fold our tents and steal away. We'll be at full-scale operations for a maximum of a year. Maybe it will go for . . . two years, but we should start selective decontrols, Phase III, at the end of the first year, even if the program goes on for two years."

I cite these to show that in the PC we believed that: (1) we should decontrol at the first opportunity after reaching our goal, and (2) it was part of our job to think about decontrol and ways to achieve it, from the price side.

The CLC did not agree. Rumsfeld and Shultz both felt that the task of the PC was to get the inflation rate down and to leave the planning for Phase III up to someone else.

The disagreement had already surfaced in February 1972. When our top staff went to Belmont, a retreat spot outside of Washington, notes of that staff conference state:

> CLC feels that decontrol is their decision. It is. But they will need information from us and I think it should be our responsibility to provide information and recommendations, and not on the spur of the moment. We need a sophisticated group to study future possibilities without any other assignment. I don't think CLC is going to do it.

My belief that the CLC was not going to do it was based on my experience with their planning for Phase II. I felt that the pattern was likely to repeated again, and I wanted to get ready for Phase III, whether it was to be decontrol or a tighter program.

The man I assigned to the task was Bob Anthony.

Bob was a Professor of Management Control at the Harvard Graduate School of Business Administration a friend of many years. Bob had joined us as a part-time consultant immediately after I gave him a ring from Washington in the first few days. He had been extremely helpful in the early period in advising the Commission and staff on accounting problems, price control policies, and forms design.

I gave him an office, some part-time staff members, and a budget for outside contract research. His assignment was to come up with an alternative control system that would permit either selective decontrol or tighter controls, based on detailed economic analysis of industries, price leaders, concentration ratios, historical trends, cyclical patterns, and other data.

In June 1972 Bob came up with an extremely detailed four-volume analysis of all major industries, and a comprehensive system of controls that could be used either for selective decontrol or an entirely new system of industry-by-industry controls—loose or tight. As he handed me the product of his labors, I shuddered when I saw the cover, "Phase III." While some people in the PC were aware of the fact that Anthony was studying alternative control systems, it had never been labeled "Phase III." And given the fact that we all were constantly trying to avoid speculation about when Phase III might be launched, and what it would look like, the cover alone was a bombshell. The cover was changed to read: "A Price Control Strategy." It quickly became known to those associated with it as the "Anthony Report."

As Bob outlined his general strategy, it became apparent that the foundation rested on a Return on Investment (ROI) concept —at their point an anathema to the Commissioners! I knew that there was no way that they would ever consider it.

But the basic work was so good and useful for anyone using any control technique that I did not want to have it buried. I decided that it should be sent to all Commissioners and key people in the CLC—Rumsfeld, Shultz, Stein, and Burns. I wrote a very carefully worded transmittal note, assuring them that we were not about to implement the recommendations, that we did not necessarily agree with the methodology or policies of control used in the analysis, . . . and so on.

My memo was full of disclaimers to try to assure them that we were sending it along because it contained valuable information for those (whoever they were) that might be planning for the future. We were asked to keep it quiet, to restrict the number of copies, and not to give it any wider distribution.

Anthony was finished with his task, and he had other personal things he wanted to do. He concluded his relationship with the Commission in July, and the report was never acted on or referred to again, except as a reference source about industry characteristics.

This was the only formal planning exercise ever done in the PC specifically targeted toward a comprehensive Phase III. But all of us knew that our Phase II policies couldn't last forever and that some overhauling would be needed if the program continued into 1973, particularly as demand inflation became more prevalent. Some of the staff studies in the Policy Group focused on demand inflation and what it meant for our policies and controls in general. The conclusions were usually pretty gloomy: "In general, we are left with the conclusion that the Price Commission has really no sensible direct action it can take in combating a demand-pull inflation." Other staff studies focused on industry-by-industry type controls as modifications to our policies. Other studies were directed toward alterations to the profit margin rule.

Though all of these studies were future-oriented, none of them were labeled "Phase III" studies. The words were banned from policy papers.

However, many conversations were held informally at the top staff level, and in Commission meetings, about Phase III. The Commissioners agreed among themselves that we would never speculate publicly about any timetable for Phase III or its design. And inside the PC, we requested all staff to do the same. That wasn't so hard to do, for everyone was too busy trying to make Phase II work.

Speculation, however, about the date and method of decontrol began from almost the first moment we began operations. Speculation was natural and occurred all during Phase II. The press speculated. Businessmen speculated. Staff speculated. Yet, in every single public appearance or article that I wrote, I reiterated the constant theme that "we're in this to win, and we will take every step necessary to win. But when we have achieved our goal, we plan to self-destruct, and get rid of the Commission."

After finishing one such rousing speech in Philadelphia in June—"When we reach our goal, my recommendation will be that we blow up the whole program!"—Jim Elliott of our Public Affairs staff came over. "Boss," he said, smiling, "could you tone these remarks down just a wee little bit. You're making the staff mighty nervous."

Stories appeared in both the *Washington Post* and the *New York Times* in the middle of January 1972 on the subject of "Pullout on Controls?" Arguments were that the President might destroy the controls just prior to election. This kind of speculation didn't last long after the bulge appeared—people reasoned that it would be impossible to get off the tiger anytime soon.

But in summer, when the indicators began to look better, speculation began again. A June 19, 1972 *Time* roundup story quoted an economist as guessing that the chances were fifty-fifty that "after the election, the Administration will declare a victory over inflation and abandon the control program." The majority of *Time's* economists, however, figured that controls would be needed well into 1973 because of predicted rising prices in the autumn and big labor contracts coming up next year (rubber, electrical, trucking, railroad, apparel.)

By July and August, the speculation mills were grinding in full gear. *Dun's* headlined a July issue article: "More Controls Coming?" Almost any word, phrase, or action was interpreted by some reporter or leader in Congress, in business, or in labor as a sure sign that either "controls are on their way out," or "decontrol is right around the corner."

In Dallas on August 1, a reporter asked me the usual question for the nth time: "Will controls be over on April 30?" I replied, "I'm very pleased with the progress in controlling inflation to date, and the President has said that he will remove controls as soon as we have achieved our goal. I refuse, however, to predict that controls will be lifted by April 30."

Stories appeared within hours in many papers across the nation, headlined: "Grayson Hints at April 30 Controls End." Others said, "Suggests end by April 30," or "Optimistic about April 30." Any slight deviation from the normal response was immediately picked up as a highly significant indicator.

Right after the August 1–2 PC meeting in which the Commissioners decided against any drastic tightening action, I visited Shultz and Stein. I informed them of some Phase II problems (specifically of lumber and auto problems), of the need to establish interagency procedures for handling demand-pull problems, and the strategy of setting up an economic evaluation group to monitor the economy and make predictions. But the main purpose was to give them some indication of my assessment of the future. Though I discussed a "staggered" end for the PC, I recommended a sudden termination. I believed that a gradual decontrol would create more distortions than it would be worth. I also informed them that several of the Commissioners had told me privately that they might not stay much longer after the election. As possible dates for decontrol, I recommended that they consider November 14, December 31, or the President's State of the Union message.

And then I asked about the planning for Phase III. Both Stein and Shultz said that they naturally were thinking about it, but that no specific planning had been done. They suggested that the PC should do none because it would detract from enforcement of our present policies and might leak to the press. However, Shultz told me that I personally should give it some thought and pass on to him any ideas I had.

I stressed that the date they selected for a decision would have many implications for some Phase II decisions. We had to decide soon whether to revise the rent regulations, overhaul the health regulations, rework forms, renew Term Limit Pricing agreements, and develop a complex data base. Their advice was to go ahead with every decision as though controls were going to last indefinitely.

As soon as I returned to my office that August afternoon, I wrote a memo to Lou, Bert, and Pete stating how I was going to allocate the bulk of my time in the next three months:

1. Ideas for Phase III.
2. Contact with Administration officials.
3. Personal contacts with staff throughout building.
4. Productivity program.
5. Speeches and articles.
6. Major policy studies.

Though Shultz, Stein, and Rumsfeld had said that they were thinking about Phase III, we believed it probable that little would take place within the top level Administration until after the election. Administration people were already out on the circuit making speeches. And so we began to talk among ourselves about Phase III, culminating in the retreat at Charlottesville, September 30.

Not long after that meeting, I got appointments with top stabilization officials, but due to heavy travel schedules and conflicts, I did not see them until nearly mid-October. I visited with Rumsfeld, Stein, Shultz, and Burns and personally delivered my written recommendations arising out of the Charlottesville meeting.

Each said that he was glad to get them, and appeared a little surprised that I was recommending complete destruction. Burns, in particular, felt that it would be unwise to get rid of the program so soon because he felt that the inflationary psychology was not broken, and he feared the large wage negotiations coming up in 1973. I pointed out that there was still a Stabilization Agency in my recommendations that would be monitoring the economy. Mandatory authority could be delegated to them when the President chose. I did not think Congress would let the program die without the creation of such an agency.

Stein and Shultz both thanked me, asked how many copies I had made, and discussed some of the specifics. I stressed that these

180

were my personal recommendations, not those of the Commissioners. I also emphasized that I was personally convinced after a year of control experience that there was no way that any central system could more effectively allocate resources between competing demands. "Even with its imperfections, the marketplace is still better than we are."

Rumsfeld said that he appreciated the memorandum, and would see that it received due attention. He alluded to a group that was doing some preliminary thinking about Phase III, but did not name anyone. He again requested that we not make any internal studies ("run the PC, that's your job. Let us worry about Phase III where we can look at both pay and price") and don't comment publicly about any options or dates ("don't remove any of the President's options")

After turning in my recommendations, I asked Lou, Bert, and Pete to make sure that we did not let up on Phase II enforcement.

In addition, I asked them each to try to stay with the program until the end. They were now being offered new jobs with new challenges and opportunities elsewhere. But if they left, other staff would read this as a signal and assume that the program was nearly over. A run might start because of the close-knit relationships in the staff. Each agreed to stay and to try to convince others to stay who were receiving attractive alternatives in government, academia, and business. In one sense, this was unfair in that some top staff passed up good opportunities. In another sense, their leaving would have done a disservice to the country in causing the Commission to begin dissipating before the decision was made about its future.

After submission of my recommendations, further conversation and thoughts about Phase III decreased as attention increasingly focused on election day—November 7.

That is, until October 30.

The November issue of *U.S. News & World Report* (out on October 30) carried an interview with me about "What Controls Have Done to Prices." The inevitable question came during the interview:

> Q. Suppose you can hold down the annual rate of inflation to less than 3 percent for the next 3 or 4 months. Would

you feel that perhaps early in 1973 it would be safe to abandon the whole price-control program?

A. That's a decision the President of the United States will have to make—not the Chairman of the Price Commission. . . .

Q. Do you see any reason for continuing controls after the law authorizing them expires next April?

A. No . . . I don't think those arguments (wage increases and price pressures) are persuasive enough to cause me to feel that controls should be continued—once the President has made the basic decision that stability has been reached.

I picked up my *Washington Post* on Monday, October 30 and was reading it in the early morning hours. There was my picture over a headline that read "Chief Backs April Death of Controls." (I distinctly remember feeling a knotting of my stomach—"Oh, no.") The story went on to say that Grayson saw "no reason for continuing controls beyond their expiration date of April."

The story quoted me accurately. I had said it just that way, and I had reviewed the transcript before publication. I must have said essentially the same thing over a thousand times, but I had not said it exactly by the previous scripts. Instead of putting the qualifier in front—"once the President has made the basic decision that stability has been reached"—I put it last. There was my big "No" sitting there first before the qualification.

I felt sick.

The story was picked up in newspapers around the country, and our Public Affairs staff was busy trying to explain that I had basically not changed my position. I heard nothing from anyone in the Administration, probably because it was near elections and everyone was busy. But I understand that it did create some consternation.

I called Rumsfeld and Shultz in a few days to assure them that my position hadn't shifted, and that it was just the rewording that had caused the problem. They were cordial about it. "Don't worry about it. We all say something sometimes that we wish we hadn't."

The story was picked up right away by Senator Proxmire when

I appeared before the Joint Economic Committee on November 15. He and the other members of the JEC asked me to state my own recommendations about what should happen to the controls when they expired on April 30.

My reply was that I had made my own personal recommendations to the President, but that I felt that it was not proper for me to state my views or to make public recommendations until the President had weighed all of the views and considerations. I pointed out that the definition of "stability" encompassed more than just price levels, it included pay considerations, fiscal policy, monetary policy, unemployment, balance of payments, and so on.

Some people believed I was being "muzzled" by the White House. It wasn't true. I honestly believed that this was the best course of action for the program. I promised the Senators that when the Hearings were held on extension of the legislation itself that I would make my views known.

I stated in my testimony both the positive and negative impacts of controls, restated my own views that controls were self-defeating in the long run, but refused to make a specific recommendation. With this strong declaration on my part, the focus then shifted to the CLC and the White House for further signals.

A Gallup poll in late September reported that while there was dissatisfaction with controls, only 9 percent of the public wanted them removed, 45 percent said they should be more strict, and 29 percent said they should remain as they are. Cited as the main reasons were fears of fresh inflationary pressures in 1973, a surging economy, new labor contracts in 1973, and fears of a postcontrol bubble.

One of the things that surprised me during the second half of 1972 was the growing support by businessmen for continuance of controls into 1973. Support for the initial freeze and Phase II had come from a majority of businessmen, including their chief associations—the U.S. Chamber of Commerce and the National Association of Manufacturers (NAM). This support was key in making Phase II work, for without voluntary compliance by business, the program could not have been effective. What surprised me in the fall of 1972 was the extent of feeling by businessmen that controls not only would be continued into 1973, but also *should* be.

At a Business Council (leaders of top U.S. corporations) meeting in late October there was a general sentiment for the continuation of controls. This was not unanimous, however, for some felt they should be ended that day. But most both predicted and recommended continuation into "some time in 1973."

When I pressed businessmen on this issue, I learned that the deep-seated reason was their fear of union power. Having lived through the late 1960s when large contract settlements rippled through the economy year after year, many businessmen decided that the balance of power had swung to the unions, and that there was little they could do to stop wage demands, short of controls. Though they disliked the controls on their prices, they welcomed controls on wages. Most knew about the large number of wage settlements coming up in 1973, and feared that if controls were removed, there would be a fresh wave of large settlements, initiating a repeat of the upward spiral of the late 1960s.

While I welcomed any support for the Commission, I had some reservations about businessmen's reasons. My views were on the record: "The notion that you need controls to protect you from the other guy could become ingrained in our thinking. The longer this belief persists, the harder it will be to return to a competitive economy. With this disturbing 'control-us' psychology, we could find ourselves unable to do without wage-price controls."

Labor—surprisingly—also said they would support an extension of controls.

At the JEC Hearings in mid-November, Carl Madden, chief economist for the U.S. Chamber of Commerce, supported continuation of controls. Senator Proxmire responded: "I find it astonishing to see the Chamber, the citadel of free enterprise, become the champions of controls." Even the Committee for Economic Development (CED) issued a report recommending continuation through 1973, but gradual phasing down through selective decontrol.

I could see the tide turning toward a continuation of controls.

The speculation even infiltrated our birthday party on November 14, which was fun, albeit a little stiff. The PC staff had planned

184

a swinging, ribald, strong-punch evening affair to celebrate our anniversary on November 14. But word was received that the CLC wanted to hold a Stabilization-wide party at the Mayflower Hotel, and some of the plans (and strong personality jokes) were subordinated to the larger affair. The PC had its own separate lively party the next day.

However, the large evening affair did go well. Skits poked fun at the program and people—including Rumsfeld and myself. One cartoon on a wall showed two track runners simultaneously going, over a hurdle, but in opposite directions. The two runners were Rumsfeld and Grayson, saying: "Hi, Jack." "Hi, Don."

For my part in the skit, I said that there had been a lot of speculation concerning decontrol, and that I thought this was an occasion where we could be serious for a moment while I made an announcement:

> After weighing the negative and positive aspects of the control mechanism on wages and prices in America, I am recommending to the President tomorrow morning, that before the expiration date of April 30, 1973 . . .

The audience grew very quiet.

> . . . willaby forensic patton. He can obviously have no alternative than pressicate the forlor, and missicate all former massens, thereby deciding to ask the Congress to tendom.
>
> I predict that Congress, with this clear alternative so eminently vassar, will with bipartisan unanimity, effic a consan parrage of mannerils for both wages and prices, for an indefinite period into the unalterable months, whichever is shorter . . . and that the President will sign.

At the PC party the next day, we read telegrams that the PC *might have* received on its anniversary.

CONGRATULATIONS ON YOUR SURVIVAL. LET 'EM EAT CAKE.

Pillsbury Baking Company

HERE'S TO ANOTHER SPLENDID YEAR OR TWO OR THREE OF CLOSE COOPERATION.

Earl Butz

BEST WISHES FROM THE SECRET TELEPHONE BOOTH IN THE MEN'S ROOM ON THE 9TH FLOOR.

The Price Commission
"Spokesman"

CAN YOU SEND US YOUR POLICY ON LONG-TERM CONTRACTS?

Cosa Nostra

DON'T WORRY ABOUT THE RUMORS. I'M BEHIND YOU 1,000 PERCENT.

Richard M. Nixon

The tremendous election victory had thrown the government machinery into neutral. We just sat back and waited for some signal. Almost.

On December 5 I wrote a memo to the top staff:

> This morning at 5:00 A.M., I began to think about the legislative hearings that will have to be conducted one of these days on the extension of the Act.
>
> Who knows what the date will be or what the proposal will be from the President.
>
> While we have a little more time, how about thinking about that testimony and what it might look like? I feel a responsibility to point out in more detail than I did at the recent JEC Hearings some of the problems of the control program and some of the benefits.
>
> I've jotted down some of the pros and cons of decontrol now, versus later, or not at all. Clearly, I am biased, but that's the way I feel and I'd like some arguments.

The following list was sent along with the memo. It reveals not only views about continuance of controls at that time, but also my views about controls in general.

To Control or Not To Control?

Pro	Con
1. Wage settlements in 1973 may be excessively large without controls particularly in union sectors.	Real wages are up; no large catch-up required; unions no more or less powerful than before controls; businesses will get in the habit of leaving negotiations to the Pay Board.
2. Productivity will decline in 1973, and with wages still high, unit labor costs will rise.	Controls won't stem productivity decline; controls aren't the answer to keeping productivity and compensation in line.
3. Inflationary psychology has not changed.	Consumer confidence up; expectations still too high but will shift to fears of post-control bubble whenever controls lifted; will not be substantially changed until food prices are down.
4. Fiscal and monetary measures not yet sufficient to prevent resurgence of inflation.	Controls never a substitute for responsible fiscal and monetary policy and cannot remain viable in a demand-pull situation.
5. Food prices still too high and due to skyrocket this winter.	Controls can't be effective against food price increases; requires changes in agricultural policies.
6. One more year and the variables will have quieted down.	Same argument will be given one year from now.

To Control or Not To Control?
(continued)

Pro	*Con*
7. Have not reached our goal yet.	Without food, overall rate is low. Areas which we can control are at target rate; demand-pull sectors require methods other than controls.
8. Demand-pull inflation is likely next year with a booming recovery.	Controls cannot handle a demand-pull situation.
9. Distortions not so bad now; we can last another year.	Distortions will increase in 1973. Longer controls last, the greater will be the distortions.
10. Income distribution not correct in this nation— controls can help.	Controls are not the instrument to alter income distribution; danger that they will be used for this purpose.
11. Unemployment still too high.	Controls increase this problem, if they have any effect at all.
12. Market power of large unions and corporations still too high.	Controls don't tackle these issues.
13. Structural blocks to a freely functioning economy and free collective bargaining still exists.	Controls don't tackle the structural blocks.

Pro	*Con*
14. Decontrol, at this time, will undermine business and consumer confidence.	Consumers have no confidence in the current program because of food price increases; business confidence may be more impaired by a profit margin squeeze than by decontrol. Business usually reluctant to face an uncertain situation so their desire to keep controls may be an automatic reflex.
15. U.S. currently has the lowest inflation rate in the world; would be foolish to risk any increase with our balance of payments problem.	Inflation rate should not get any worse. Under continuing controls, money may be sent out to invest in foreign subs because neither their goods or profit margins are controlled. Controls may be aggravating balance of payments.
16. Decontrol will lead to a large barrage of price increases which will, in turn, rekindle the wage-price spiral.	There is a danger of this occurring whenever economy is decontrolled. However, under present program, costs have been passed through with historical margin so there is less reason for a bubble. Furthermore, for competitive reasons many companies have not even used full authorized amount.

Pro	*Con*
17. Business profits rising too rapidly.	Not concerned with controlling profits but with controlling prices; profit squeeze would impede recovery.
18. Public favors controls.	Danger of controls being the easy way out and being looked at as the solution rather than a temporary stop gap.
19. Buy time to correct economic ills.	People develop dependency on controls; no incentive to correct economic ills.
20. Program working — why stop a good thing.	Economic factors moving in right direction to sustain continued reduction in inflation without controls: real earnings up, unemployment rate down, productivity up, still in business cycle upswing. Investment may be diverted from cyclical and visible industries. Longer controls continue, more numerous evasions and more difficult compliance monitoring. Will lead to market distortions — already occurred with #2 heating oil, zinc, molasses, potash, etc. Increasing likelihood of contradictions between controls and aims of other agencies.

Only a week later, on December 12, the President announced that he was going to request an extension of the Stabilization Act. The announcement came as a complete surprise. We had guessed that he would come forward in the Budget Message, his inaugural address, or the State of the Union address—all to take place in January.

The President's announcement stated that all agencies of the program were to conduct extensive consultations with business, labor, academic leaders, and the general public. We called in businessmen, association executives, economists, and listened; their recommendations were sent on to the CLC. The general view was that controls should be extended until most of the big labor settlements were out of the way in 1973, and that the profit margin rule should be altered in some way. Concern was expressed about where further controls were taking us, but the good side of controls seemed to outweigh the bad in their minds.

On December 15, the Commissioners and top staff went over to the White House to give their views in person to the CLC, just as outside groups did. We assembled in the Roosevelt Room and spent about an hour with Herb Stein. Stein asked each Commissioner what he thought should be done.

Though each said something, most felt it was largely a waste of time—that the CLC was going through the motion mostly out of nicety, and that what was said would not be of great importance in the final decision anyway. They felt that the CLC had almost already made up its mind, but would not tell us from lack of trust.

Another reason for the flatness of the session was that the majority of the Commissioners were planning to resign right after the President's decision in January or just before April 30, and felt that the policy setting and administration were not likely to remain at the PC anyway, but at CLC. We had, in our opinion, largely burned our bridges with the CLC and lost our effectiveness.

When my turn came to speak, I said that I had already submitted my views in writing and that they had not changed. I didn't repeat them. (The Commissioners had not seen my views in writing, though I had told them verbally in an earlier Executive Session in October what the substance was.) "I do have one thing to add," I said. "It's a four-letter word." I held up a piece of paper on which I had scribbled while Stein was conducting the round robin. On it was written: FOOD.

I pointed out what I had written to Rumsfeld in memos in October and November:

> I thought you might like to see two recent Daily Decision Lists reflecting large percentage price increases granted for food.
>
> We have held up these increases for as long as we can under our regulations. All . . . are completely cost justified, but the numbers are alarming. All of these represent supply and demand situations. I asked why some of these were so large and I received a short list of natural disasters. It seems there are a lot of disasters these days.

In another memo, I had forwarded to Rumsfeld some summaries of pending food cases.

	Requests	Average Increase (Percent)
Cereals	92	16.28
Fish	151	12.9
Candies	10	5.16
Flour (Russian wheat sale not yet reflected)	51	4.04
Canned Fruits and Vegetables	98	6.43
Coffee	150	7.60

The list went on.

I pointed out to Stein in the White House meeting that the situation had not changed since those memos.

"Do you have any ideas?" he asked.

"Nope. Not beyond drastic measures, or working on the supply side, and that takes time."

Stein thanked everyone for coming. We adjourned and went home.

I called Shultz for a meeting on December 29. I had not heard from him, or any other member of the Administration, since I made my recommendations in late October. I wanted to know what had happened to my recommendations, and also to give Shultz some last-minute information about some other factors that they should consider when making the final choices.

Shultz opened our meeting by saying that he had personally presented my recommendations to the President, who was surprised, and pleased, that someone in the Federal bureaucracy was recommending the destruction of his own job. Shultz indicated that the President had not yet made up his mind, but that he was likely to come down somewhere near the present control system, but largely self-administered. Then when it was working smoothly, and largely by itself, the program would be ended.

I said that if present policies were adopted, a lot of work was needed in certain areas: revision of profit margin rules, revisions of health and rent regulations, retail regulations, forms, hearings on steel and oil, and many others. Further, I urged him to ask the planners to seek out PC staff for their advice, since it would be a crime to ignore their expertise. I said that I knew that there was some fear of PC press leaks, but that with the President's announcement about wanting consultations, there was no longer a problem. Our staff should be consulted just as outside groups were. Shultz asked me to call Rumsfeld and tell him that we had that conversation and to work out arrangements.

I also informed him that at least four of the Commissioners were planning to resign within the next four months, regardless of what was decided. I also indicated their restlessness; their feeling that they no longer were needed and had little to do.

I stressed that while morale was high in the PC staff—amazingly high considering the circumstances—it was becoming unstable and could easily be lost.

Whenever the decision was made to wind down the Commission, I urged that the government not only recognize the valuable service they had rendered, but also not overlook their unusual competency and experience. Special attention should be given to their "placement" back in their own agencies through reemployment rights and/or through absorption into a new agency. The transition period would be rough, I knew, given the high identification of the staff with the PC, and the distance, distrust between our staff and that of the CLC.

193

George said he would keep me informed and I would hear before the press announcement was made. "Think of what you are going to say," he said.

George wished me a Happy New Year.

I was in New York City on January 10 in the offices of Wilson Newman. The phone rang. It was Rumsfeld's secretary.

"Could you please get right back to Washington? Mr. Rumsfeld would like to meet with you and Judge Boldt in his office this afternoon just as soon as possible."

This was it.

Wilson said to keep him informed, and though I could only tell him that I was called back to Washington, he knew.

Rumsfeld told the Judge and me that a decision had been reached, and he outlined the program that was essentially Phase III.

We should plan between now and tomorrow morning what we would say to the press and to our staffs. Shultz was to make the announcement at an 11 A.M. press conference. But nothing was absolutely sure until it was uttered, so no advance information should leak about the nature or content of the announcement. We could tell only the very top staff so that they could prepare for the internal announcements. He said that he was telling us first, and now had to make phone calls to tell other members of the CLC.

On the way out the door, Rumsfeld indicated that if Lou and I returned later that evening, we could see advance copies of the details of Phase III, and might have some last-minute thoughts.

Lou and I did return that evening.

The Phase III regulations were very similar to Phase II. Some modifications were made, but the major change was that the regulations were now to become largely self-enforcing. It was about 11 P.M., and clearly the major decisions had been all made.

Lou and I suggested only two changes. First was a strong request for a transition period of ninety days instead of the planned thirty days for staff personnel adjustments. Not only did we feel that the CLC would need PC staff expertise, we simply didn't think it was fair to force the phase-down in thirty days. We sensed even then that the CLC would "take over" and put all of

194

their people on top. It would not be pleasant. Rumsfeld agreed to the ninety days.

The other suggestion involved the retail part of the regulations. We convinced Rumsfeld that retailers had been squeezed so far that they needed relief on at least one aspect of our regulations —additional cost pass-through of governmentally mandated costs, particularly if minimum wage laws passed. He agreed, and woke Stein up to see if he had any objections. He didn't. It was done.

Then Rumsfeld thanked us, and we were done.

We left CLC's offices about 1:30 A.M., as their lawyers continued their regulation writing. At the parking lot, Lou and I looked at each other.

"It's been great," I said.

He smiled. "You take care, you hear."

The morning of the eleventh we called a meeting of all top PC staff people for 11 A.M. in our Conference Room. No one was told why, but clearly they were expecting an announcement.

At exactly the same time that Shultz began talking in the White House, I told the staff. They were stunned.

Almost to a man, they had expected that controls would be extended and that the Price Commission would continue. I tried my best to tell them that the battle was not over, that they had done an outstanding job, that they would be needed in the transition period of ninety days just as much as they were now, that there was no staff like them anywhere in the world, in my opinion, that they would be taken care of in helping them to find positions in the new organization, other agencies of government, or on the outside, that . . .

But in their faces was one stark, unavoidable, sickening fact. The Commission was finished.

Part four

The aftermath

In the hindsight of Phases I, II, III and IV, my views on where we are going.

Was Joseph Schumpeter right?
Have we taken the big stride toward the perfectly planned economy?

I hope not. And I most certainly argue that we should not.

11

What price, controls?

*In other words, price control may result in a surrender of
private enterprise to public authority; that is, in a big stride
toward the perfectly planned economy.*

Joseph A. Schumpeter
Capitalism, Socialism, and Democracy

That sentence was not written in 1973, 1972, or even 1971.

It was written late one evening in 1949 by Joseph Schumpeter,
a leading economist. It was literally the last sentence he ever
wrote.

He died the next morning.

For almost fifteen months, I exercised control over most of our
nation's price system. From this experience, and from what has
happened since, I am personally convinced that our economic
system is steadily shifting away *from* private enterprise and a
free-market, and toward central direction and public control.

Admittedly, we have had, since 1930, some regulation of private enterprise—a public-private mix. But since then the mix has
steadily—and ever faster—turned toward central control. The
price and wage controls of the seventies have helped to quicken
the rate of this change. At some point, possibly in fifteen or twenty
years at the present rate, the essential characteristics of a competitive, private enterprise system (nonregulated prices, profit motive,
risk taking, collective bargaining) will no longer be character-

istic of the American economy. Call it what you will—managed capitalism, socialism, a planned economy, a postindustrial state —in the end, it will mean the virtual elimination of the free-market system as we now know it.

No traffic lights. No signposts.

But if you look closely, there are indications—subtle ones because they have not sprung up overnight. Business and labor too often seek to reduce, rather than encourage, competition in their markets. Continuing price and wage controls make central planning and control seem superior, mandatory, and desirable. Americans, in distrust of the market system, are demanding more economic benefits from the federal government and are seeking ways to insulate themselves from the impact of economic change. In addition, the economy can no longer be contained by political boundaries—interdependence on a global scale prohibits such isolationism. As recent problems with balance of payments and exchange rates demonstrate, closed economies are a thing of the past. Inflation can be exported and imported—like a disease—increasing the call for more centrally coordinated economic policies among nations as well as within them.

The eventual system will probably not mean widespread public ownership of production and distribution. But it will mean public control. General Motors won't die, but neither will it remain a capitalistically motivated and directed enterprise. Rather, it will operate as an organization designed to implement the economic, political, and social policies of the government.

Because I strongly believe in our present system, and because of the effect its loss would have on the social character of the American people, I must regard this current trend as a threat to our free, competitive economy.

How did this change come about? Why? Why is it a matter of concern? What can be done about it?

Ironically, the impetus hasn't come from revolutionists, and only partly from leftists, liberals, radicals, intellectuals, or socialists. Instead, it has come from the public at large, from Congress, and, perhaps most surprisingly, from many labor and business leaders.

In the free market, competitive behavior is required not only of business but also of labor. There must be *competition* in wages as well as in prices. More and more, however, it's not turning out that way.

Consciously and unconsciously, businessmen add to the probability of greater centralization by seeking ways to reduce market competition—the very keystone on which the capitalist system rests.

Normally, competition is curtailed either by private monopoly or by government protection. It is still unclear whether large corporations have sufficient power to control markets, reduce competition, and "administer" prices. Our internal studies at the Price Commission did not provide any evidence that prices were being administered by corporations. But, clearly, we did not have sufficient time to make a full study of this issue. We did have time, however, to observe innumerable instances in which business turned to government to seek forms of assistance which, in effect, would reduce competition—for example, asking for imposition of subsidies and tariffs, occupational licensing, fair trade laws, and import quotas.

Excerpts from letters written to me at the Price Commission by businessmen serve as illustrations:

> I do not advocate any program of isolation, but I do think it is good business for us to protect our national economic situation in the face of stiff and competitive foreign trade. (A steel company)

> We need government protection because we can't compete against the big companies. (A consumer goods company)

> If you break our fair trade laws, the market will be chaotic. (A cosmetics company)

> We can't survive if you let cheap products in from foreign countries. (A shoe manufacturer)

> We must have minimum milk prices if we are to have an orderly market. (A dairy products company)

> If we allow liquor prices to fluctuate freely, competition will be ruinous and the Mafia might move in. (An alcoholic beverage company)

Another way some businesses are hampering the free-market system is by not using the age-old competitive tool of reducing prices.

Again, to quote from my 1972 mail:

> In all my years in business, I have never reduced prices to hurt a competitor. (A retail food supplier)

> Why did I raise my prices? My competitor did. I always go up when he does. (A chemical company)

Of course, such attitudes are not shared by all businessmen. After the Price Commission authorized a cost-justified price increase, one businessman told me, "You gave us a price increase. I wish the market would."

My point, however, is that far too few companies are exploring market flexibility by reducing prices. And yet, when we ordered some companies to reduce prices because they had violated regulations, several reported that they experienced increased volume and a higher total profit.

But the reluctance to reduce prices is also understandable. Several heavy-industry companies reported that they feared competing too aggressively on price because they would capture a larger market share, drive out smaller companies, and fall subject to Justice Department or competitor antitrust suits. Efficient stevedoring companies argued they would drive out smaller businesses if they held prices down. And after the Russian wheat sale drove flour prices up, small bakeries urged us to *force* large bakeries to *raise* their bread prices!

The threat of continuing price controls has compounded the price reduction problems. Many companies report hesitancy to reduce prices for fear of being caught with a low "base price" in future freezes and phases. This was clearly demonstrated in Phase III, when freeze "talk" actually accelerated price increases.

Finally, I was surprised to find that the majority of businessmen with whom I talked wanted Phase II controls continued. The most commonly stated reason was fear of union power. The argument ran that the balance of power has swung so far toward the unions that businessmen can no longer negotiate successfully. Accordingly, they chose price controls over wage disputes; they preferred regulation to the problems freedom poses.

Like big business, big labor tries to use government or private power to protect itself against the natural effects of competition, such as layoffs, dislocations, wage reductions, and advancement by competition.

Whether labor has too much power was not an issue we studied at the Price Commission during the control period. But we did receive reports of many instances in which noncompetitive labor practices were driving costs up—for example, featherbedding in railroads and docks, restrictive work rules in construction and shipping, and restrictions on the use of more efficient methods in construction and printing. An October 1971 staff report of the Bureau of Domestic Commerce estimates these extra costs for selected industries as follows:

Industry	Estimated Annual Costs
Construction	$1,000,000,000 to $3,000,000,000
Railroads	700,000,000 to 1,200,000,000
Printing	400,000,000 to 600,000,000
Supermarkets	250,000,000 to 400,000,000
Trucking	275,000,000 to 400,000,000
Total	$2,625,000,000 to $5,600,000,000

These restrictive, noncompetitive work practices are usually defended by labor on humanitarian grounds. Without judging the merit of that position, I can definitely say that these practices drive costs up and usually result in higher unit labor costs, higher domestic prices, and reduced competitive abilities abroad.

Just as business too often resists price reductions, labor resists wage reductions, despite the natural relationship between the productivity levels and the wages that a company can afford to pay. Companies report mounting pressure from labor for increased compensation, regardless of the productivity of individual workers or of the nation as a whole. Labor's typical demands include increased minimum wage levels, "catch-up" wage increases, fixed output rates, tandem wage agreements, and annual pay increments. To return to the coal miners' settlement as an example, productivity in that industry had actually *decreased* in the years prior to their 16.6 percent increase in wages.

The coal companies, however, were held to a 5.5 percent pass-through, as were other companies. As a result of this "5.5 rule," some companies suffered reduced profits, but others bargained harder at the table because they knew that they could not "pass on" more than 5.5 percent. In fact, some companies reported privately that they were pleased with the government intervention because it gave them a bargaining weapon greatly needed to withstand labor's pressures.

There is little question that if labor settlements, on the average, rise faster than overall productivity, the result will be inflation, unemployment, or both. Increasing productivity is one answer —and we tried that. Our 5.5 percent limitation was an attempt to at least partially offset the imbalance by forcing price increases to reflect no more than the long-term 3 percent national productivity gain plus the 2.5 percent "allowable" inflation rate.

We also heard arguments by labor that economic justice demands that wages be increased, that wages should be based on need rather than on competitive reality.

But those who argue this line sometimes end up taking contradictory positions, as was illustrated during the debate over the minimum wage. At the same time that many labor leaders and members of Congress were loudly protesting price increases in Phase II, they were also fighting equally hard for increased minimum wage levels and extended coverage. Without entering into the merits of the economic justice argument, the Commission computed that the various proposed bills on the minimum wage before Congress in 1972 would have increased the Consumer Price Index that fall anywhere from 0.3 to 0.8 percent. Since no productivity gains would have ensued, the increased costs either would have come out of profits or would have been passed on in prices.

Both labor and business too often seek, through private market power or government help, to reduce the effects of competition. I can only point out that by so doing, they invite the danger of permanent central control over the economic system.

Without competition, wage-price controls may become not an option, but a necessity.

True, such controls can attack inflation in the short run by

204

(*a*) reducing inflationary expectation, (*b*) intruding on the discretionary market power of business and labor, and (*c*) influencing the timing of price and wage decisions. But, by their very design, such controls interfere with the market system and hasten its metamorphosis into a centralized economy. I can spot seven ways this occurs:

First, wage-price controls lead to distortions in the economic system, which can be minimized only in the short run. The longer controls are in effect, the harder it is to discern real from artificial signals. No matter how cleverly any group designs a control system, distortions and inequities will appear. It happened in European control programs; it was beginning to happen in Phase II.

For instance, lumber controls were beginning to lead to artificial middlemen, black markets, and sawmill shutdowns. Companies trapped with low base-period profit margins were beginning to consider selling out to those with higher base periods, sending their capital overseas, or reducing their efforts. Instances of false job upgrading—which were actually "raises" in disguise—were reported on a scattered but increasing basis. To keep away from profit-margin controls, companies were considering dropping products where costs, and thus prices, had increased. And shortages of certain products (e.g., molasses and fertilizer) were appearing because artificially suppressed domestic prices had allowed higher world prices to pull domestic supplies abroad.

Exceptions and special regulations can handle some of these distortions, but the task grows more difficult as each correction breeds the need for another.

Second, during a period of controls, the public forgets that not all wage-price increases are inflationary. In a freely competitive economy, wage and price increases occur because of real consumer demand shifts and supply shortages. The resulting wage and price increases signal to business "MAKE MORE"; or to labor, "MOVE HERE"; or to the public, "USE LESS."

Controls interfere with this signaling mechanism. An artificially suppressed price can eventually cause shortages; natural gas is an example. Similar examples can be found in labor where suppressed wages do not attract labor to areas in which there are shortages of skills or of workers.

But with wage-price controls in place, the public believes that all increases are inflationary—almost antisocial—and the clamor is for no, or very small, increases.

"You can eliminate the middleman, but not his function"—this applies equally to our economic system. We live in a world of scarce resources, and, as much as some would like to repeal the laws of supply and demand, it can't be done. Some system must allocate resources, we hope, to the most efficient use for society. If wage-price controls, other government regulatory rules, or business-labor monopolies prohibit the price system from performing its natural function, then another rationing system (such as central planning and control) must be used.

You can eliminate the price system, but not its function.

Third, during a control period, the public forgets what profits are all about. Even before the recent wage-price controls, the public believed profits were "too high," though they actually declined from 6.2 percent of GNP in 1966 to 3.6 percent in 1970, and increased only to 4.3 percent in the boom year of 1972. And with profit increases raised to the top of the news during the recovery of 1972 and early 1973, the negative public sentiment against profits increased. Why? The control system itself heightened the public's negative attitude toward profits at a time when capital regeneration, the fuel of the capitalist engine, was already alarmingly low.

Fourth, wage-price controls provide a convenient stone for those who have economic or political axes to grind, particularly those interested in promoting a centralized economic system.

For example, in 1972, Ralph Nader argued that the control system should be used to prohibit automobile companies from raising their prices to reflect style changes. Others argued that price increases should not be given to companies that employ insufficient numbers of minorities or pollute the environment. Nor should wage increases go to uncooperative unions. And so on.

Fifth, wage-price controls can easily become a security blanket against the cold winds of free-market uncertainties. They tell people what the limits are; they help employers fight unions; and they provide union leaders with excuses to placate demands for "more" from their rank and file. The controlled become dependent on the controllers and want regulations continued in preference to the competition of a dynamic market. At the same time, the controllers themselves can become so enamored with their task that they also don't want to "let go."

The public begins to fear what will happen when controls are ended, and seeks continuance. Witness the fears of moving from Phase II to Phase III, and the public (and Congressional) pressure for the freeze to replace Phase III. Even Wall Street seemed terrified at the thought of returning to supply and demand in the market.

It is much easier to get into controls than to get out.

Sixth, under controls, business and labor leaders begin to pay more attention to the regulatory body than to the dynamics of the marketplace. They inevitably come to the same conclusion, summed up by one executive: "We know that all of our sophisticated analysis and planning can be wiped out in the blink of a Washington controller's eye."

Seventh, and most dangerous, wage-price controls misguide the public. They draw attention away from the fundamental factors that affect inflation—fiscal and monetary policies, tax rates, import-export policies, productivity, competitive restrictions, and the like. The danger is that attention will become permanently focused on the symptom-treating control mechanism rather than on the underlying problems.

Additionally, the public is also strengthening the trend in a number of ways.

For one thing, the public has lost much of its faith in the ability of both business and labor leaders to operate our economic system. In recent years, poll after poll has reported the growth of this tendency in public opinion. For instance, over the last seven years, Louis Harris and Associates has established that (*a*) corporate executives share with bankers and educators the largest loss in public respect, declining from 55 percent in 1966 to 27 percent in 1973, and (*b*) confidence in labor leaders shrank from 22 percent to 15 percent in the same period.* A 1971 Opinion Research Corporation study revealed that 62 percent of the public favored governmental controls over prices, 60 percent of all stockholders believed competition could not be counted on to keep prices "fair," and fully one-third of the public believed that Washington should set ceilings on profits.†

My personal mail, and my experience in numerous interviews with newspaper editorial boards and others, confirmed that the public feels there should be more, not less, control of business and labor. And Congress reflects this mood in asking for more controls, tighter regulations, and more public agencies. Time and again, when I was testifying before Congressional committees, I was told that we had to have more controls because the private enterprise system "didn't work."

Such sentiments do not make me optimistic about continued public support for our free enterprise economy.

Nevertheless, the growth in the public's disenchantment with the private enterprise system has been matched by an increase in the public's demand on that system. The public wants, for instance, higher pay for teachers, policemen, and women; a clean environment; better schools and medical care—and all without increases in prices or taxes.

At various Price Commission public hearings and in meeting with public groups and congressmen, I heard many of the same demands: increased pollution controls, but at the same time, lower transportation prices; increased health benefits, but lower hospital costs; increased mine safety, but lower coal prices; decreased insecticide usage, but lower food prices; protected forests, but lower lumber prices; and so on. The demands are outrunning what we, as a society, can afford.

We cannot have it all ways without increased productivity. And, more and more, the public is not willing to wait for the market to provide remedies. Instead it is seeking centralized solutions to obtain the desired benefits—*now.*

* Louis Harris, "The Public Credibility of American Business," *The Conference Board Record* (March 1973), pp. 33–38.

† Thomas W. Benham, "Trends in Public Attitudes toward Business and the Free Enterprise System," White House Conference on the Industrial World Ahead (February 1972).

Finally, the move toward a central system is being aided by the public's desire to make people the same, both in ability and in susceptibility to economic change. The market system is founded on competition, monetary reward, excellence, and change. The current attitude stresses stability, cooperation, egalitarianism, and income equality enforced by a central authority.

"Can we be equal and excellent too?" queries John Gardner in the subtitle to his book *Excellence.** It is a question which he discusses thoroughly but does not answer. Everyone might like to be both excellent and equal, but the competitive system works on the notion that those individuals and institutions outperforming others are not and should not be rewarded equally. But now, more people are seeking and getting protection—through tax reform, income redistribution plans, promotion by seniority, and so on—against "differences" generated by the operation of the competitive system.

Society's insistent cry for economic stability poses three dilemmas for our capitalistic system.

First, if the business cycle becomes too stabilized by government policies, we run the risk of eliminating capitalist system's ability to adapt to changing circumstances and to encourage risk-taking—its principal features. Complete stabilization removes not only the negative sanction of failure, but the incentive of success as well.

Second, the goal of "maximum employment" has been interpreted to mean low unemployment, and the arguments have centered on definitions of "low" (2 percent, 4 percent, 5 percent) and "unemployment." But stimulating demand to achieve low unemployment risks inflation.

The issue boils down to whether we can simultaneously achieve low unemployment, growth in the economy, price stability, and a favorable balance of payments. This unemployment-inflation trade-off is perhaps one of the most critical economic issues for modern societies. I do not know the answer to the question, and it seems that no one really knows. Pessimists say "No." Optimists say "Yes." Pragmatists say "We'll try hard."

In recent years, however, societies in the United States and

* John Gardner, *Excellence* (New York: Harper & Row, 1961).

Europe have been opting for setting the primary goal as very low unemployment by stimulating demand. Not knowing how to "fine tune" the system, the typical result has been an overkill, with inflation resulting. Rising inflation has, in turn, triggered the cry for wage and price controls. There isn't very much indication in the political or economic system that we can yet find the proper balance or break the cycle.

And the problem is growing more difficult even as I write.

Third, central economic planning holds a great deal of logical appeal for many economists, intellectuals, and businessmen. If planning works so well in corporations, particularly with the computer and new scientific management tools, why shouldn't we do a better job by having the federal government do the planning for the economy? If physical technology can conquer space, surely we can use the same "rational" decision making to conquer the economy. A planned economy is surely better than an unplanned one.

It has appeal. The centralists (and an increasingly large number of the public, Congress, and businessmen) are coming around to believe that "there must be a better way." They reason that with our complex technology and conflicting social demands, we need central solutions rather than what they feel are "fragmented, uncoordinated, individualized" market actions. It sounds more ordered and rational. It is comforting to think that some intelligent Olympian-like men have the facts, the techniques, and the wisdom to relieve us of the burden of chaotic decision making.

And who knows for certain? Maybe it can be done. One day. But I say with some emphasis that *we aren't there now. And I personally doubt that we ever will be.*

The tradeoffs in our extremely large, tightly linked, and interdependent economy are too complex ever to be done efficiently on a centralized basis. Each time you try to optimize one goal, it produces in our highly interdependent economy effects besides those intended. Adjustments lead to further adjustments. Jay Forrester of M.I.T. with his Industrial Dynamics simulation of even one company, has shown that an economic system which begins to oscillate can become even more unstable when further attempts to control it are made.

Our attempt in the Price Commission to control lumber prices is a good illustration. Log prices were not controlled because raw agricultural products were exempt. Log prices rose faster than lumber prices because of demand, and thus developed a cost-price squeeze on domestic firms attempting to supply the booming housing market. Black markets and shortages appeared, hampering the housing industry. Also, in some cases, log price contracts were based on lumber prices. As lumber prices rose, log prices went up, and so on. In the end, as we tried to hold down the rate of increase in lumber prices, we tended to either reduce production, or we encouraged export sales which helped the balance of payments but reduced U.S. supplies.

This example illustrates in a small way what tends to happen when man alters any cybernetic (e.g., ecological) system held in balance by unknown adaptive responses. When one variable is purposefully altered, side effects—often undesirable and unexpected—are created. The controller attempts to minimize the variable, only to discover that he has altered two other seemingly unrelated or conflicting variables. And so on, with the number and complexity growing in geometric progression.

People assumed that in the Commission we were using highly sophisticated econometric models to "fine tune" the economy. This was not so. We looked at such models, but the builders were the first to admit that they did not have the macroeconomic models on which to base economy-wide or even industry-wide control parameters. All we could get were broad indicators at the highest level of aggregation, useful for general policies perhaps, but absolutely no use in "planning" a detailed control system. My view is that such tools are not likely to be forthcoming in the future.

The second reason for my skepticism about a planned economy is that the greater the number of variables in the environment and the more rapid the rate of change, the more a system must be one of *infinite* responses. Ross Ashby,* a systems theorist, calls this the "Requisite Law of Variety." He postulates that only a cybernetic system is capable of such variety and adaptive behavior. The market system can be viewed as such a cybernetic system of "infinite responses" in that it *is* responding every day in infinite ways to the micro decisions proceeding from individual values.

* Ross Ashby, *Design for a Brain* (Scranton, Pa.: Barnes & Noble, 1966).

Even if one would make the heroic assumption that the system could be pruned down to manageable proportions for "enough" central control, then who supplies the value judgments for the operation of the model?

An elite?

Authoritarian systems have a lot of appeal for planners (as in the Soviet Union) because "they" can supply the value function for allocation decisions on "behalf of all the people." *I have to concur with Friedman that the market system is consistent with individual freedom.* An authoritarian system is consistent with an elitist group planning for others.

And a final note. If such a planned system would result, it would take away the economic gains motivating an individual to take risks, and be innovative. As centrally planned systems of other nations have shown, the byproducts are often defeating: low morale and productivity, delays, antisystem creativity, bottlenecks, poor quality, and the like. The planned system tends to hold down the disturbances from random inputs of creativity and to become a closed system. I doubt that it could ever be as adaptive, motivating, and efficient as the cybernetic market system.

I also doubt that the planners will give up.

What does this all add up to? Where are we headed? Is the system actually doomed?

There are many who have said, *yes.*

Karl Marx predicted that capitalism would destroy itself; Joseph A. Schumpeter flatly stated that capitalism cannot survive;* and Robert L. Heilbroner concluded: "The change [away from capitalism] may require several decades, perhaps even generations, before becoming crystal clear. But I suggest that the direction of change is already established beyond peradventure of doubt."† Even Mr. *Supermoney,* 'Adam Smith,' observed that the consensus is moving away from the market as decision maker and from the business society.‡

Clearly, in my opinion, the factors I have cited *are* carrying us

* Joseph A. Schumpeter, *Capitalism, Socialism and Democracy,* 3d ed. (New York: Harper & Row, 1972), p. 61.

† Robert L. Heilbroner, *Between Capitalism and Socialism* (New York: Vintage Books, 1970), p. 31.

‡ 'Adam Smith' *Supermoney* (New York: Random House, 1972), p. 226.

farther and farther away from the market system and toward a central economic one. I cannot prove that we have or will go "too far," but I can point to figures substantiating the trend: Our National Income accounts show a shift in governmentally directed expenditures from 15 percent in 1930 to about 40 percent today. And the federal—as opposed to state and local—proportion has risen from 5 percent in 1930 to about 26 percent in the same period.

I am *not* saying, however, that the private enterprise system is doomed, nor that continuance of the trend toward central control is inevitable and irreversible. Nor do I feel that government has no role in the economic allocation system. It clearly does and should. I believe, rather, that we are very near the point where further centralization will change our present system into one that can no longer perform its function efficiently.

I view this trend with alarm because I favor retaining the very powerful features of the market system. I hold this position, not out of blind faith in an ideology, but for the following reasons:

Demonstrated economic superiority. The economic record clearly reads that the American free-market, private-enterprise system has produced the highest standard of living in history and has demonstrated a remarkable ability to adapt to changing conditions.

Political freedom. The principles of democracy and personal freedom are most compatible with a decentralized market system.

Personal experience. I have experienced the difficulties of trying to allocate resources by centrally directed price controls. These difficulties have convinced me that it is impossible to improve on the system in which billions of daily market decisions by the public determine our resource allocations.

Before some brand me a chauvinistic throwback to Social Darwinism, let me quickly add these points: Our present system does have competitive imperfections on both the price and the wage sides. It has never been, and never will be, as theoretically competitive as the original Adam Smith's description. Government vigilance and action *are* required to prevent the natural monopolistic tendencies of the system. There *are* social problems and inequities in our present system which need correction. The central government should play a role in this task.

The difference between the centralists and myself is that I do not think that the best solution is always to increase the size or degree of control by the central system. *Rather, the difference is in a better functioning of our private competitive system and a better quality, not quantity, of public control.*

The question remains: How can this be accomplished?

One clear statement I am making is that the real answer to fighting inflation is not wage-price controls. The lessons of history seem pretty clear. Centralized efforts to fight inflation were started before Christ was born. Rome, for example, fought inflation by various means, for centuries. Finally, in A.D. 301, the Emperor Diocletian imposed the first extensive price-wage control program. His Edict (referred to as "commanded cheapness") set schedules for 76 different wage categories, and for 890 different price categories (222 of these were for food!). The penalty for an offense was death. Thirteen years later, the program, in shambles, was abandoned. In the thirteenth century, the great Mongol, Kublai Khan, decreed maximum prices. And Medieval Europe had a "just price" code.

Not many people are aware of it, but the United States began some attempts at wage/price controls during its early years. The American Puritans imposed a code of wage and price limitations in 1636, in which those who violated the code were classed with "adulterers and whoremongers." The Continental Congress set price ceilings even before the Declaration of Independence. A few states enacted price control laws. Inflation became so severe that General George Washington complained in April, 1779 that "a waggon load of money will scarcely purchase a waggon load of provisions." The control attempts were sporadic, highly controversial, and not comprehensive. All efforts were largely abandoned by 1780.

Most modern nations have instituted wage/price controls during periods of war, but it was in Europe right after World War II, that almost every European nation tried some form of comprehensive peacetime controls (remembering the inflation that had torn apart European economics after World War I). Some European nations had success with their "incomes policies" for a period of time. Some had short lives. Some were started, stopped, and reinstated in another version. But none have lasted continuously.

Though specific "lessons" are difficult to transfer across international boundaries, and even difficult to use in one nation from one time to another, it was helpful to us in the Commission to view their experiences—generally negative—in Europe. (A set of general observations about European experiences is given below.

One overriding lesson, however, is obvious: wage and price controls have never worked satisfactorily over an extended period of time. Consequently, I strongly believe the trends toward wage-price controls and a centralized, or government-controlled, economy should be halted.

But I do not believe, as some free-enterprisers do, that any of my suggestions should do away with the social achievements of the past forty years. I believe that much, if not most, of the social legislation passed by the U.S. Congress protects the unprotected and provides social equity in economic terms that are consonant with the spirit of our political life and law.

I deeply believe in equity.

I do not believe, however, in inequity. It is the inequities, rigidities, bureaucratic stiflings, and actual absurdities that we must attack. But it is a question of *how*.

General Lessons From European Incomes Policies

1. If either labor or business does not cooperate, a wage/price controls program will not work.
2. Incomes policies do not work for long. They erode with time.
3. Getting into controls is easier than getting out.
4. Rising profits drive wage demands up.
5. Neither business nor labor is very satisfied with any given distribution of their share of income at any given time. Both will seek to improve their share.
6. Voluntary incomes policies have been limited in success and in time. The tendency is toward mandatory policies.
7. Labor nearly always believes that the government figure for estimated productivity in setting wage guidelines is low. History shows that labor is generally right.
8. A wage "drift" occurs over time as business and labor cooperate to break many of the wage guidelines.

215

9. Efforts to restrain business and labor through education and exhortation has very limited success.
10. If wages are to be controlled, then so must prices be. The only exception is France which has had a limited price control program, but not a wage control program.
11. Cost of living escalators accelerate inflation.
12. Less productive labor groups eventually demand comparability in wages with the more highly productive labor sectors, thereby eroding the wage guideline.
13. Expectations feed inflation.
14. Increasingly interdependent world trade can intrude and upset another nation's income policies.
15. Incomes policies are increasingly difficult to make work as demand increases and unemployment decreases.

This list is a set of general observations from readings and personal conversations with individuals concerned with European incomes policies.

Businessmen, labor leaders, legislators, and administrators have the power to slow or alter the trends I've cited. By doing so, we may be falsely labeled right-wingers or reactionaries, but we should not be daunted. If a goodly number of us do not try to stop the present trends, we may, even within this decade, end up with an economy we simply cannot manage.

Here are some things we can do to avoid that.

Selective deregulation. Obviously, not all regulation in the public interest should cease: For example, control in the areas of safety, product quality, pollution, and health should remain. But many economists can make a good list of those regulations that are interfering excessively with the competitive model, such as subsidies, quotas, tariffs, and competition-limiting labor and business practices referred to earlier in the chapter.

Monopolistic vigilance. Both business and labor have innate tendencies to seek monopolistic positions, and therefore they must be restrained. The same message also goes for professions (e.g., accounting, law, medicine) that build up anticompetitive practices in the name of "professionalism."

The Sherman, the Robinson-Patman, and the Clayton Acts, all designed to bring about these goals, were written many years ago.

216

Each needs continued enforcement and should be examined for possible revisions and oversights in their application.

Three branch overhauls. Just as physical systems need periodic checks and overhauls, so do our social institutions. Government is no exception. Many of our procedures and institutions at the local, state, and federal level were designed for an agrarian society with slow communications and an isolated domestic economy.

At a minimum, I suggest regularized (say, every three years) public procedures for a review of the organizational and administrative procedures of government.

Political involvement. We live not just in an economy but in a political economy. Our economic system does not only operate according to the classical laws of supply and demand but also, through the interaction of power and politics with economics. If business and labor leaders wish to steer the system in the direction they believe best, they cannot simply deplore, fume, curse, and hire a Washington lawyer or lobbyist. They must get directly involved by holding public office, personally visiting regulatory bodies and Congress, participating in citizens' affairs groups, and allocating time for employees to participate in local, state, and national politics.

Public advocacy. Related to the need for political involvement is the need for public advocacy of all views about our economic system. Those supporting increases in government's role are currently more vocal than are the advocates of the private enterprise system. The reason, I suspect, is that advocacy of private enterprise is often ridiculed as mossback in viewpoint, antiintellectual, socially insensitive, and on the side of the greedy vested-interests and the "fat cats."

Nevertheless, those believing in the private enterprise system must speak out, not bombastically but intelligently. Every avenue should be utilized—speeches, articles, participation in local affairs, appearances at schools, employer-employee discussions, and so forth.

Economic education. If people are to make intelligent choices about the nature of our economic system, they must understand more economics. My experience at the Commission has convinced me that economic understanding in this nation is low, much lower than it should be for people to make wise choices.

Education to promote understanding should begin with our young people and extend through adult life, emphasizing not a partisan view but a clear presentation of various economic fundamentals and systems.

Better economic tools. The economic policy tools of taxation, budget, and monetary supply, by which government manages the overall economy, are very crude and require overhauling. The econometric models are weak, the implementation process rigid, and the needed data often not available. For instance, decisions were made in Phase II with a frightening paucity of economic information. At the very least, this situation could be corrected by funding the many excellent economic research organizations to enable them to come forward with recommendations for the Congress and the President.

Business schools. Business schools should turn out students who understand both the strengths and the weaknesses of the private enterprise system, as well as its responsibilities to society. Too often, technicians are being graduated who are narrow professionals and blind ideologists.

One particular recommendation is that more schools encourage entrepreneurs. The entrepreneur is the life-blood—the innovator, creator, pusher—of the private enterprise system; without him, the system will tend to become change-resistant and bureaucratic.

At the business school of Southern Methodist University, where I am dean, we are trying explicitly to turn out such individuals. We are creating a new kind of educational program at SMU designed to turn out managers who are action-oriented, risk takers, change-oriented, self-reliant, believers in the competitive market system, and socially conscious. I do not think these kinds of people are being generated in the traditional schools.

Department of Economic Affairs. There is a lack of *coordinated* and *accountable* economic policy making, especially little relationship between foreign and domestic strategy and policies. The process is balkanized. Part of President Nixon's proposed departmental reorganization program is the creation of a new Department of Economic Affairs. In the Price Commission, we saw numerous instances in which the dispersal of economic policy matters in various parts of government inhibited the formulation of an integrated and consistent program.

218

I support the proposed new department, which would gather together under one head the economic branches of various departments and agencies, e.g., Transportation, Commerce, Labor, the Small Business Administration, and others.

Productivity. I have proposed in speeches and articles a nonprofit organization, funded and operated by the private sector, that would focus solely on increasing American productivity.

Why? Because labor expects, and has been getting, annual wage increments well above our 3 percent long-term productivity growth rate. Business seeks expanded profit margins—but faces challengers in world markets with higher productivity growth rates and lower prices. And the American consumer/citizen wants ever-increasing social and economic benefits.

But there is no way to enlarge the pie for labor, business, and society without an increase in the key factor—*productivity.*

And nowhere in the entire U.S.—as far as I know—is there a single organization, association, or instrumentality of any significance whose basic effort, objectives, and expertise are devoted specifically and solely to improving American productivity in the years ahead. There isn't one national clearing house for the collection of productivity data. There isn't one organization providing a source of information, publications, or education about productivity for American labor, business, and the public. And there isn't one nonprofit organization supplying expert assistance to labor and business desiring to create programs to increase productivity.

Japan has developed such an organization, the privately run Japan Productivity Center: a 300-man educational, data-gathering, research, informational, and counseling organization for both labor and management. It has a $7.5-million annual budget, which was originally—and ironically—set up by foreign aid and U.S. experts. West Germany has such a center, the RFK, with a staff of 250. Even tiny Israel has developed the 300-man Israel Institute of Productivity.

But the United States which is still the most powerful and productive nation on earth, has only a 20-man National Commission on Productivity in Washington, whose annual working budget is about $2.5 million—an insignificant amount in a $300 billion national budget.

Compared to what other countries are doing, this is almost a total void. And on a matter so important as productivity, it is astonishing.

At this moment in our national history, it is particularly alarming. Our productivity gain in the last decade has been the lowest in the modern industrial world. Europe and Japan especially have far outstripped us in recent years. They've not only gained on us; they've passed us in some areas. After Britain, our rate of investment in fixed assets is the lowest in the modern world; our investment in research and development has also slid to the bottom. Problems of balance of payments, formal devaluations, dollar weaknesses—all signal deterioration in our international economic leadership. And Phases I through IV generate the very real specter of permanent wage-price controls and a more centrally directed economic system, unless competition and productivity from the private sector can contain inflation.

An *American* Productivity Center, totally dedicated to improving productivity—in both its social and economic sense—is critically needed and overdue.

Urgent tasks await such an organization. It could tackle the messy problems of definition and measurement. The economists' definition that productivity is the ratio of "physical output to physical input" raises more questions than it answers. *Output* involves both quantity and quality. How do you measure the quality of an improved TV set, a new drug, or an improved stepladder? How do you measure the nonphysical output, for example, of a university, a doctor, a tax assessor? Equally difficult, what is *input?* Is it time, materials, wages, land, capital, effort, brains, attitudes? And how do you separate the contribution that each input makes to output? We must get beyond the present practice of settling for the partial productivity factor of "output per manhour," which is inadequate and inapplicable for many businesses.

And those are the questions arising from only *one* definition. There are many others. Financial people argue that productivity improvement is a matter of capital investment. Industrial engineers say it is better work methods and measurement. Behavioral scientists view it as motivation—teamwork, incentives, involvement of people, self-actualization, and new workplace organization. Management scientists and consultants tout more efficient management techniques. Labor leaders say it really means harder work by the work force—more sweat, more speedup from already overworked and dehumanized workers.

Productivity is some of all of these, no doubt. Regardless of the method, however, it really means getting more quantity and quality out of each unit of capital and labor going through the economic system. The Center could group its work into these two large baskets: capital productivity and labor productivity.

Impartial research and policy recommendations will be urgently needed to indicate where—at the national level—capital investment is needed to at least maintain our current leadership, as well as to give early warnings of lagging sectors and challenges by international competitors. Policy alternatives could be laid out for government tax policies and direct investments. At the corporate level, research, information, and advice could be given on capital budgeting, management systems, innovation in organization, marketing, and management, and technological trends.

Collected in the capital area would be the work of economists, financial officers, bankers, tax experts, statisticians, and accountants. Tools in this area would be money, materials, technology, systems—all expressed in quantitative language.

Similarly, ideas and recommendations are needed to stimulate labor productivity—ideas in the area of human behavior, attitudes, and motivation.

The currently exploding attention to human factors in the workplace is a relatively new Western phenomenon. I believe it will have as profound an impact on our ways of performing and regarding work as the phenomenon of capital investment did during the Industrial Revolution. So far, though, it has emerged more extensively abroad than in the United States. It manifests itself in the groups called Quality Control Circles in Japan, and at Olivetti in Italy, Norsk-Hydro in Norway, Imperial Chemical Industries in Britain, and in the U.S. in companies such as AT&T, Procter & Gamble, Corning Glass, and Texas Instruments.

Collected in the labor area would be sociologists, psychologists, labor relations experts, industrial relations officers, union leaders, plant managers, and the like. Their tools would be training, organization development, job redesign—usually expressed in qualitative terms.

221

Clearly, capital and labor productivity interact—the familiar two sides of the same coin. But today that interaction is occurring in a distrustful adversary setting—each playing ritualistic games, often neutralizing the other in a suicidal manner. The Center must point out the common grounds and mutuality of interests of those two apparently disparate areas.

The Center could provide a place for labor, business, and the public to turn for counsel as to how to improve both capital and labor productivity. It could provide a full resource of economic and social productivity data in a computerized system national in scope. It should constantly research and report the state of the art of productivity—new developments, new suggestions, new theories and hypotheses. It could provide a focus for expert advice on "how to get started" or "how to improve." Such assistance would range from educational and referral services to on-site, long-term counseling in getting productivity improvement programs started and continued. The Center would supplement, but not compete with, private firms advocating particular methods.

In international and in domestic firms, the chips are down. But I believe there is something in the American character that always has and always will respond in situations of importance.

There *must* be an American Productivity Center.

It is already late. Time is short to get such a Center organized, funded, developed, and developing.

And it is up to the private sector to bring such a Center into existence.

All these recommendations advocate continuation of a private enterprise competitive market system with these essential characteristics:

- --The price system.
- --Private ownership.
- --Collective bargaining.
- --The profit motive.
- --Freedom of entry.

Capitalism is more than a system of economic voting by buying a can of peas. It is a system of values and attitudes—a way of life that permits individual motivation, excitement, personal freedom,

222

variety, and excellence. It has produced the highest standard of living in the world. In the world of rapid change that we are increasingly living in, the private capitalistic system is capable of faster adaptation and innovation than any other.

I do not see these attributes flourishing nearly so well in a centrally planned and controlled system.

Yet I am not denying a role to central government. Government can help to ease transitions caused by change to help stimulate or contract the economy, and to inform the public of the cost benefits of various alternatives: e.g., pollution control versus higher prices, caribou protection versus energy supply, unemployment versus inflation.

Government also has the function of setting and monitoring the rules of the economic game within which business and labor can compete. Clearly implied are some restrictions on the free operation of the market place, principally to keep competition alive and to protect the general public interest when ignored or threatened. Examples: anti-trust, product quality, pollution control, safety standards, and so on.

The key issue is, at what point do such activities and restrictions on the private enterprise system inhibit its workings to the point of rendering it effectively inoperative?

Where are the limits?

The tug between laissez-faire and central regulation has been going on for centuries. Both are valid approaches and applicable under appropriate conditions, yet neither is of universal application for all purposes. Each has its limits and should not be carried out to excess in total disregard of the other.

Laissez-faire probably was what this country needed in its infancy, as was the case in England in the beginning of the Industrial Revolution. Perhaps our growth could not have started, or started so well without a large amount of economic freedom, for no one knew what the effects would be, or what government controls would be needed. Society soon learned of some of the undesirable byproducts, the neglect, spawned by completely unregulated private enterprise; and a new tack of state regulation was taken in the 1930s. The trend has been steadily in that direction since then, and as I have tried to argue is approaching even more quickly the opposite limit.

Revising the trend does not mean returning to "pure and perfect" competition, which never really existed. The fact that we have moved toward a more centralized system does not mean that the trend is irreversible. Centrally dominated societies (Russia, Yugoslavia) are moving toward a market system, but that doesn't suggest that they will end up with a private enterprise capitalistic system. We seem to advance by over-accentuation of one principle at a time, like a sailing vessel that is first on one tack and then on another, but is making to windward on both. It is important, therefore, not to hold too long on the same tack.

There is no reason to suppose that the limits between laissez-faire and centralism will ever reach a permanently stable position. Conditions change more rapidly than ever with man's growing control over his environment, his self understanding, and his heightened expectations. The true (i.e., our best) mean lies between the vices of deficit and excess of either system, and this varies with the conditions. It becomes ever more important, therefore, that the debate and subsequent decisions are made not as to ultimate truths, but as to what is best for society under the conditions we see, or can reasonably foresee.

As Ralph Lowell points out in his *Conflicts of Principle,* a danger is that each person advocating a belief asserts his to be absolute and universal. He strives for a complete philosophy, struggles for victory over the other, and refuses to consider limits of proper application. Labels are attached: "Socialists, greedy capitalist, bleeding-heart liberal imperialist, fat cat, pinko." Revolted by the opposition, the advocate then asserts opinions and seeks action more drastic than he would if he reflected less heatedly. If we are to choose between the shoals of the limits, we must not assume that the other is absolutely wrong.

What we must do is seek the balance between opposing principles, realizing that it is almost impossible to frame a comprehensive and universally applicable economic system. Decisions will be made on the basis of experimentation and observation of practical results, and it is extremely likely that the chosen path will not be the same forever, but will shift from time to time. We are searching for economic limits, just as we have searched in the sixties for social and political limits.

If you asked people whether they would like to do away with

private enterprise, most would say "no." Recent polls by Lou Harris, published by The Conference Board, report that people don't want the government to take over. But the danger I see is that the general public, including business and labor leaders, will erode the market system, in steps, without realizing what they are leading to.

My view is that we are increasingly regulating the market system to the extent that it is being burdened and regulated beyond its power of endurance, and to where mere differences in degree are becoming differences in kind.

Wage-price controls accelerate the trend, via a cyclical process.

Once controls have been imposed in peacetime—even on a temporary basis as a sort of "inflation interruptus"—the probability of their being reimposed in the future is increased. (As Senator Proxmire said on August 15, 1971, "Things will never be the same again.") The political pressure to freeze and reimpose controls will be much faster and greater if inflation rises again. Every experience with controls lessens our future will to avoid them. Witness Freeze II and Phase IV.

Some argue that the public increasingly will call for controls over business and labor as protection against inflation, and that if inflation subsides, so will these cries. If true, then it becomes all the more important to conquer inflation. This is why I place so much emphasis on moderating inflationary pressures—the number one problem facing this nation and the world. Inflation will lead to further and faster regulation of the market system and, eventually, its transformation.

Removal of controls will present an opportunity—an opportunity for labor, business, and government to demonstrate that the private sector can manage the market and fight inflation without further government intervention. If not, then I don't think that labor, business, or the public will like the controls that will be imposed on our freedoms in the future, and we will have helped to build our own cages.

This is not a pessimistic view, for as Schumpeter stated, a report that a ship is sinking is not defeatist. It is defeatist if the crew sits and drinks. They can also rush to man the pumps.

In every sense, it's up to each of us.

Epilogue: A guide for the wage-price controller

I think I can safely make two assumptions about the future.

One, the peacetime price control system initiated in 1971 will, in time, become the subject of thousands of pages of articles, books, dissertations, and memoirs. These works will range from detailed economic analysis to pure historical narratives, and their purpose will be to provide some helpful insights to the planners of any future controls program, should controls again be necessary.

Two, if controls are ever imposed again, the controllers will *not* have the time to read these thousands of pages of articles, books, dissertations, and memoirs.

With those two assumptions in mind, I have written a very brief "Guide for the Wage-Price Controller" which contains some basic *do*s and *don't*s of creating an Economic Stabilization Program. Hopefully, this short essay will be of use to the next group of men and women who are given the task of regulating what may then be a multi-trillion dollar economy.

These suggestions are not intended to be economic absolutes. The dynamics of our society make it impossible for the conditions that prevailed in Phase II to duplicate themselves exactly at any time in the future.

And that leads me to my first and most important recommendation—BE FLEXIBLE!

Planning

The conditions necessitating the imposition of wage-price controls add up to a national emergency—whether it be during war or peace. Consequently, policy and implementation questions must be decided *quickly,* leaving little time for detailed study and evaluation.

Since the actual decision makers will not have the opportunity to do much research on their own, it is extremely important that a quick-response research staff be available to provide economic data and policy option papers as needed. The group should be comprised of: (1) economists to supply facts and analysis, (2) experienced accountants to discuss customary business financial practices, and (3) industry experts to analyze the feasibility of fitting different control mechanisms to different sectors of the economy. It is important that this group be set up and ready to begin work before the policy makers start their deliberations. By the first meeting, the research staff should have an array of the various regulatory options, together with a list of the pros and cons of each.

It is also important to have at least the skeletal framework of a General Counsel's office. In addition to providing advice on legal matters, the lawyers will have to determine whether or not the policies adopted can be converted into enforceable regulations. The rent policies of the Price Commission, for example, seemed relatively simple in theory; but once spelled out on paper, they were not even comprehensible to lawyers, let alone to the general public. Furthermore the General Counsel's office will be able to point out some of the more specific policy questions and inconsistencies that must be dealt with before regulations can be published. If these problems are ironed out before the program is announced, much confusion, misinformation, and uncertainty can be avoided.

A small staff of operational people should also be available to begin work on any forms, questionnaires, or procedures that will be needed to implement the control policies. Like the General Counsel's office, they too will be able to point out issues that must be resolved before the program gets under way.

Finally, an Executive Director, senior administrative staff, and necessary administrative authority should be available immediately to begin dealing with organizational problems such as personnel, correspondence, space, and supplies.

Organization

If at all possible the entire program should be handled by one agency. Both policy making and operation can be much more effective and consistent when handled by a single organization.

Phase II worked with separate pay and price organizations, and this may again be necessary to secure political constituencies. But better policies, from an economic standpoint, could have been created by the same policy body so as to avoid situations where wage increases are high, and price increases low, or vice versa.

The members of the single board or commission should—again, if possible—be public members. A body comprised of men and women who represent a particular interest group cannot often respond quickly enough to the demands of an emergency program. Moreover, such a group can at times convey a very divisive posture to the public at a time when unity and cooperation are extremely important.

The operational and field division *must* be part of the policy-making agency. When new and complicated regulations are being issued every day, it is vital that those familiar with the policy be able to disseminate information and respond immediately and directly to field offices. When more than one agency is involved in this process, countless approval and coordination procedures have the effect of tieing up information for days and, sometimes, weeks. Thus, agents in the field are unable to deal efficiently with the public. The net result is a loss of public confidence and worker morale. I cannot emphasize too strongly this need for direct communication between the policy agency and its field offices—not only for the above reasons but also because of the need of the national headquarters to obtain rapid feedback on the effects of its policies.

The internal organization of the control agency should include

228

a policy and economic analysis division, a General Counsel, an exceptions division, an operations division, a field response and coordination division, as well as the traditional administrative offices. The size of each will vary depending on the nature of the control program adopted.

Policies

The policies suitable for a given controls program will depend on the degree and nature of the inflationary problem (cost-push versus demand-pull), as well as the general state of the economy. Even though there is no one set of policies to fit all situations, there are certain guidelines which are generally applicable.

A basic policy problem affecting all decisions is the trade-off between simplicity and fairness. We found that simple policies led to many inequities; conversely, equity led to complexity. A balance between the two is desirable but very difficult to achieve. A simple standardized control mechanism, such as a freeze or a percentage limitation, can be used for a brief period of time. If the program lasts more than a few months, however, it will probably be necessary to develop specific policies for specific economic sectors. The alternative is severe distortion of the marketplace.

The level of specificity can range from item-by-item control to industry-by-industry standards—or, as was chosen for Phase II, division of the economy by size and function. The first method requires a huge bureaucracy; the second presents difficult definition problems. The third has the advantage of being specific enough to sustain a program without being so specific as to necessitate the formation of a mammoth control organization. If public sentiment permits, most small firms should be exempted.

The third method was selected in Phase II with separate regulations for manufacturers, service organizations, retailers and wholesalers, rents, health services, insurance, and public utilities. The following are some recommendations for developing policy for each of the areas:

Manufacturers and Service Organizations

Manufacturers and service organizations were permitted to pass through incurred (but not anticipated) increases in costs along with their traditional markups. Such firms were also subject

229

to a productivity offset and a limit on their overall profit margin.

In general, this policy worked very well except for demand-pull situations. The greatest controversy involved whether or not to allow the firms to take a markup on their increased costs. Our majority felt this was necessary at a time when the economy was emerging from a recession. In fact, in the few instances where we did restrict firms to dollar and cents pass-through, there was very little difference between the price charged and the price that would have been charged if a markup were added.

Cost justification was satisfactory in a cost-push situation, but I would not recommend it for use in a demand-pull economy.

A more simple approach, which we applied on a selective basis, was Term Limit Pricing. TLP agreements permitted firms (mostly manufacturing but some service) to have an average aggregate percentage increase for all their products. However, firms still had to cost-justify the overall percentage increase and obey the profit margin limit. They were also prohibited from raising the price of any one product by more than 8 percent.

TLPs cut down tremendously on the amount of paperwork processed by the Commission. In a future controls program, a TLP approach applied on a mass scale would have not only the advantage of minimizing paperflow but also of providing the business community with a simple, easily understandable program that permits long-term planning.

The TLP approach could be further simplified by allowing all firms in a given sector to have a certain percentage increase, i.e., 1.5 percent, without cost justification or a profit margin limit. Companies requiring more than that amount could apply for an exception.

Retailers and Wholesalers

This area is highly competitive, and therefore, generally speaking, not inflationary. If at all possible, it should be exempted. Realistically speaking, however, the need for public credibility and support may require control of the retail and wholesale sectors.

In the latter situation, regulations should be based on control of the firms' gross margins at some aggregate level—a control number for each firm, for each store, each category in a pricing zone, and so on. These figures are computed regularly and are easily monitored. Without going into any further detail, let me say that any other type of control leads to excessive red tape and enforcement problems.

Rents

Rents, like retail, were not inflationary on a national scale. Ideally, they should not have been controlled. Rent controls are very popular and tend to perpetuate themselves. Public pressure may require some type of regulation.

If so, the controllers should opt for more simplicity and less equity. An equitable system, as the Price Commission painfully discovered, is extremely complex and completely incomprehensible. As a result, the public support—which was the reason for controls in the first place—is lost and all that is left is a serious problem area which demands more than its share of available resources. Therefore, a flat percentage cap or a freeze is really the only feasible form of control. In either of these cases, be prepared for plenty of exception requests.

Health Services

The nature of the health services industry has changed tremendously during the past decade and will probably change even more during the coming decade. Thus, I deem it wiser to suggest a general approach to regulation of health care rather than enumerate specific policies.

A health care unit should be set up both to recommend policies and to implement and administer the day-to-day program. The people in this unit should be health specialists with a few generalists in charge of overall management.

Instead of devoting equal concentration to all types of providers and all sizes of institutions, as did the Price Commission, a control program should focus more on institutional providers and should develop a tier system similar to that used by the Price Commission in other sectors of the economy. This would permit better utilization of manpower in the areas where the real problems are.

Another suggestion is to develop regulations which do not require a massive exceptions procedure. In this industry, in particular, regulations should be realistic and easily enforceable. Otherwise, they can be potentially dangerous.

Insurance and Public Utilities

The approach taken by the Commission in both insurance and public utilities, I feel, was a wise one. These sectors are already subject to regulation by people far more numerous and knowledgeable than any group that could be established by a controls agency. It would be futile, then, for a new agency to attempt to impose a second layer of controls. Rather, the Price Commission chose to "regulate the regulators" by furnishing them with a set of criteria and putting them in charge of seeing that the criteria were met. This allowed the regulatory agencies to continue to do their job with only minor modifications and freed the Commission to concentrate on other areas.

Profit Margins

The profit margin control was the foundation of control for several sectors of the economy.

For a cost pass-through approach, it is particularly useful as a second line of defense. Although firms were not permitted to estimate costs, they were required to estimate the effects of volume increases on fixed costs. In cases where there were sizable underestimates, the discrepancy would show up in the profit margin report. The necessity of reporting quarterly profit margins also made it more difficult for a firm to submit inaccurate data on price increase requests.

On the con side, the profit margin did restrict firms which had exceeded the limit more for reasons of better productivity than for reasons of higher prices. In addition, certain firms were caught with low base periods, but not low enough to qualify for loss/low profit treatment.

It worked well for Phase II in the short run, but could create serious distortions if kept for a long-term program.

Productivity

Any controls program should incorporate a productivity provision, for increased productivity is one of the primary anti-inflation weapons.

The Price Commission used standard industry productivity figures as an offset to allowable costs. This not only helped to keep

232

prices down but also promoted a new and very much needed productivity-consciousness in the business community.

Miscellaneous

When the provisions of the program are made public, the policies will probably be of a general nature since only day-to-day interchanges will reveal the areas which need further detailing.

Several questions, however, will arise in all control programs and should be addressed, if at all possible, prior to the announcement of the general policies. These include seasonality, long-term contracts, loss/low profit firms, new products, new firms, custom products, formula-determined leases, cost reach-back dates, export sales, mergers and acquisitions, and the definition of when a transaction occurs.

When visited by officials from other nations observing our program, I always gave them a list of "essential elements" of any control program:

- --Broad and complete authority over prices.
- --Independence from political influence.
- --Support of business and labor.
- --A flexible, not specific, authorizing law.
- --Decisiveness and swiftness of action.
- --Staffing by competent and experienced people.
- --Field organization.
- --Public education.
- --Adequate size, funding, administrative authority.

Emergency Procedures

The government is ill equipped to facilitate the setting up of emergency units. Time honored and detailed procedures of the Federal government—for example civil service hiring, procurement, space, payroll—do not and cannot respond in a "now" environment in which emergency organizations such as the Price Commission must operate.

Such organizations, designed to meet emergency situations, would be dead in the water if they followed all of the ponderous and lengthy procedures, none of which were designed to meet a crash project.

The Office of Management and Budget and the Civil Service

Commission could take the lead and design a set of simple, short-cut systems that could be put into operation right away. This might require a set of special authorizations for the first year of a new organization. Then the leaders of the next crash operation could focus on the program issues rather than devoting half of their energy to the frustrating, no-win game of how you work with administrative systems designed for normal operations.

Summary

In order for controls to succeed, they will have to be supported by the public. For no matter how many people are employed by the regulatory agency, they will never be able to check all, or even a significant percentage of, the prices in the economy. Controls can work only if the public chooses to make them work.

Controllers should therefore keep two things in mind: First, Americans are willing to sacrifice a great deal as long as they feel everyone is sacrificing equally. As soon as they feel some are carrying less than their share of the burden, they withdraw their support. Second, a controls program which seeks to change customary business practices may look good on paper but will never work in practice. Red tape and widespread evasions will eventually undermine the effectiveness of the regulations.

Finally to our successors—and, unfortunately, I am sure there will be some—*good luck!*

Appendixes

Appendix A: Legacy of the freeze*

I. Introduction.
1. Days into freeze
2. Days to go
3. Volume during freeze
   a. Inquiries
   b. Complaints
   c. Exemption requests
4. Current nature of inquiries
II. Positive contributions of the freeze.
1. Has halted inflation (WPI and CPI).
2. Increased prospects for achieving a more favorable balance-of-trade
3. Provides skeleton framework for administering Economic Stabilization Program. Can draw on expertise, personnel, and experience of various agencies involved in the freeze.
4. Internal Revenue already familiar with the monitoring techniques and public information process.

* Outline of a presentation by Lou Neeb for the Price Commission and Pay Board Members to review as they were designing Phase II.

237

5. Public acclimated to wage-price controls. Expect tough treatment. Generally, all sectors of the economy willing to cooperate.
6. Awareness of important needs of the economy.
7. Aware of policies that have created problems during the freeze and need to make adjustments for them in the post-freeze period.

III. General minuses of freeze.
1. Has not totally reversed the inflationary psychology.
2. We have yet to see any significant decrease in unemployment rate.
3. Effects on balance of trade deficit not known.
4. Surcharge adds to CPI and WPI.
5. Many sectors are in a precarious position because of squeeze from wage-price freeze policies.

IV. Problem areas during the freeze.
1. Prices.
   a. Abnormal cost-price relationships.
      i. Should price increases be allowed for industries facing increased costs due to legislative requirements (e.g., anti-pollution laws)?
      ii. Should utility rates be permitted to increase to cover increased costs?
      iii. Should industries whose costs rose prior to freeze be permitted to raise prices?
   b. Definition of "transaction" and "substantial volume of transactions."
   c. Definition of "raw agricultural products." Should processors of raw agricultural products be allowed to pass on cost increases?
   d. How many base periods? Can the base period differ from industry to industry?
   e. Should uniform price scales be permitted within an industry.
   f. How large a profit margin should be allowed?
   g. Dues for non-profit organizations. (Hurray for Girl Scouts!)
   h. What policy should be adopted regarding price increases that were announced or effective prior to

the freeze, with no transactions taking place? Problem of catalogs published in advance.
  i. Definition of "new products."
  j. Long-term purchase contracts.
  k. What percentages should be permitted for price increases?
      i. Should there be a uniform percentage rate for all industries?
      ii. Should the percentage rate allowed vary from industry to industry?
  l. Insurance rates. Will the public support increases based on experienced-rated formulas?
  m. Commodity market prices.
  n. Corporate merger-related prices.
  o. Definition of comparability.
  p. Specific problems.
      i. Tuition and room and board.
      ii. Advance ticket sales to sporting events (Atlanta Falcons).
      iii. Advertising rates for the media (violation of First Amendment?).
      iv. Price increases for 1972 automobiles.
2. Wages.
  a. Equalization of wages of employees.
      i. Occupying same position in same firm.
      ii. Occupying comparable position in plants in the same area.
  b. Exemption of certain fringe benefits such as vacations, pensions, etc.
  c. Should deferred wage increases announced prior to the freeze be permitted to become effective?
  d. How should low wage persons be treated?
  e. Should incentive, merit, longevity, or increment wage increases be permitted?
  f. Exercise of stock options.
  g. Payment for Americans working abroad for American owned subsidiaries.
  h. Wage increases given for productivity increases— should they be allowed?

      i. Should a flat percentage increase be allowed for different industries?

      j. Policy toward wage increases reached during the freeze.

      k. Retroactivity.

      l. Executive compensation.

      m. Specific wage problems.

            i. Teacher salaries (failure to communicate; legal contract problems). What should be the policy towards teachers who signed contracts many years ago guaranteeing them a wage increase every year?

            ii. Construction industry salaries (Davis-Bacon Act).

3. Rents.

    a. Policy toward rent-controlled areas.

    b. Should pass-through-tax rent increases be permitted?

    c. Cost-rent squeezes.

4. Miscellaneous.

    a. Compliance checks.

    b. Policy toward record-keeping.

    c. Restitution.

    d. Phasing out controls.

V. Transition.

1. Staffing will be able to draw on temporary staff detailed from other government agencies to the Office of Emergency Preparedness (OEP) during the freeze. Will also work with a transitional task force from OEP.

2. Need to establish criteria for price, wage and rent adjustments after the freeze.

3. Establishment of appeal procedures necessary.

4. Criteria for exceptions and exemptions. During the freeze, OEP National Office denied 529 requests for exceptions and exemptions. Regional OEP Offices denied 1,846 such requests. Four requests were granted out of a total of 2,379 received. Of the four granted, three involved health insurance (Columbia County,

Florida; Texas Public Employees Association; joint request from the Missouri State Department of Education and the Missouri Teachers' Association.) The fourth allowed an increase in water and sewage rates for Cresco, Iowa. Our criteria were stringent. Obviously, the standards developed by the Pay Board and the Price Commission will have to be more flexible.

5. Problem of handling large volume of correspondence. OEP had 22,000 items.

6. The need for liaison between CLC, Pay Board and Price Commission.

7. Expanded IRS/Justice preparation of cases for litigation necessary.

8. The need for determining what areas should be completely exempted from wage-price restrictions?

9. Let staff know where they stand.

10. Work with your lawyers.

11. People have learned to send their problems to more than one office and follow the answer they like.

Appendix B: Statement by the Price Commission*

The policies of the Price Commission announced herein are designed to achieve a goal of holding average price increases across the economy to a rate of no more than 2.5% per year. This is in line with the President's goal to stabilize the economy, reduce inflation and minimize unemployment, and with the Cost of Living Council's objective of reducing the rate of inflation to not more than 2 to 3% by the end of 1972.

These policies rely heavily on voluntary compliance, but they impose close supervision on those segments of the economy which substantially affect price levels. Specific regulations implementing these policies will be issued in the next few days.

Prices may not exceed their freeze period levels except as changed by published regulations or on orders of the Commission.

The basic policy is that price increases will not be allowed except those that are justified on the basis of cost increases in effect on or after November 14, 1971, taking into account productivity gains. While price increases, in the aggregate, must not exceed 2.5%, some will be above 2.5% as justified on the basis of cost

* Press release by Price Commission, November 11, 1971, announcing Phase II policies.

242

increases and other factors. Price increases will not be granted to any individual or firm to provide retroactive relief for the impact of the August 16–November 13, 1971, freeze.

Reporting procedures for price increases vary depending on the amount of annual sales or revenues reported by a firm in its most recent fiscal year.

a. Firms with sales of $100 million or more must prenotify the Price Commission on proposed price increases. Unless the Commission advises otherwise within 30 days after the notification is received, the notified price changes may take effect.

b. Those firms with sales of between $50 million and $100 million must make quarterly reports to the Price Commission on changes in prices, costs and profits.

c. All other firms are not required to prenotify or report on a regular basis, but will be subject to the standards and criteria that the Price Commission will establish.

Different economic sectors will be subject to different rules and regulations. These sectors are:

a. Manufacturers.
b. Wholesalers, retailers, and similar commercial enterprises.
c. Service industries and the professions.
d. Others.

Manufacturers

Prices charged by manufacturing companies may not be increased over freeze period levels, except as the following provisions may apply:

1. Allowable cost increases in effect on or after November 14, 1971, reduced to reflect productivity gains will serve as a basis for price adjustments; and

2. Price adjustments shall not result in an increase in a firm's pretax profit margin (as a percentage of sales) as established during its base period.

Retailers/Wholesalers

Retail and wholesale prices are to be controlled on the basis of customary initial percentage markups which are applied to the cost of the merchandise or service. These customary initial percentage markups cannot be higher than those in the base period. Moreover, a firm may not increase its prices beyond that amount which would bring its net profit rate before taxes (as a percentage of sales) to a level greater than that in the base period.

Retailers are to post prominently their freeze period prices for all covered food items and for many other selected items other than food as will be specified in the regulations. Until all such selected prices are posted, retailers are not permitted to increase any prices. In any event, such freeze prices must be posted no later than January 1, 1972.

Service Industries and the Professions

Prices charged for services may not be increased over freeze period levels, except:

1. As a result of allowable cost increases in effect on or after November 13, 1971, reduced to reflect productivity gains, and
2. In any event, price increases shall not result in any increase in a firm's pretax profit margin (as a percentage of sales) as established during its base period.

The Commission recognizes there is a multitude of different service industries, characterized by widely varying types of costs and market conditions, possibly warranting more specific forms or regulation. The Commission is considering more specific regulations.

Until the Commission publishes specific regulations for nonprofit organizations and Government units, the prices of services supplied by such organizations may be adjusted for allowable cost increases in effect on or after November 14, 1971.

Base Period

For purposes of these regulations, base period shall mean the average of any two of the past three fiscal years of the firm ending prior to August 15, 1971.

Rents

Guidelines for rents will be developed after consultations with the Rent Board. In the interim, the freeze will continue with some rule changes amending freeze-period definitions which resulted in hardships. Landlords are required to record and make available upon request both the unit-by-unit freeze period rent and the basis for any adjustments. The Rent Board will develop basic rent guidelines for consideration by the Commission.

Regulated Industries

For prenotifying firms the relevant regulatory agencies shall submit all existing and new requests for rate increases to the Price Commission. These regulatory bodies will also notify the Price Commission upon approval of rate adjustments which will be reviewed by the Price Commission. For reporting firms, the regulatory bodies will report approved rate adjustments for review by the Price Commission. The Price Commission will retain the right to implement more stringent standards.

Some regulated firms proposed rate increases have been approved by regulatory authorities, but were not allowed to become effective because of the freeze. Such increases may go into effect; however, the appropriate regulatory authority shall review such increases for consistency with the goals of the Economic Stabilization Program.

Correction of Inequities

Inequities arising as a result of certain definitions and rules promulgated under the freeze or for other exceptional reasons will be handled as follows:

1. Changes will be made to amend certain definitions and to correct inequities created by the operation of rules promulgated under the freeze, but none of these changes will permit retroactive price increases. On or after November 14, freeze-period prices may be adjusted pursuant to such changes. Specific price adjustments are subject to review by the Commission. In such cases, the Commission will determine whether the increase is significantly inconsistent with the goal of reducing the rate of inflation.
2. Prenotification firms must file with the Commission any proposed price increases based on the modification of freeze-period rules.

3. Firms which can demonstrate a continuing gross inequity not ameliorated by the rules of the Price Commission may request an exception through local IRS Offices.
4. Firms must retain records supporting price increases that are made pursuant to the modified rules, and reporting firms must file reports of these changes with the Commission.

Windfall Profits

Windfall profits refer to those profits which would not have existed except for unique conditions created by the operation of the Economic Stabilization Program. The Price Commission is determined to take those measures necessary to achieve the goal of reducing the rate of inflation to 2–3% by the end of 1972. Therefore, in the administration of the stabilization program the Commission will at certain times issue such regulations as necessary to cause windfall profits to be converted into price reductions.

Other Considerations

Notwithstanding the foregoing, in making determinations based on the standards set forth in this statement, the Price Commission will take into account whatever factors it considers relevant to an equitable resolution of that case and considers necessary to achieve the overall goal of holding average price increases across the economy to a rate of no more than 2.5% per year.

Appendix C: Agendas of Price Commission November 22, 1971 to December 20, 1971

Monday, November 22, 1971

72-hour Filings
Local Rent Authorities
IRS—Rent
Coal
Stopping the Clock
Volatile Prices
Loss/Low Profit Firms
Third Party Interventions
Regulated Utilities

Tuesday, November 23, 1971

Autos
Posting
Federal, State, Local Governments
Deals and Allowances
Third Party Intervention

Coal
Loss/Low Profit Firms
Volatile Prices
Regulated Utilities

Monday, November 29, 1971

Status Report—Operations
72-Hour Cases
IRS Relationships
Commission Staffing
Rent Advisory Board
Commission Forms
Regulated Utilities
Base Period Calculation
Prenotification Requirements
Volatile Prices
Autos
Steel
5.5 percent Pass-Through

Tuesday, November 30, 1971

Commission Systems Development
Markup or Dollar Pass-
Through
Coal
Steel
U.S. Chamber Meeting
Allowable Costs Definition
Rent Advisory Board
Joint Ventures
Acquisitions and Spinoffs
Profit Margin Text
Exceptions Backlog
Loss/Low Profit Firms
Weighted Average Agreements
Price Increase Requests—
Limit?
Financial Institution Fees
Forms Revision

Monday, December 13, 1971

Retail Compliance
Markup v. Dollar Pass-
Through
Weekly Internal Reports
Policy v. Case Decisions
Speaker's Bureau
Rent Advisory Board
Regulated Utilities
Term Average Price
Status—Economic Stabiliza-
tion Act

Health Industry Committee
Postal Rates

Tuesday, December 14, 1971

Posting
Consumer Price Index
Long Term Contracts
Catalog Sales—Posting
Government Purchasing
Rent Advisory Board
Unemployment
Forms Revision
Loss/Low Profit
Cost Reachback Date
Health Industry Committee
Term Limit Pricing

Sunday, December 19, 1971

Executive Session
White House
PC Certification Process
Category Overages

Monday, December 20, 1971

Chairman McCracken
Status—IRS and CLC
Rent Advisory Board
Insurance
Long Term Contracts
Loss/Low Profit
Stopping the Clock
By-Product Pricing
Blue Cross/Blue Shield
Productivity
Wholesalers/Retailers
Term Limit Pricing

Appendix D: Agendas of Price Commission January 4, 1972 to November 14, 1972

Tuesday, January 4, 1972

Public Affairs
Businessmen's Conference
Internal Revenue Service
Cost of Living Council
Exceptions Criteria
Economic Stabilization Act
Rent Advisory Board
Program Operations Case Load
Decontrol
Long Term Contracts
Guidelines for Low Profit
  Firms
Tuition Fees of Colleges
  and Universities
Time Limit for Allowable
  Costs
General Counsel Report

Tuesday, January 11, 1972

Forms
Internal Revenue Service
Public Affairs
Executive Session
Cost of Living Council
Rent Advisory Board
  Recommendations
General Counsel
Liability of Buyers
Contract Pricing
Coverage and Classification

Wednesday, January 12, 1972

Coverage and Classification
Sugar Act Exemption
IRS Disclosure
Low Profit Firms

251

TLP—Reduction of Upper Limit
Profit Margin Limitation
Penalties for Failure to File Forms
Rent

Wednesday, May 3, 1972
Food
Profit Margin
Utilities
Small Firm Exemption
3 Percent Cap for Service Industry
Productivity Progress Report
CPI Report
CLC Weekly Report

Tuesday, May 16, 1972
Multi-Industry Firms and the Reporting Entities
5.5 percent Rule
Shoe Industry
Dollar for Dollar Pass-Through
Service Sector Cap
Confidentiality of Information
Consumer Confidence Figures
"Rent Reconsidered" Letter from Senator Clifford P. Case
Civil Damages for Price Violations
Remarks of Herb Stein Before Economic Club of New York
Letter from Senator Proxmire
Utilities

Tuesday, June 6, 1972
Public Affairs

252

Retail Pricing Procedures
Price Reductions
Health Care Services
Minimum Wage
Shoe Industry
Disclosure of Information
Food
Pay Board/Price Commission Joint Meeting

Wednesday, June 21, 1972
Reestimation of Impact in 1972 of Profit Margin Limitation
Stevedore Exceptions
Auto Pricing
Services Cap
Food
Jawboning

Tuesday, August 1, 1972
Demonstration of New Conference Room
Operations Update
Economic Overview
Demand Pull Inflation
Inflation Matrix Discussion
Long Term/Short Term Interest Rates
Price Redistribution Plan
Service Cap
Labor Cost Pass-Through

Wednesday, August 2, 1972
Long Term/Short Term Interest Rates
Price Redistribution Plan
Service Cap
Labor Cost Pass-Through
Utilities Status

Jawboning
Federally Mandated Costs

Monday, August 14, 1972

Joint Pay Board/Price
   Commission Meeting
Jawboning
Rent
Vending Machine Prices

Tuesday, August 15, 1972

Program Distortions
Professional Services Cap
Pricing Redistribution Plan
Retailing
Commodity Prices Action
Construction Industry

Tuesday, September 26, 1972

Economic Models
Lumber
Exceptions Criteria
Consumer Budget
Auto
Rent
Price Reduction Plan
Price Posting

Tuesday, October 10, 1972

Automobile Pricing Issues
Exception   Procedures—$2.75
   Wage Rates
Prevailing Price Concept
TLP Planning
Cement Industry
Food
Profit Margin Impact

Tuesday, November 14, 1972

Liaison Status
Health Regulations
Long Term Interest
Lumber
Food
Automobiles
Steel
Economic Overview
TLP
Gold and Silver
Unit Pricing
Anomalies

Appendix E:
Pricing formulas*

1. *Cost Reimbursement*—(dollar and cents pass-through)—pass-through to selling prices of the dollar and cents increases in specific costs between some base date and the current date.

2. *Margin Maintenance*—reimbursement for percentage cost increases which have occurred between a base period and the current date, plus a historical rate of operating profit.

3. *Fixed Percentage (Flat Rate) Formula*—ceiling prices for products and services could be increased at a percentage rate, from the freeze period in monthly or quarterly increments or at other periodic intervals.

4. *Unit Price Control Formula*—the Price Commission sets specific selling prices on certain products which are sold typically by many different vendors in a large number of transactions at uniform prices; i.e., chewing gum, a quart of milk, a bag of cement, a package of regular sized popular brand cigarettes, a gallon hi-test gasoline, etc.

5. *Net Profit Formula*—a company could raise prices to a point

* Excerpted from "Report of Certified Public Accountants Advisory Committee" prepared as a background paper for the Stabilization Program, October, 1971.

permitting it to earn the same percentage of net profit (before tax) to sales which it earned during the base period.

6. *Return on Investment Formula*—permit price increases sufficient to permit a company to earn the same percentage profits on net worth as the business earned in a "base period"; i.e., the same Return on Investment (ROI) as the firm had in the base period.

Index

Index

261

WE'VE COME A LONG WAY SINCE PHASE ONE